Building Leadership Character

This book is dedicated to the many Cornell students who have demanded
more from me and challenged me to improve—to continuously develop
my own character to become a better educator and a better person.

SAGE PUBLISHING: OUR STORY

We believe in creating fresh, cutting-edge content that helps you prepare your students to make an impact in today's ever-changing business world. Founded in 1965 by 24-year-old entrepreneur Sara Miller McCune, SAGE continues its legacy of equipping instructors with the tools and resources necessary to develop the next generation of business leaders.

- We invest in the right **authors** who distill the best available research into practical applications
- We offer intuitive **digital solutions** at student-friendly prices
- We remain permanently independent and fiercely committed to **quality, innovation, and learning.**

Building Leadership Character

Amy Newman

Cornell University, USA

Los Angeles | London | New Delhi
Singapore | Washington DC | Melbourne

FOR INFORMATION:

SAGE Publications, Inc.
2455 Teller Road
Thousand Oaks, California 91320
E-mail: order@sagepub.com

SAGE Publications Ltd.
1 Oliver's Yard
55 City Road
London EC1Y 1SP
United Kingdom

SAGE Publications India Pvt. Ltd.
B 1/I 1 Mohan Cooperative Industrial Area
Mathura Road, New Delhi 110 044
India

SAGE Publications Asia-Pacific Pte. Ltd.
3 Church Street
#10-04 Samsung Hub
Singapore 049483

Acquisitions Editor: Maggie Stanley
Editorial Assistant: Alissa Nance
Production Editor: Karen Wiley
Copy Editor: Rachel Keith
Typesetter: C&M Digitals (P) Ltd.
Proofreader: Theresa Kay
Indexer: Maria Sosnowski
Cover Designer: Candice Harman
Marketing Manager: Amy Lammers

Copyright © 2019 by SAGE Publications, Inc.

Printed in the United States of America

Library of Congress Cataloging-in-Publication Data

Names: Newman, Amy, author.

Title: Building leadership character / Amy Newman, Cornell University, USA.

Description: Thousand Oaks, California : SAGE, 2019. | Includes bibliographical references and index.

Identifiers: LCCN 2017049583 | ISBN 9781544307855 (pbk. : alk. paper)

Subjects: LCSH: Leadership. | Character.

Classification: LCC HD57.7 .N495 2019 | DDC 658.4/092—dc23
LC record available at https://lccn.loc.gov/2017049583

This book is printed on acid-free paper.

18 19 20 21 22 10 9 8 7 6 5 4 3 2 1

Brief Contents

Detailed Contents

Acknowledgments

I am most grateful to Maggie Stanley, my editor at SAGE, who contacted me about a project three years before we agreed on this one. I appreciate her patience and guidance, particularly in finding ways to incorporate reviewers' feedback. I have always felt supported in trying to achieve the goals of this book.

I am also grateful to the terrific team at SAGE: Alissa Nance for her thorough review and timely communication, Karen Wiley for her keen organization, and Rachel Keith for her eagle-eye editing.

Reviewers for this book have been instrumental in shaping complex concepts and making the unique approach with real examples work. Their time and dedication are evident in their thoughtful comments, which have enriched the book as a useful learning tool. I would like to thank the following reviewers: Mitchell R. Alegre, Niagara University; Paul Barker, Bresica University College; Josh Bronstein, Bank of America; Rochelle Brooks, Viterbo University; Abigail Charpentier, Aramark; Christine R. Day, Eastern Michigan University; Janie Harden Fritz, Doquesne University; Diana D. Galbraith, Slippery Rock University; Corday T. Goddard, St. Norbert College; Keeok Park, University of La Verne; Pedro David Perez, Cornell University; Risa M. Mish, Cornell University; Robert Waris, University of Missouri–Kansas City; Herbert Z. Wong, John F. Kennedy University; Robert M. Yawson, Quinnipiac University; Xia Zhao, California State University, Dominquez Hills; and Jeff Zimmerman, Northern Kentucky University.

I am appreciative of my affiliation with Cornell University and the many "hotelies" I have had the opportunity to know. Their openness and interest in learning impresses me every day, and I know I'm lucky to work in a place where people want to be and where service to others is paramount.

Finally, I haven't always displayed the best character during the writing process, as my partner and editor, Eric Clay, will attest. He has been everything I could want, adding depth and insight and tolerating my frustrations along the way. With a master of divinity, a Ph.D. in urban and regional planning, and 30 years of practice in multi-faith settings, he's the perfect writing and life partner. His voice throughout the book tempers my corporate, professional teachings.

Writing a book on character is both a curse and a blessing. A chronic self-scrutinizer by nature, I am worse now. The premise of this book is that we can all develop character to become better people—and I am doing my best without holding the bar so high that, at 60 inches tall, I can never jump over it.

But we do learn what we teach. My hope is that this book provides examples and a path for developing leadership character—for each of us.

Introduction

Developing Character Is One Way to Become a Better Leader and a Better Person

Most people want to live good lives and to do well by others. Whatever your role—student, coworker, community organizer, CEO—you can build leadership character and have better outcomes for yourself and for those around you. Our roles dictate how we behave in certain situations, and these expectations are important for meeting professional standards. But character is about our humanity—how we live in the world and relate to others in every aspect of our lives. We demonstrate character in almost everything we do, in our interactions with others, and in our decisions and communications. To use the vernacular, character is "what we are really made of."

Character is developed over a lifetime, and this book offers a path. We analyze company examples to learn how to develop character within ourselves. A leader's communication offers a window just big enough to illustrate character dimensions, such as accountability, integrity, courage, and authenticity. We'll see leaders communicating and miscommunicating—demonstrating character and showing us how it could be stronger.

The company examples bring research and theory to life, and then our work begins. Developing character requires an understanding of ourselves and others—our ideas, emotions, and visceral reactions. Self-reflection exercises, assessments, and activities throughout the book offer resources for personal development. We practice developing our own character to improve how we operate in the world and how we affect others.

Leaders Demonstrate Character When Communicating During Difficult Situations

In crisis situations, we see leadership character on full display. During what may be the most pivotal event in a leader's career, we see that person exposed. We hang on every word of a leader's message, hope for an apology we may never get, make jokes, and post about it everywhere. We are often disappointed.

Yet human beings are behind the organization's messages. They know that public perception depends on their response, and they know they cannot reasonably satisfy all constituencies: employees, shareholders, the board of directors, customers, the media, and particularly, the social media mob. Sometimes they have to choose who gets priority—a difficult choice because of competing loyalties and self-interests that test their character.

As one example, a *New York Times* article blames Wall Street for recent airline failures. Increasing pressure to improve profits has made stock price "the only criterion for executive pay." Bonuses are based on financial performance rather than, for example, reducing lost baggage or customer complaints.[1]

Such incentives don't help our corporate leaders make good ethical decisions. Why did United Airlines CEO Oscar Munoz, at first, try to justify dragging a man off the plane? Dr. David Dao was asked to give up his seat, and he refused. Employees and airport security officers followed specific procedures, and Munoz defended his employees despite physical injury to the passenger. We have sought mechanistic ways to measure and guide performance. But regulations, policies, and procedures—such as incentives based only on financial performance—force compliance, bar good judgment, and do nothing to build character.

When pilot Chesley Sullenberger landed a US Airways flight on the Hudson River in New York instead of following procedures to reach a nearby airport, he demonstrated courage. "Sully" credits the decision with instinct he developed over 42 years of flying, and he admits it felt routine—what he had trained for during his entire career. During a congressional hearing, he warned airlines about decreasing the salaries and pensions of experienced pilots—again, sacrificing people for profits.

We need goals that value better outcomes for more people. Then, we can rely on leaders—at all levels of an organization and in their personal lives—to build character from within and to inspire others to do the same.

Corporate Work and Teaching Have Inspired This Book

For most of my career, I worked in leadership development roles for large, global companies, developing and implementing selection processes, performance management systems, and training programs. My responsibilities included helping to orchestrate layoffs—giving leaders tools to decide who would leave the organization and helping them communicate their decisions. It wasn't the highlight of my career, and I eventually left.

I have seen good and questionable leadership character at all levels of the organization. I know firsthand that failures of communication and failures of character are sometimes hard to distinguish. When a manager decides to lay off an employee—*when the employee is in midair*, flying across the country to relocate for her new position—is that poor communication or poor character? When an employee mutes a conference call to make a distasteful joke about the person speaking on the other end, how do we classify that? I have witnessed these behaviors and consider them to be failures of both communication and character.

For the past 13 years, I've had the honor of teaching students at the Cornell SC Johnson College of Business in The Hotel School. My focus is business communication, and I'm proud of the work I do and my students' dedication to improving their writing and presentation skills. They also learn about strategic communication, understanding their audience, crisis communication, making ethical communication choices, and more.

But as I developed relationships with students and revised my textbook, *Business Communication: In Person, In Print, Online*, now in its 10th edition, I wanted to focus on character in addition to competence. How do students bring their whole selves to their communication? What do their messages say about them as people and as leaders? How can they communicate in ways that contribute to an organization as well as provide value to others and to society?

Two articles put responsibility on business education. A 2009 article by Daphne Jameson, a former colleague at Cornell University, questioned the role of business communication faculty in the economic crisis.[2] In addition, a 2013 article by Mary Crossan et al., "Developing Leadership Character in Business Programs," hit home:

> [T]he role of character resurfaces time and again as a contributing culprit in the apparent decline of ethical leadership, particularly in the business sphere. More troubling is that the responsibility for this morass is increasingly being assigned to the business schools' pumping out a staggering number of so-called leaders, to populate not only corporate America, but also multinationals worldwide.[3]

Since 2010, stories about communication in the news on my blog, Leadership Character and Communication (amynewman.com), have enriched my classes, illustrating for students how leaders communicate successfully and, more often, when they fall short. This book builds on this approach to focus on leadership character as a developing area of research.

This Book Presents a Path to Develop Leadership Character

Character development is a messy enterprise. Rarely is there one "right" or "best" solution to an ethical dilemma, and we have many different ideas about morality. More important is how we improve our self-awareness and develop our ability to engage others over time.

The goal of this book is to develop what Mary Gentile at the University of Virginia Darden School of Business calls "moral muscle memory."[4] In the same way a musician or athlete remembers physical moves, the more skilled we become in carrying out good decisions, the more often we will choose a right path. The more we choose a right path, the easier it becomes. For example, taking action that defies convention or "how it's always done around here" becomes our norm.

Chapter 1 defines and presents a case for leadership character and puts character in the context of leadership theory and ethical decision making. In Chapter 2, we see the value of learning from failure and explore ways to exercise judgment to learn from our own failures.

The remaining chapters begin with a major company situation in which we see leaders failing to demonstrate one of the character dimensions. We then learn the dimension definition, explore relevant research, see positive examples, and end with reflections and activities for self-development.

This approach certainly isn't the only way to learn about and develop leadership character. But by seeing character in action, exploring the dimensions within ourselves, and practicing applying the dimensions, we can, over time, become better leaders in any position and in any organization.

Leaders' Successes and Failures Illustrate Seven Character Dimensions

We examine company situations because they involve failures of both character and communication. A lack of character is often easier to spot than good character. We can probably agree that people who put their own self-interests above others' needs—for example, prioritizing money over people—don't demonstrate good character. Their character is evident through their communication—in emails to employees, videos, corporate statements, tweets—and in a lack of any communication at all.

As we'll see in Chapter 2, failures are a necessary part of success, and they offer terrific learning opportunities. By understanding others' failures, we come to understand our own. In hearing about others' missteps, we learn how to avoid them in our own careers.

We'll look at seven major crisis situations to illustrate seven dimensions or aspects of leadership character:

Leadership Character Dimension	Crisis Situation
Vulnerability: Risking Exposure	Volkswagen Emissions Defeat Device
Authenticity: Living as Yourself	General Motors Ignition-Switch Recall
Integrity: Being Consistent and Whole	FIFA Corruption
Accountability: Responding to Others	Wells Fargo Fake Bank Accounts
Courage: Standing Up	Samsung Phone Recall
Humility: Learning From Others	Uber Leadership Issues
Compassion: Caring for Others and Ourselves	SeaWorld Response to *Blackfish*

Each chapter also provides many positive examples from leaders in industries around the world. Their strength is a model for our own character development.

With a storytelling approach and a natural writing style, the book is a cross between a casebook, a textbook, and a "good read." The lessons don't offer tired advice or trite steps to follow; they explore universal principles for leaders to live better, more meaningful lives.

We are fortunate that character is not a fixed trait. We can improve—to become better people for ourselves and for those around us.

1

Leadership Character in Context

Chapter Overview

Leadership character is cultivated and developed over time. We'll start this chapter with a leader's communication during the Great Recession to illustrate a failure of both character and communication—one of many exemplified throughout the book. From this situation and from positive examples, we'll see that character is a combination of values, virtues, and traits and an important part of ethical decision making. Seven dimensions of character focus our efforts for self-development, which happens through reflection and practice. In the end, our goal is to live better, more meaningful lives and to support others in doing the same.

Leaders Choose Character

Before defining leadership character, we'll see an illustration of a character failure. Leadership character is a matter of choice and not position; every one of us can demonstrate and develop character. Yet we don't choose character just to "appear" to be better people; we want to live better lives and create better outcomes for more people in organizations.

Financial Industry Example

The financial crisis of 2008/2009—the Great Recession—threw 8 million Americans out of work[1] and led to almost 4 million home foreclosures in one year.[2] Eight years later, 6.7 million Americans are still "underwater," meaning they owe more than their home is worth.[3]

As people were desperate to refinance their mortgages, hoping to stay in their homes, some sought external counsel and learned language they could use to appeal to their lenders, such as Countrywide Financial. When CEO Angelo Mozilo received customer emails, he got angry, and instead of forwarding one email, he accidentally hit "reply" with the message shown in Figure 1.1.[4]

In Mozilo's communication, we see a failure to acknowledge others' hardships and to demonstrate empathy. Critics of the banking industry said borrowers were misled about their loans and didn't understand the risks of an adjustable-rate mortgage. But Mozilo blamed those who were struggling and failed to acknowledge the bank's role.

Six years later, when the U.S. Attorney's Office in Los Angeles was planning a civil lawsuit against Mozilo, he still didn't understand his responsibility. In an interview with *Bloomberg News*, he said he had "no idea" why the government was pursuing a suit; he also blamed real estate for the collapse: "No, no, no, we didn't do anything wrong. Countrywide or Mozilo didn't cause any of that."[5] Although one reporter calls Mozilo "a pioneer of the risky subprime mortgages that fueled the financial crisis," the U.S. Justice Department decided not to pursue a case against him after all.[6] Bank of America acquired Countrywide and later paid almost $17 billion in settlements because of faulty mortgages.[7]

Figure 1.1   Bank CEO criticizes homeowners

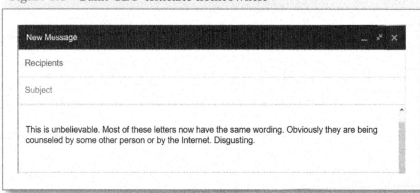

The Role of Character

Since the recession and other corporate scandals, educators and ethical corporate leaders have been asking, "How can we prevent another crisis?" Mary Crossan, Gerard Seijts, and others at the Ivey Business School in Canada researched the financial industry and identified leadership failures in competence, commitment, and, particularly, character as causes of the crisis.[8]

Competencies and commitment are important leadership components. Competencies are skills, abilities, and knowledge, for example, evaluating a mortgage application and understanding regulatory procedures. Commitment represents how much effort people put into using their competencies. Do they aspire to do good work? How engaged are they? What are they willing to sacrifice?[9]

Although competencies and commitment are important, Crossan and her colleagues identified character as the distinguishing factor for companies that "survived, or even prospered during the meltdown."[10] Through their research and interviews, they found character to be the driving force for building competencies and demonstrating commitment.[11]

Character Defined

Character is the collection of traits, values, and virtues that define a whole, complete person. We see character in everything we do: how we think, feel, and behave. When we evaluate character, we take a holistic view to determine how that person is known to others.

Much of the groundwork on character is from positive psychology, which emphasizes living a fulfilling life. In their foundational book, *Character Strengths and Virtues: A Handbook and Classification*, Christopher Peterson and Martin Seligman identified character strengths that "contribute to various fulfillments that constitute the good life, for oneself, and for others."[12,13]

We choose character to contribute to the world and those around us in positive ways. Leaders at all levels of an organization choose, for example, how they interact with people on their team, whether they reward someone for taking initiative, how they assign work, and so on. They decide what is important to them and to those around them. Leaders have tremendous opportunities to impact the lives of others—to create good outcomes for the people they serve.

Our impact on others transcends our role in an organization and in society. Character is more than our position or status as a middle-manager, accountant, sister, or brother. Although companies assign employees a place on an organizational chart, we can lead from any position within an organization. Character-based leadership is about the choices we make.

Leaders with strong character take on issues beyond themselves. They are willing to step outside their role and engage in conflict to challenge institutions and "the way things are done around here." They pursue greater goals for more people. Next, we'll describe how virtues, values, and traits relate to character.

Virtues, Values, and Traits

Crossan and her colleagues adapted Aristotle's virtues to create a model of leadership character in organizational decision-making contexts. Virtues are generally thought of as representing good moral behavior and are believed to be universal. All behaviors associated with character are considered virtuous; they become vices when they are deficient or when used in excess. For example, too much courage leads to recklessness and too little leads to cowardice.[14]

Values are individual, deeply held beliefs, such as loyalty. Values are formed by our religion, family, education, peer group, and other factors and may change over time. Crossan says values "are usually associated with words like 'should' and 'ought,' as in 'Leaders ought to treat everyone with dignity and respect.'"[15] Mary Gentile argues that values and virtues are both about goodness, but that values are also about what we desire. For example, we value loyalty and aspire to be loyal to others.[16] These are subtle differences, and both authors acknowledge an overlap in definitions.

Although values vary among individuals, researchers and others argue that values, like virtues, are surprisingly consistent across cultures. As Peterson and Seligman describe, "We argue that these are universal, perhaps grounded in biology through an evolutionary process that selected for these aspects of excellence as means of solving the important tasks necessary for survival of the species." In his book *Moral Courage*, Rushworth Kidder cites many studies showing consistently held values across continents and among prisoners, students, world leaders, and executives.[17]

Unlike values, traits, such as introversion or extroversion, are aspects of personality that may be inherited and are typically stable over time. Traits are believed to be more fixed than character, and they may influence our character. For example, if we're conscientious, we may be more willing to be held accountable, one of the character dimensions we'll explore in this book. Our focus in building leadership character is on behavior.[18]

Our Choices

Because character can be developed, we can choose to behave and communicate in new ways that demonstrate stronger character. Over time, we develop new habits and communication approaches to achieve "moral muscle memory," as discussed in the Introduction.

Overarching questions begin the journey, such as how we define success and what we see as our purpose at work. Many of us think of external accomplishments that go on a résumé. David Brooks, author of the bestseller *The Road to Character*, instead asks us to consider the virtues that someone might describe in a eulogy at our funeral (Figure 1.2).

Brooks encourages longer-term thinking about ourselves and our impact so that we can lead richer, more meaningful lives. He suggests asking deeper questions:

> [Y]ou don't ask, What do I want from life? You ask a different set of questions: What does life want from me? What are my circumstances calling me to do?[19]

This perspective—asking what the world needs from us instead of what we can get from the world—is a shift from thinking about careers. Choosing where to work and what to do is perhaps a future leader's first step in developing character.

Figure 1.2   Cultivate character rather than build a professional résumé

We live in a society that encourages us to think about how to have a great career but leaves many of us inarticulate about how to cultivate the inner life. The competition to succeed and win admiration is so fierce that it becomes all-consuming. The consumer marketplace encourages us to live by a utilitarian calculus, to satisfy our desires and lose sight of the moral stakes involved in everyday decisions. The noise of fast and shallow communications makes it harder to hear the quieter sounds that emanate from the depths. We live in a culture that teaches us to promote and advertise ourselves and to master the skills required for success, but that gives little encouragement to humility, sympathy, and honest self-confrontation, which are necessary for building character.

– David Brooks

Source: David Brooks, *The Road to Character* (New York: Random House, 2015), p. xiii. Used by permission of Random House, an imprint and division of Penguin Random House LLC. All rights reserved.

Criticism

Although we choose how to be, critics warn against merely *appearing* to be virtuous. In 2015, James Bartholomew, author of *The Welfare of Nations*, coined the term "virtue signaling," meaning taking a stand just to look good.[20] According to Bartholomew, people often criticize a politician's actions not so much to uphold a cause but to show their own goodness. This tendency is perhaps most apparent on social media, where it's easy to react to an issue or position while doing nothing about it.

Also in 2015, Jeffrey Pfeffer at Stanford's Graduate School of Business wrote *Leadership BS*. He argues that decades of teaching leadership hasn't produced better leaders; they are still generally untrustworthy. From his research, he suggests that, instead of trying to be authentic, a concept covered extensively in this book, leaders need to focus on gaining power. Perhaps unlike Bartholomew, Pfeffer believes leaders need to "put on a show."

These critics have much to contribute to the discussion of character and leadership. We are exploring complex topics, and we operate in complex organizations in a complex society. No answers are easy.

Yet we can't fake character; it is what we become, and people typically see through deceit. In addition, a common theme in *Building Leadership Character* is achieving a greater understanding of ourselves and of others— for the good of ourselves and for others. Our assumption is that we want to do well and to continue to improve. To live by our values, we don't deceive others, and we try to catch ourselves taking action just to be *perceived* as good people.

We'll explore more criticism throughout the book, particularly in Chapter 4. First, we'll see how character has become more prevalent as leadership theories have developed over time.

Leadership Theories Have Evolved

Older theories viewed leadership as a fixed trait, but more recent research argues that leadership—like character—is developed over time. We'll explore definitions of leadership and a timeline of leadership theory.

Leadership Defined

Traditional definitions of leadership include managing people. Many leaders in organizations have employees who report to them, but we're using a broader definition here.

Although definitions are varied and have changed over time, scholars typically agree that leadership involves four components:

- *Process.* Leadership is not a trait but an interactive event that affects followers who may be your peers, those who report to you, or even those to whom you report.
- *Influence.* Leaders affect others.
- *Groups.* Leadership occurs within a group of people.
- *Common goals.* Leaders work toward achieving something.[21]

Author Kevin Kruse gives us one definition of leadership:

Leadership is a process of social influence, which maximizes the efforts of others, towards the achievement of a goal.[22]

The definition works because it doesn't require authority over others. A line-level employee can lead by influencing others—for example, to work harder or to join a union. Leaders don't need a particular title. At the same time, leaders encourage others to work toward a goal, so they have an intended outcome—for instance, producing more or improving benefits for the team.

We prefer leaders who work in positive ways, but we don't include this criterion in our definition. People can be good leaders or bad leaders and can achieve good or bad outcomes. For our purposes, we examine the specific successes and failures that help us learn to become better leaders.

Leadership Theory and Character

The definition of leadership has evolved with the formulation of new theories (Figure 1.3). We'll explore a few major milestones in leadership theory next and see how the role of character is emerging.

We have come a long way from the "Great Man" theory that holds that leaders are born, not made. In the early 1900s, leaders were considered heroes, and their characteristics were thought to be intrinsic. Leadership focused on power and control, and in the 1930s, the focus was on determining which personality traits and characteristics contributed to successful leadership.

The 1940s framed leadership in groups, which continued in the 1950s with a focus on shared goals, relationships, and effectiveness. In the 1960s, a popular definition of leadership emphasized behavior, and the 1970s brought an

Figure 1.3   Leadership theories focus more and more on character

			1980s–1990s	
		1960s	Transformational and	
	1930s	Behavioral	Servant Leadership	
	Trait Theory	Theory	Theories	
Early 1900s	1940s–1950s	1970s		Early 2000s
Great Man	Group Theory	Organizational		Authentic
Theory		Behavior		Leadership Theory
		Approaches		

Data source: Peter G. Northouse, *Leadership: Theory and Practice*, 7th edition (Thousand Oaks, CA: SAGE, 2016).

organizational behavior approach. The Situational Leadership model prevailed during this time. The model focused on leadership styles and instructed leaders to behave according to follower readiness in different situations.

In more recent leadership theories, we start to see the importance of character dimensions. In the 1980s, new themes emerged in leadership theory. Definitions included getting done what the leader wants, influencing others, and traits (reemerging earlier ideas of leadership). Since the 1990s, leadership theories have focused more on relationships and contexts than on characteristics and competencies.[23]

For example, transformational leadership has emerged from the 1980s as a popular theory. The focus is on developing followers for the good of the organization.[24] Motivation and morality are components of this definition. Transformational leaders differ from transactional leaders, who use their authority and a system of rewards and punishments to get followers to complete tasks.[25] They do use charisma, motivation, intellectual stimulation, and individual attention to influence followers, but the focus is on outcomes for the organization.[26]

The concept of servant leadership has also become popular. Servant leaders prioritize others above themselves and organizational goals. Their primary focus is directed toward followers—they operate in service to others. Rather than focusing on outcomes, servant leaders focus on the service itself.[27]

Research shows a correlation between servant leaders and character traits. A study of leaders and followers in three organizations found ratings of servant leaders positively related to their followers' ratings of their empathy and integrity, two elements of character we'll discuss later.[28] At General Motors, CEO Mary Barra said, "It's one thing to be a strong leader and have a vision, but . . . it's your concept of followership. If you haven't won the hearts and minds of the team, and so they're not with you, you're not going to get very far."[29]

More recently, Bill George, author, former CEO, and senior fellow at Harvard Business School, popularized the concept of authentic leadership. In this theory, we see clear connections to character. In his book *Discover Your True North*, George credits revered leadership expert Warren Bennis for saying, "Leadership is character," and for identifying leadership as a "lifelong process of self-discovery."[30] George advocates a "natural way of leading":

> No longer is leadership about developing charisma, emulating other leaders, looking good externally, and acting in one's self-interest, as was so often the case in the last twentieth century. Nor should leadership be conflated with your leadership style, managerial skills, or competencies. These capabilities are very important, but they are the outward manifestation of who you are as a person. You cannot fake it to make it, because people sense intuitively whether you are genuine.[31]

Crossan and her colleagues argue that by developing character, leaders can be more versatile, so they can adapt to different situations and contexts. Rather than following a Situational Leadership model, for example, which tells leaders how to act in certain circumstances, and figuring out what a leader should *do*, we can ask a deeper question: "What kind of a person do I want to *be*?"[32] *Then* we can ask, "What skills do I need to get there?"

Frances Hesselbein, author and former CEO of the Girl Scouts, agrees with Crossan's view. She confirms that leadership is about "how to be, not how to do."[33] As she says, "in the end, we know it is the quality and character of the leader that determines the result."

Next we'll explore dimensions of character and how to develop character over time.

Dimensions Focus Our Efforts to Develop Character

This book focuses on seven character dimensions, which are introduced here, and we see a positive example from Adidas.

Seven Selected Dimensions

Character models offer many dimensions from which to choose. Work by Christopher Peterson and Martin Seligman, Al Gini and Ronald M. Green,

Fred Kiel, David Levine, and others is worthy of consideration. To keep the number of dimensions manageable, this book examines seven, most selected from Crossan and her colleagues' work.

The dimensions were selected because they are central to helping leaders manage through difficult situations. These dimensions focus our attention on what leaders can address and change to improve their communications and develop their character. Using abundant and rich illustrations, we can analyze leaders' actions and, more specifically, their messages. Then, we build character by recognizing and changing our own behavior. How we communicate offers an obvious way to start forming new habits.

Four of the seven dimensions are included in the Leadership Character Framework developed by Crossan and her colleagues from Aristotle's 12 virtues: *integrity, accountability, courage, and humility*.[34] Three additional dimensions are *vulnerability* (one of the behaviors supporting humility), *authenticity* (a behavior supporting integrity), and *compassion* (a behavior supporting humanity). These are elevated in this book to recognize their importance in leadership communication, particularly during difficult situations and times of change. The seven dimensions are defined briefly below and shown in Figure 1.4.

- Vulnerability: Risking Exposure
- Authenticity: Living as Yourself
- Integrity: Being Consistent and Whole
- Accountability: Responding to Others
- Courage: Standing Up
- Humility: Learning From Others
- Compassion: Caring for Others and Ourselves

Some dimensions are interdependent with others, and we will see more than one dimension illustrated by leaders' examples. For example, we demonstrate vulnerability and courage when we are accountable; we demonstrate humility when we show compassion.

Although we focus on seven dimensions that can be illustrated in communications, it's worth acknowledging that leaders need to use the full complement to avoid overusing some dimensions and underusing others. Additional dimensions in the Leadership Character Framework are collaboration, drive, humanity, judgment, justice, temperance, and transcendence. Three of these are particularly important in crisis situations. Transcendence allows leaders to see possibilities for the future, which

Figure 1.4   Leaders' communication failures illustrate seven leadership character dimensions

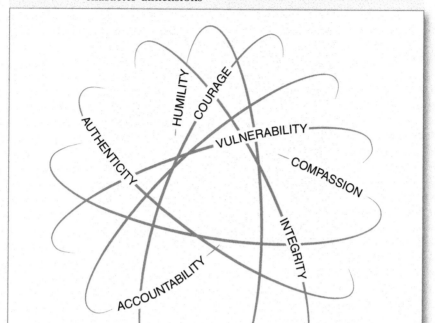

elevates their judgment. Judgment, a topic discussed later, is central in the Framework as the leading cause of bad decisions. Finally, temperance helps leaders remain calm and composed.[35] In Chapter 2, we'll discuss how leaders, particularly when facing failure, find hope, use good judgment, and regulate their visceral reactions.

Adidas Example

As a positive example, an Adidas apology demonstrates both accountability and compassion. Adidas sent an email to 2017 Boston Marathon participants with the subject line "Congrats, you survived the Boston Marathon!" The writer wasn't thinking about the terrorist attack four years prior, when two bombs killed three people and left several hundred injured.[36] Criticism came quickly, but so did Adidas's apology (Figure 1.5).[37]

Figure 1.5   Adidas apologizes

Source: Adidas. (2017, April 18). [Tweet]. Retrieved from https://twitter.com/adidasUS/status/854422872944771073?ref_src=twsrc%5Etfw&ref_url=http%3A%2F%2Fwww.npr.org%2Fsections%2Fthetwo-way%2F2017%2F04%2F19%2F524692534%2Fadidas-apologizes-for-congratulating-2017-boston-marathon-survivors

In this brief example, we see more than a crisis communication tactic. We see the glimmer of leadership character. Adidas's North America president Mark King spoke openly about the incident and, as in the apology, didn't blame anyone or excuse away the decision.[38] The message is simple and clear: the email was thoughtless.

The company managed to avoid further damage—to the victims and to the brand—by admitting the mistake and recognizing the impact. The social media response to Adidas's apology was positive because it demonstrated strong character and genuine concern for the impact of the mistake.

Leadership Character Has Organizational and Personal Benefits

Leadership character, demonstrated partly by communication, is important to a company's reputation and has additional benefits for organizations and individuals.

Corporate Reputation and Leader Communication

Communication may be the distinguishing factor in how leaders handle difficult situations. All organizations and leaders make mistakes. How leaders respond may impact a company in the long run more than the crisis itself. GM CEO Mary Barra recognized this in an email to employees during the company's ignition-switch recall trouble: "Our company's reputation won't be determined by the recall itself, but how we address the problem going forward."

Reputation reflects how people feel about a company's products and services and is correlated with stock prices, market valuation, and stock volatility.[39] To limit reputational damage during a crisis, crisis communication theory instructs leaders to use different approaches for different situations. For example, the situational crisis communication theory (SCCT) by Coombs and Holladay recommends apologizing when a crisis is perceived as preventable, which means the organization is likely responsible.[40]

In addition to managing the *organization's* reputation during a crisis, more and more, people care about a CEO's *personal* reputation. According to a Weber Shandwick study, 83% of executives believe a strong CEO reputation can protect the company against crises.[41]

Consumers agree with executives about the impact of a CEO's reputation on a company's reputation, and they point to a CEO's communication more specifically. In Weber Shandwick's survey, 59% of consumers responded that company leader communications are very or somewhat influential on their opinion of the company.[42] At no time is a leader's communication more visible than during a crisis.

At some point in a crisis situation, perception becomes reality. The biggest problem for the company is not the passenger removed from his seat or the faulty car brakes; it's the public's perception of the company and the perception of the leader, as GM's Mary Barra noted. The leader's focus shifts from solving the initial problem to limiting unnecessary damage to the brand. Crisis situations give leaders an opportunity to show the best of themselves and their organizations, and this requires good character and good communication.

Additional Organizational Benefits

In addition to helping a company manage through a crisis, leaders with strong character benefit their organizations in other ways. Although an emerging area of research, character has tangible, positive effects on organizations. KRW International in Minneapolis, led by Fred Kiel, has identified a "Return on Character™ Curve." Between 2006 and 2013, KRW researched 84 U.S. CEOs and compared data from 44 businesses. They found that leadership teams who rated highly on character aspects, such as integrity, responsibility, forgiveness, and compassion, had about five times the return on assets over a two-year period and 26% higher employee engagement than leaders who weren't rated well.[43,44]

Although Kiel admits his study doesn't prove causation, a *Harvard Business Review* writer summarizes the research:

> If Kiel's experience (and his clients') is any indication, character isn't just something you're born with. You can cultivate it and continue to hone it as you lead, act, and decide. The people who work for you will benefit from the tone you set. And now there's evidence that your company will too.[45]

Crossan's Leadership Character Framework is based on research from 1,817 leaders.[46] If failures of character contributed to the financial meltdown, and demonstrations of character helped companies withstand the recession, we can see powerful business implications for the future.

Throughout the book, we'll see research about additional organizational benefits of character dimensions and elements, such as authenticity, accountability, and integrity.

Personal Benefits

At all levels of an organization, leaders who demonstrate character have a positive effect on the people around them. Kiel describes the impact of character:

> Each of us constantly makes decisions about how to interact with other people, and each of those decisions has the potential to either harm or enhance the other person's well-being. So it would seem logical to assume that we are moral and have strength of character when our behavior enhances the well-being of others, and we are immoral and have less strength of character when our behavior harms or detracts from the well-being of others.[47]

For us personally, developing leadership character helps us live more meaningful lives as we do better for others. For example, we'll learn how vulnerability allows us to make connections with others, and we'll see the importance of authenticity for accepting who we are as people.

We approach character development through a process of self-reflection and self-development. We develop character as we develop ourselves—striving to be the best leaders and the best people we can be. Next we'll see the importance of judgment to ethical decision making and developing character.

Judgment Contributes to Ethical Decision Making

By developing leadership character, we become better equipped to manage through challenging ethical situations. Judgment is critical to good decision making, yet some organizational efforts to manage ethics do the opposite: they remove employees' ability to exercise good judgment. We see an example from United Airlines.

Ethical Challenges

Michael Lewis has been writing about the financial industry since 1986, when he worked as a "bond salesman" ("fixed income salesperson" today). His book and the 2015 movie *The Big Short* tell us more about what happened during the financial recession. In one scene in the movie, mortgage brokers brag about their big bonuses from making "NINJA" (no income, no job) loans. Unfortunately, these loans left people struggling to pay their monthly bills and inspired the email the former Countrywide CEO received.[48]

Even today, reports about risky loans continue, and the latest concern is student loans. The *New York Times* identified subprime loans sold by Navient—with the knowledge of government agency Sallie Mae. Attorneys general in Illinois and Washington have sued Sallie Mae for "predatory lending," calling the loans a "baited hook" and "designed to fail."[49]

In an article for *Bloomberg*, Michael Lewis warns of "occupational hazards of working on Wall Street," particularly the short-term focus and pressure not to question:

> The question I've always had about this army of young people with seemingly endless career options who wind up in finance is: What happens next to them? People like to think they have a "character," and that this character of theirs will endure, no matter the situation. It's not really so. People are vulnerable to the incentives of their environment, and often the best a person can do, if he wants to behave in a certain manner, is to choose carefully the environment that will go to work on his character.[50]

Lewis has a point: social norms are powerful. Studies show how susceptible people are to lying, cheating, and hurting others, given the right circumstances and context.[51] In addition, what is encouraged and rewarded in one group is not acceptable in another. Behavior accepted in a restaurant kitchen is quite different from that required in a corporate law firm or not-for-profit organization.

Of course, the financial sector isn't the only one suffering from what Crossan and her colleagues call "an apparent decline of ethical leadership."[52] In the Introduction, we saw airlines' failures, and throughout *Building Leadership Character*, we'll see examples from the automotive, technology, sports, service, and entertainment sectors. We can also find plenty of examples in politics. Leaders are tempted to do bad things in every country, in every company, and at every level of an organization.

Short-term thinking, for example, isn't exclusive to the finance industry. When hospitality managers were asked in a survey, "What do you consider to be the most pressing ethical challenges facing hospitality organizations today?" the top response was taking a short-term view.[53] Although not everyone would share Michael Lewis's cynicism, researchers and educators agree that organizational factors influence ethical decision making and that judgment is key to creating a path for doing better for more people.

The Role of Judgment

Crossan and her colleagues consider judgment central to "controlling when and how we choose to behave."[54] Elements of demonstrating judgment include being situationally aware, cognitively complex, analytical, decisive, a critical thinker, intuitive, insightful, pragmatic, and adaptable.[55] Judgment helps us decipher complex and conflicting information, which influences how we respond.

Leaders with good judgment understand the nuances in situations and have good instincts for how to handle challenging ethical dilemmas. When leaders demonstrate good judgment, they display the following behaviors:

- Consistently make good business decisions
- Add insight, direction, and clarity to problem-solving discussions
- Don't make assumptions or jump to conclusions
- Tailor solutions to the situation[56]

Crossan's team argues that character is "foundational for effective decision making." Although they acknowledge that some mistakes are made because of insufficient competence (for example, not having the skill set to perform a job), they assert that the "root cause" of mistakes is more likely a failure of character. Character is required, for example, to admit shortcomings, listen to other perspectives, and address discrimination.[57] These leadership functions require character and, more specifically, judgment.

James Rest and others have identified four psychological processes that someone who is "behaving morally" will perform. In each of these, we see the importance of judgment:

- Know the possible courses of action, who is affected, and the impact on each.
- Determine which courses are morally correct.
- Prioritize moral values over personal interests.
- Have the strength and skills to follow through.[58]

Although organizations try to manage ethical behavior, some efforts remove judgment and good decision making from an employee's job. In a review of 141 articles about business ethics, researchers identified many organizational factors that affect ethical behavior. Rules, rewards, policies, location of power, organizational climate, and communication are just some of the external forces that drive decision making.[59]

Some of these efforts may have a positive effect, but Stephen Cohen at the University of New South Wales warns against too many rules and regulations. Organizations' efforts to "systematize judgment" can be counterproductive, taking responsibility away from individuals and relying on organizational controls that ultimately fail.[60] Next and throughout the book, we'll see how this type of control often has the opposite effect of what is intended.

United Airlines Example

United Airlines CEO Oscar Munoz's communications illustrate how situational pressures and a dependence on procedures impede ethical decision making. One example of his communication is a tweet following the situation described in the book introduction (Figure 1.6). He posted the message after millions of people saw the video of the passenger, Dr. Dau, being dragged down the aisle of a United Airlines flight, unconscious with his bare belly showing. We hear his screams first and then passengers yelling in the background. Later, we learned that Dr. Dau lost two teeth and suffered a concussion and a broken nose, which explains the bleeding.

By all accounts, the CEO, Oscar Munoz, did not respond well. His tweet used jargon and didn't reflect any meaningful apology, particularly to Dr. Dao. In a leaked email to employees, Munoz referred to Dr. Dao as "disruptive and belligerent," which made the situation worse.

In his communication, we see competing pressures. As discussed earlier, airlines are under pressure to cut costs, which may explain why gate agents

Figure 1.6   Organizational factors affected United Airlines' response

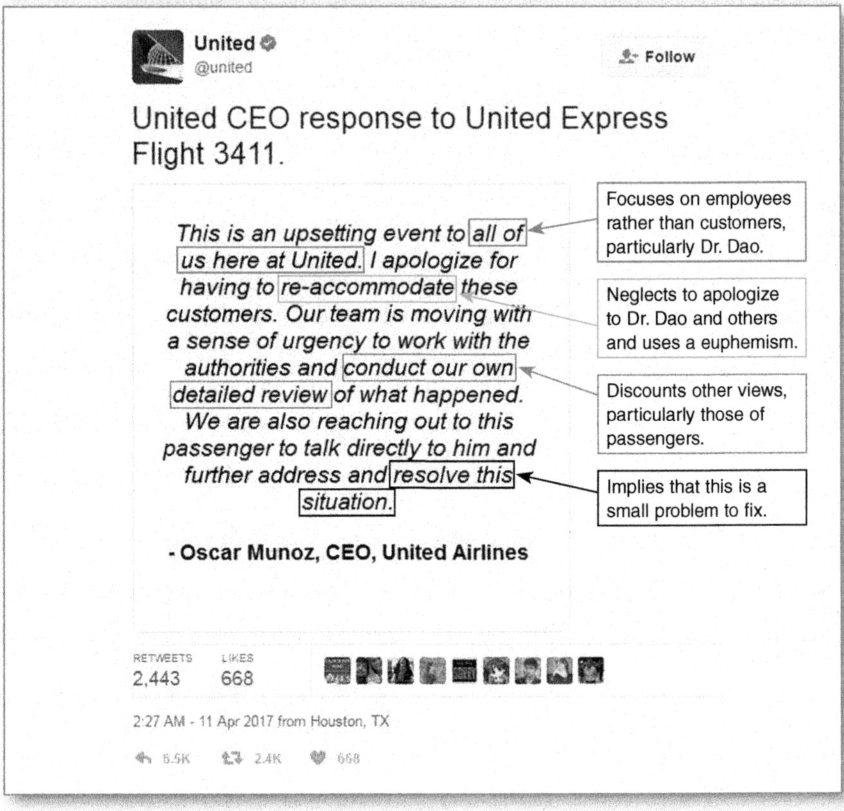

United ◎
@united   ⚷ Follow

United CEO response to United Express Flight 3411.

This is an upsetting event to all of us here at United. I apologize for having to re-accommodate these customers. Our team is moving with a sense of urgency to work with the authorities and conduct our own detailed review of what happened. We are also reaching out to this passenger to talk directly to him and further address and resolve this situation.

- Oscar Munoz, CEO, United Airlines

Focuses on employees rather than customers, particularly Dr. Dao.

Neglects to apologize to Dr. Dao and others and uses a euphemism.

Discounts other views, particularly those of passengers.

Implies that this is a small problem to fix.

RETWEETS   LIKES
2,443   668

2:27 AM - 11 Apr 2017 from Houston, TX

↩ 6.5K   ↻ 2.4K   ♥ 668

Source: United (@united), "United CEO Response to United Express Flight 3411," Twitter, April 10, 2017, https://twitter.com/united/status/851471781827420160, accessed May 9, 2017.

didn't offer passengers more money to take another flight. Munoz also defended his employees; perhaps unions created more pressure. In an email, Munoz wrote,

> Our employees followed established procedures for dealing with situations like this. While I deeply regret this situation arose, I also emphatically stand behind all of you, and I want to commend you for continuing to go above and beyond to ensure we fly right.[61]

Standing by his employees is commendable—and more than we'll see, for example, at Volkswagen and Wells Fargo, whose leaders almost immediately blamed their line-level employees.

But, by some accounts, United and airport employees have strict rules to follow and, as a result, failed to follow their conscience.[62,63] In a later email,

United admitted, "It happened because our corporate policies were placed ahead of our shared values. Our procedures got in the way of our employees doing what they know is right."[64]

This is precisely Cohen's concern: we are systematizing decision making rather than helping people use good judgment to make better ethical choices. Famous for its customer service, Nordstrom provides employees with one overarching rule: "Use good judgment in all situations."[65] Although this may be a simplification, Nordstrom associates are more likely to feel empowered to "do the right thing" in challenging customer situations. By encouraging judgment over following procedures, companies allow employees to put the customer first and consider many factors before making a decision.

Researchers of ethical decision making believe ethical breakdowns are a process—not an event.[66] With deteriorating ethics, people aren't given the chance to develop the judgment it takes to practice making better decisions and to develop leadership character.[67] Under pressure to follow written and informal rules, people live out of fear—afraid of not fitting in, not performing well enough, or losing their job.

From his years of experience, Chesley Sullenberger, the U.S. Airways pilot who safely landed the plane on the Hudson River, chose hope and faith instead of fear. In a congressional hearing, "Sully" said, "There's simply no substitute for experience in terms of aviation safety." His 42 years of flying certainly helped him make a good decision, but he also used good judgment. Despite recommendations to land at nearby airports, Sully took a risk and trusted in himself, his copilot, and his equipment to land safely in the water.

Sully embodied the elements of judgment identified by Crossan. He made a decision he could successfully carry out in the midst of a potentially catastrophic failure. Although not a guarantee of success, using good judgment means we make a sound decision by analyzing information, applying our insight, and adapting to the situation.

Corporate Failures Teach Us About Character—and About Ourselves

With judgment and ethical decision making as foundational concepts, we'll explore company failures to learn about character. Leaders' communications illustrate a great deal about their character and, more important, teach us about our own. The goal is to develop character by analyzing examples, understanding concepts and research, reflecting on our own strengths and areas for development, and practicing new behaviors.

Learning From Corporate Failures

The book profiles seven major communication failures—one for each dimension—in Chapters 3 through 9. In addition, we'll see many examples of leaders demonstrating good character both in *responding* to events and in *initiating* good business practices.

You'll recognize the companies featured in the book; most have solid brands, and all have been in the news for bad behavior. We can learn from each of them.

Vulnerability: Risking Exposure

This chapter will start with an overview of the Volkswagen emissions scandal, focusing on the executives' unwillingness to acknowledge the possibility of intentional deceit. Former CEO Martin Winterkorn will be featured in most detail.

Authenticity: Living as Yourself

General Motors' leader gave us both strong and weak examples of authenticity when the company delayed ignition-switch recalls. As a new CEO, Mary Barra may not have had the authority to do what she thought was right, but she eventually led the turnaround by showing the public who she really is and intends to be.

Integrity: Being Consistent and Whole

FIFA made headlines when officials were arrested for taking bribes and fixing the games. Despite a clear code of ethics, the coverups and lies at the most senior levels of the organization caused a loss of public trust, hurting athletes and fans across the world.

Accountability: Responding to Others

Former Wells Fargo CEO John Stumpf and the board didn't admit that a systemic compensation system pressured employees into opening accounts for customers who didn't request them. The company shirked its management responsibility and fired line-level employees instead.

Courage: Standing Up

When Samsung's Galaxy Note 7 phones were catching on fire, the company did recall them; however, replacement phones also exploded. The recall decision was hasty—a sign of wanting the trouble to simply go away—and was not handled with courage. The company was eventually forced to stop production, but only after further negative publicity and loss of consumer confidence.

Humility: Learning From Others

Uber will star in this chapter. CEO Travis Kalanick built a successful company but failed to see a view outside his own. Company decisions and embarrassing moments—for example, the video of Kalanick's interaction with an Uber driver—caused customer campaigns like #DeleteUber and led to his resignation.

Compassion: Caring for Others and Ourselves

Perhaps no company in the last few years was more oblivious than SeaWorld, which ignored criticism after the movie *Blackfish*. Social media backlash called on SeaWorld to answer for its treatment of captive orcas and related trainer deaths and injuries, but the company took years to respond in any meaningful way.

Respecting and Learning From Failure

Social media puts our character flaws on display—holds them up to the light for others to criticize and mock. All the leaders profiled in this book have been the subject of embarrassing late-night talk show monologues, memes, and tweets. Our intent isn't to throw more daggers.

No one wants to see his or her company in a crisis situation. Leaders called to respond during difficult times may do so reluctantly, and we can understand why. In some of these cases, the leaders got caught doing what they should not have done; in others, the leaders were willfully ignorant, rude, or insensitive; in still others, they may have been in the wrong place at the wrong time. Regardless of the circumstances, they were forced into what were often impossible situations. Given the breadth of their jobs and the magnitude of their constituencies, leaders will all disappoint someone. Unless we have had a similar experience, we cannot imagine the stress.

We also are not the final judge. For these companies, leaders' communications illustrate a failure in some respects and a success in others. We certainly can't conclude that any of the dozens of leader examples in the book either have character or do not. Character is not a dichotomy, and we see only a small window into these leaders' lives.

Emotional intelligence—an ability to understand ourselves and others—is critical to strengthening leadership character. We analyze these cases and communications and come to understand leaders' strengths and needs in our own terms. Through self-reflection and practice, we hone our ability and develop an approach for self-development.

The value of analyzing leaders' failures isn't merely to judge or gawk. It's to understand—with compassion, which will be the final character dimension covered in the book. And our critique isn't without purpose: we hope to do better for more people in our own lives. We learn from others' and from our own failures. In the next chapter, we'll look at failure as a powerful tool for learning.[68]

SUMMARY

We demonstrate character in nearly everything we do and develop character over time. Character-based leadership means seeking goals beyond our own interests. We strive for positive outcomes for others.

Researchers have identified character as the distinguishing factor in effective leadership. Competencies and commitment are important, but character drives ethical decision making.

Judgment is key in how we interpret information and make decisions. As we'll see throughout the book, too many rules and procedures remove people's ability to use good judgment. Instead, leaders need to give and receive the leeway to make good choices and to build character.

We'll explore seven character dimensions and will see positive and negative illustrations of each. Our journey to develop leadership character begins with understanding each dimension, analyzing others' communications, reflecting on our strengths and areas for development, and practicing new behaviors.

In the next chapter, we'll see the importance of failure to success and as a learning opportunity.

EXERCISES

Concept Review Questions

1. What is character, and how does it differ from competencies?

2. How is character developed?

3. What is the value of leadership character to organizations and to individuals?

4. Describe the role of judgment in ethical decision making.

Self-Reflection Questions

Self-reflection questions at the end of each chapter help you apply concepts to your own life. Understanding yourself is critical to developing leadership character.

1. Do you know someone you would describe as having strong character? How would you describe this person, and how does this example illustrate or contradict the definition in this chapter?

2. What would you like included in your obituary? It might help to think of who you are when you're at your best. How would you like others to remember you?

3. For your current or next job, how would you describe your purpose? Again, try to think beyond tactical outcomes, such as selling. What value do you or will you bring to the organization, your coworkers, customers, etc.? What impact do you or will you have on others?

4. Think about a time when you used good judgment. How did you add insight, avoid jumping to conclusions, and tailor a solution to make a good decision in the end?

5. At this point, how motivated are you to build leadership character? What is inspiring you, and what is discouraging you?

Mini-Cases

At the end of each chapter, you'll apply concepts to work-related scenarios. By practicing what to say and do in these cases, you will develop new habits in responding to difficult situations. This practice is one way to develop "moral muscle memory," such that making good ethical decisions and speaking up when necessary become the norm.

On your own or with a partner, discuss the best course of action in each case. What would you do, and what factors into your decision?

Scenario 1

You have landed a job interview with your favorite company. At the end of the interview, the hiring manager tells you that part of the job involves impersonating customers to get information about competitors. For example, you would pose as a customer to find out pricing for custom services; this information isn't available to the public but would help your prospective employer accurately price similar services. You know that many people in the industry do this, but you consider it unethical. One of your values is honesty, and you wouldn't feel comfortable giving a fake name or other information. Everything else about this job sounds great. What will you say during or after the interview to address the disconnection between your values and this company practice?

Scenario 2

A coworker or another student asks about a project team you're leading. She wants to join the group, but you have worked with her in the past and didn't have a good experience. She missed deadlines, and you had to rewrite much of her work. You value quality work and don't want her to be part of the team. How will you handle this situation?

Scenario 3

Your first day on a new job, two of your coworkers are telling you about one of your client accounts. They call the client a "whiner" and say she complains about everything. You want to meet her and form your own opinions, and you don't like the way your new coworkers are talking about a company client. What will you do in this situation?

Individual or Paired Activity

For this activity, you'll compare two examples from your work or other experience.[69] The purpose of this exercise is to see how you have taken action in a situation that conflicted with your values. Then, you will analyze a time when you didn't take action to see how you could have handled the situation differently.

Individual Planning Questions

1. First, think of a time when you were expected to do something that conflicted with your values, and you spoke up or acted in some way to address the situation.

   a. Briefly describe the context.

   b. What inspired you to do something?

   c. What did you do and how did it impact others?

   d. What are some things that would have made it easier for you to take action in this situation? Which of these were under your control, and which were outside your control?

   e. In retrospect, how did you do? You don't need to be too self-critical, but think about what would have been ideal in the situation.

2. Next, think of another situation in which you did not speak up or act when you were expected to do something that conflicted with your values or ethics.

   a. Briefly describe the context.

   b. What prevented you from speaking up? What would have motivated you to take action?

   c. What are some things that would have made it easier for you to take action in this situation? Which of these were under your control, and which were outside your control?

   d. In retrospect, what could you have done differently?

Partner Feedback

If you can work with a partner, discuss your responses and learn from each experience.

When talking about your own situation, you don't need to defend your actions or be too critical. When you listen to your partner's situation, you can ask clarifying questions or share similar experiences, but try not to judge the decision. Like you, your partner may be sensitive about actions taken or not taken.

At the end of your conversation, summarize the main learning points. What would you like to do more of in the future to develop leadership character?

2

Learning Character
Lessons From Failure

Chapter Overview

This chapter explains the importance of failure for success, the value of learning from failure, and the approaches we take to manage through failure. Throughout the book, we analyze leaders' failures in character and communication as one way to develop our own character. Although painful, failure presents an opportunity to build leadership character, which we do through self-reflection and by honing our judgment. We can manage failure intellectually, emotionally, and physically through reflection, mindfulness, and physical activity.

Failure Is Critical to Success

Rarely is success a straight line. We fail along the way, which inspires us to learn from our mistakes and to do better next time. In this section, we'll see an example at Amazon and will compare everyday failures to corporate crisis failures.

Amazon Example

In almost every letter to shareholders, Amazon CEO and founder Jeff Bezos emphasized failure. In a recent letter, he wrote, "I believe we are the best place in the world to fail (we have plenty of practice!)." We think of Amazon as a successful company, but it has had a string of failures: a hotel booking site called Destinations; an auction site called Amazon Auctions; and a smartphone, Fire Phone. Regarding the Fire Phone, Bezos boasts, "If you think that's a big failure, we're working on much bigger failures right now. And I am not kidding. And some of them are going to make the Fire Phone look like a tiny little blip."[1]

Bezos sees failure as part of invention, calling them "inseparable twins." He believes innovation involves being misunderstood for a period of time. Believing people learn from failure, Bezos hired former executives from a defunct online grocery delivery service to launch Amazon Fresh, Amazon's venture into grocery delivery.[2]

Common and Uncommon Failures

Everyone fails sometimes. As kids, we fall off our bikes and wet our pants; in middle school, we strike out in baseball and lose the spelling bee; in high school, we're not elected to class council and our girlfriend dumps us; as adults, we lose a job and get divorced. We also fail to take action: try out for the football team, ask the boy out, or stop a crime. We fail because we don't meet others' or our own expectations.

Although everyone experiences failure, in this book, we see company leaders fail colossally, publicly. In some ways, we are all the same: company leaders feel fear and anguish the way each of us does throughout our lives. But their failures are bigger, affect more people, and are more visible. People on social media, lurking throughout a crisis, will pounce and call something an "epic fail" just to get a laugh.

Leading and communicating during a crisis may be a leader's most significant challenge—whether the situation was created by the company's own doing or by external factors. Fortunately for us, we can analyze what went wrong in leaders' decisions and communications to learn about ourselves. Such failures are critical to success, giving us an opportunity to learn and to grow. At the same time, no one wants to fail. Next, we'll explore why that is the case.

People Fear Failure Because of the Pain

Failure can cost us time, money, and physical and emotional pain. Although these are tempting reasons to avoid failure, embracing failure opens more opportunities for us to live fulfilling lives and, as we'll see later, to build character.

The Pain of Failure

We can't get too much further without the obligatory, motivational quotes about failure (Figure 2.1).

These quotes are all true, of course, and this book *is* about learning from failure. But what is missing from these quotes is the *pain* and the *suffering*. Failure is painful: physically when we fall off a skateboard and emotionally when we lose a game. Failure can be embarrassing and humiliating—and can cause permanent damage to our bodies, our relationships, and our self-esteem. For a company, failure can mean the loss of reputation, revenue, market value, and jobs.

Most people avoid failure because they don't want to suffer. Particularly during crisis situations, what leader wouldn't rather hide than face the cameras, employees, investors, bloggers, and previously loyal customers? Leaders prefer to win at business—they have reached senior-level positions because they have won in the past.

Instead of suffering, we may be overwhelmed by fear, which serves as a protective shield. Fear of coworkers' criticisms, for example, may stop us

Figure 2.1   Motivational quotes about failure

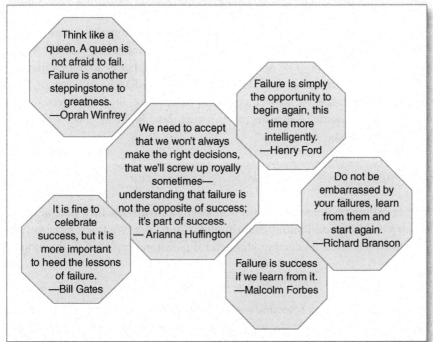

Source: Brainy Quote, "Failure Quotes," https://www.brainyquote.com/quotes/topics/topic_failure.html, accessed June 4, 2017.

from speaking out against wrongdoing. Fear of needing to change may prevent us from seeking feedback from others. Next, we'll see how one executive learned to embrace failure and face the lessons of suffering.

Shonda Rhimes Example

You might think the creator of hit TV shows *Scandal, How to Get Away With Murder, The Catch,* and *Grey's Anatomy* had it all together. Called "TV's Savior" by *The Hollywood Reporter,* Shonda Rhimes is a successful leader, but she experienced fear just like the rest of us. Because of her social anxiety, Rhimes declined opportunities that made her uncomfortable. Rhimes preferred to live in the world of fictional characters she created.[3]

In her TED Talk and book *Year of Yes,* Rhimes talks about the "hum" of work. She describes the hum as a drug and as "God's whisper right in my ear." She admits to using the hum—being a workaholic—to avoid disappointment and pain. She says, "I just know that I'm not built for failure, and I just know that I love the hum."[4] Over time, Rhimes learned to accept social and other opportunities that made her uncomfortable. She began to put people before work to live a more fulfilling, meaningful life.

People who try to avoid the pain of failure usually make things worse. The receptionist at a real estate company who hid under her desk for a half hour when the media came saw photos of the top of her head in newspapers and on websites the next day.[5] The CEO of a Canadian health care organization who refused to answer reporters' questions—insisting, repeatedly, "I'm eating a cookie"—lost his job the next day.[6] We'll see more examples in the coming pages.

Learning From Failure Builds Character

Facing failure is one path toward developing character, which begins when we are children and continues throughout our lives. We'll see how failure relates to the seven leadership character dimensions explored in this book.

Character Development in Children

Some elementary and secondary schools are emphasizing character in addition to academic success. Dominic Randolph, the head of the Riverdale Country Day School in New York City, talks about "fragile thoroughbreds"—kids who think life is easy. To promote character instead, he focuses on helping students leverage failure and learn from mistakes.[7] Other schools, such as KIPP, emphasize character as a critical part of college success.[8]

In other schools, some teachers focus on character development, including learning from mistakes. In his book *How Children Succeed*, Paul Tough profiles Elizabeth Spiegel, a junior high school teacher of a winning chess team. He explains, "Spiegel tries to lead her students down a narrow and difficult path: to have them take responsibility for their mistakes and learn from them without obsessing over them or beating themselves up for them." She can be harsh:

> Look, if you make a mistake, that's okay. But you do something without even thinking about it? That's not okay. I'm very, very, very upset to be seeing such a careless and thoughtless game.[9]

Spiegel is starting children on a path of self-development. She encourages reflection and learning from mistakes, cornerstones of developing character.

Failure and Character

Mistakes teach us how to succeed, and those are useful lessons. The kid who fell off his bike got back up; the middle schooler who lost the spelling bee studied harder; the woman who lost her job found a better one. As the saying goes, "If at first you don't succeed, try, try again."[10]

This is good advice, but failure offers more important lessons than success. Failure is a test of character, and it's an opportunity to build and rebuild character—the whole of how we think, feel, and act. Will we be resilient? Can we withstand it? Rise above it? Walk through it? Or do we collapse under the weight? Do we hide, or worse, hurt others to avoid getting hurt ourselves?

Failure teaches us to embrace complexity. When we're young, we tend to see things in terms of right and wrong. As we develop, we see more nuance instead of the false dichotomies of good and evil. We also take more responsibility for our actions and see the consequences of our behavior on others. With Spiegel's coaching, students see the impact of their behavior on the game—and on themselves. She's teaching them to use their judgment to improve.

Surviving failure—or better, learning from it, thriving from it—requires all of the character dimensions we'll discuss in the book, shown in Figure 2.2.

Success is important, but we have deeper lessons to learn and more to give as leaders and as people when we learn from failure. As we'll see next, a learning orientation helps us view failures as opportunities for self-development.

Figure 2.2   Learning from failure requires and builds character

- **Vulnerability** allows us to be open to failure, to risk emotional exposure and not fear failing.

- **Authenticity** brings us back to the core of who we are, which failure may help us find or renew.

- **Integrity** is tested by failure, to confirm we are truthful, trustworthy, and whole.

- **Accountability** ensures we learn the lessons we need from failure and share those lessons with others.

- **Courage** involves taking calculated risks that may cause failure and will help us face failure when it inevitably happens.

- **Humility** is a lesson from failure, to prevent us from becoming arrogant and to keep us open to learning from others.

- **Compassion** is kindness for others and for ourselves, a welcome result of failure.

Leaders Adopt a Learning Orientation

How do leaders respond when they encounter a failure? Our tendency may be to deny failure entirely. In addition, blaming and shaming people who fail is common, but adopting a learning orientation helps us weather the disappointment and focus on development.

Denying, Blaming, and Shaming

Our first reaction to failure may be denial. The Stanford Graduate School of Business's Advisory Council identified denial as the biggest obstacle to becoming a better leader.[11]

In his book *Adapt: Why Success Always Starts With Failure*, Tim Harford identifies typical reactions to failure: denying it happened, trying to undo the damage but making things worse, downplaying the mistake as insignificant, and reframing failures as successes.[12]

None of these reactions contributes to learning or developing leadership character. Learning from failure can be a painful process, but denial keeps us stuck where we are.

We also have to guard against blaming and shaming. Although convenient ways to control people, these tactics also prevent learning.

Amy Edmondson, a researcher at Harvard Business School, interviewed executives and found that they worried about allowing too much freedom for people to make mistakes. If people aren't blamed for failures, will they still perform at their best? When Edmondson showed executives several reasons failures happen, they admitted that only 2% to 5% really deserve blame (for example, intentionally violating a company policy), but "after a pause or a laugh," they said 70% to 90% would be "treated as blameworthy."[13]

Unfortunately, blaming and shaming tends to shut people down. They become disengaged and despondent, feeling that the mistake defines them. In the next chapter, on vulnerability, we'll see the devastating effects of shame.

Leaders get better results when they don't punish failure. In a 2015 Boston Consulting Group survey, 31% of respondents said a risk-averse culture—in which people fear making mistakes—prevents innovation.[14] A study published in the *Journal of Applied Behavioral Science* found a correlation between companies' tolerance for mistakes and revenue and profit growth over a five-year period.[15]

Edmondson found that leaders who, instead of blaming, focused on humility and curiosity encouraged people to admit mistakes. We'll explore these qualities and forgiveness in later chapters.

In addition to encountering blame from managers, we tend to blame and shame ourselves. We have little patience for failure. We want to get it right the first time, but an easy win doesn't inspire learning. Ongoing success without setbacks may mean we're not stretching ourselves. We need to push beyond success to expand what we know and how we work, and this often results in failure. With a learning orientation, we view failure as part of life.

Seeing Opportunities

When leaders focus on learning instead of blaming, they see possibilities for the future. Some leaders are achievement oriented (motivated by performance and material success), while others are learning oriented (motivated by opportunities for development). The latter group typically handles adverse situations better because they see events as opportunities instead of mere threats.[16]

With an inclination to reflect and learn from events, these leaders see what could be improved instead of what else could go wrong.[17] They acknowledge what happened and the impact on others, but they focus on the future. David Brooks introduces the idea of a "stumbler":

The stumbler doesn't build her life by being better than others, but by being better than she used to be. . . . The stumbler scuffs through life, a little off balance. But the stumbler faces her imperfect nature with unvarnished honesty, with the opposite of squeamishness. Recognizing her limitations, the stumbler at least has a serious foe to overcome and transcend. The stumbler has an outstretched arm, ready to receive and offer assistance. Her friends are there for deep conversation, comfort, and advice.[18]

The stumbler embraces failure to become a better person. Friends and coworkers can help us approach failure as learning opportunities. Offering comfort, admiration, and encouragement tells others we're rooting for them. This is one example of leading from any position: we support people in times of failure.

Learning From Success

In addition to failure, success offers a learning opportunity, but leaders sometimes miss the chance. Harvard Business School researchers Francesca Gino and Gary P. Pisano explain "why leaders don't learn from success":

- *When we succeed, we tend to give too much credit to our talents and our model or strategy and too little to external factors and luck.*
- *Success can make us so overconfident that we believe we don't need to change anything.*
- *We have a tendency not to investigate the causes of good performance.*[19]

Leaders have to be careful: too much success—the very thing that makes people rise through the corporate ranks—makes them overconfident. We attribute success to intelligence or to other factors we consider innate and disregard useful lessons. Asking questions about why the project turned out well or how we exceeded sales goals helps us recognize the many factors that contribute to success.

Remembering the Lessons

Companies also may learn from failure—and forget. Research on British Petroleum's Deepwater Horizon oil rig disaster and pharmaceutical firms found that a company's focus on safety, for example, is short-lived. During an initial focus on improvement, innovation falls. Then, after some time, the company succumbs to management and external pressures and safeguards decline. Companies cycle through these periods over time,[20] unable to maintain learning *and* innovation. We might say failure to learn and to retain learning are also failures of character.

A learning orientation helps us remember the past, to put the parts of our lives and character back together again and prepare to face the next challenge. Some organizations create a culture that fosters this process.

Forward-Looking Organizations Value Failure

While some companies avoid and punish failure, others value and reward it. Like Amazon, forward-looking companies understand the importance of learning from failure and know that taking risks, by definition, is a part of the process. We'll see more examples in this section.

Google X Example

The organizational culture at X, Google's innovation lab, encourages failure. The group works on "moonshot" products, such as driverless cars, Google Glass, and glucose-monitoring contact lenses. A *Fast Company* reporter calls the lab a "cult of failure" and quotes Rich DeVaul, the head of the project evaluation team: "Why put off failing until tomorrow or next week if you can fail now?" This philosophy is also evident on the company's "About" website page (Figure 2.3) and is a good lesson for leaders. Astro Teller, who leads the company, says he "sometimes gives a hug to people who admit mistakes or defeat in group meetings."[21]

Teller is describing the learning orientation we discussed for managing failures. This same mindset is valuable to organizations wanting to innovate; as Amazon's Bezos believes, invention and failure are closely related.

Figure 2.3   Google's X innovation lab encourages failure

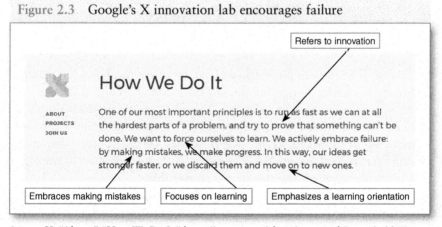

Source: X, "About," "How We Do It," https://x.company/about/, accessed June 12, 2017.

Celebrating Failure

Some companies and people not only value but publicize and celebrate failure. One of NASA's innovation awards is called the Lean Forward, Fail Smart Award.[22] Advertising agency Grey boasts a "culture of creativity" and has a Heroic Failure Award.[23]

In Sweden, an entire museum is dedicated to failure. The Museum of Failure features products you probably never heard of: Coca-Cola's BlāK, a coffee-flavored soft drink; Crystal Pepsi, a clear soda; Harley-Davidson cologne; and a Donald Trump board game.[24]

A Princeton University professor posted his "Failure CV," highlighting the academic programs he didn't get into, the journals that rejected his articles, and the funding he didn't receive. He summarizes the long list with a "meta-failure": "This darn CV of Failures has received way more attention than my entire body of academic work."[25]

These examples take the shame out of failing. The more we normalize failure as part of life, the more we can learn from it. Next, we'll see how the practice of self-reflection helps us deal with failure.

Self-Reflection Helps Us Learn From Failure

Being part of an organization that values failure helps leaders focus on self-development. We experience and process failure with our minds, hearts, and bodies. The practice of self-reflection helps sharpen our intellectual accuracy, emotional honesty, and visceral expression. Honing our judgment, developing emotional intelligence, and practicing two types of reflection help us accurately assess and learn from failure.

Honing Judgment

In Chapter 1, we saw the importance of judgment to ethical decision making. Judgment is equally important for self-reflection. Through reflection, we notice what is going on around us—the thoughts, emotions, and actions that influence us and others. By nature, we are judgmental. We know a common negative use of the word, as in, "You're so judgmental." But, by definition, everything is judged, or intuitively perceived, in some way—for example, as positive or negative, pleasurable or not pleasurable.

We try to accurately identify what we observe and experience, but we are prone to misinterpretations. For example, we may overreact to negative feedback or miss social cues. By sharpening our judgment, we can improve how we take in and react to information.

One approach to honing our judgment is to take a holistic perspective. We need a larger perspective for two reasons. First, at all ages, we tend to perceive our suffering as more serious than that of others who have gone through the same or worse. Second, we perceive our personal efforts as having been more determinative of our success or failure than is realistic. We need to keep ourselves and our failures in perspective.

To take a more holistic perspective, we judge, but we see ourselves and others in context, as part of a larger system, and we engage others in the process. This process involves emotional intelligence, which is the ability to observe our emotional reactions, thoughts, and actions and to interpret them from many points of view. Then, our self-reflection can be more accurate.

Developing Self-Awareness

In this book, we develop self-reflection first by reflecting on others' successes and failures. We study the character and communications of leaders as a way to learn about ourselves—and to develop emotional intelligence.

From interviews with 125 leaders, researchers identified the most important aspect of being an effective leader as self-awareness. Self-awareness also was identified as "the most important capability for leaders to develop" by the 75 members of the Stanford Graduate School of Business's Advisory Council.[26]

Author of the book *Emotional Intelligence*, Daniel Goleman identifies self-awareness as the first component. With a deep understanding of emotions, strengths, and weaknesses, we improve our self-awareness and can be honest with ourselves and with others—neither "overly critical nor unrealistically hopeful."[27]

To learn from a failure, this balance is critical. We don't deny failure, but we can't self-flagellate either. Leaders who are self-aware rise above problems rather than seeing themselves as victims or punishing themselves; they are not defined by failure. Particularly in difficult situations, leaders have to lead; people depend on them to figure out what happened and to find solutions. By being introspective and learning from our experiences, we can try on different ways of being and behaving, particularly when our old ways no longer work for us or those around us.[28]

Practicing Reflection

Self-reflection allows us to critically examine our actions and our relationships with others. We practice reflection in two ways: reflection *on* action and reflection *in* action. Reflecting on action requires us to step back from a situation and ask ourselves tough questions—for example, "How did I fail my friend and myself so badly when I didn't intend to?" "How did I manage to do that well today when I have never done it well before?" "What is my role in the project delay?"

Reflection *in* action means interpreting information in real time. How are people reacting to you? Is your approach getting you what you need? This process is about assessing feedback loops—how people respond to each other.

Whether reflecting alone or in a group, try to assess intellectual, emotional, and physical effects. We want to get the facts straight so we can accurately interpret actions and reactions. We want to be honest about our emotional experience, so we let ourselves feel what we need to feel instead of denying our emotions. And we want to be aware of visceral reactions that explain what happened or should have happened. For example, if you had a job interview that didn't go well, you might review the questions and your responses, let yourself feel disappointed or upset, and assess the interviewer's physical reaction to you and your physical reaction to the disappointment. The better you are at judging or interpreting these signals, the more value you'll find in self-reflection to develop leadership character. Next, we'll look at tools for practicing self-reflection.

Reflection Prepares Us Intellectually

When we fail, we want an explanation that's reasonable, that makes sense. We want to avoid the mistake in the future and to achieve the goal we missed or try to achieve a new, more realistic goal. Many methods can help us develop reflection and identify opportunities for improvement. Two are presented here with a recommendation for making time for reflection.

Post-Event Review

Most major organizations have a crisis communication plan for the inevitable, and they typically include time after the event to reflect on how the crisis was handled and to plan for the next one. In its comprehensive plan, JetBlue includes evaluation questions, recognizing that nothing will go perfectly. For example, to evaluate the team, questions include the following:

- Were there certain members who should have been put "behind the scenes" or on the "front lines" (speaking to the media, etc.)?
- Should any members be replaced should another crisis occur?
- Did all team members perform well under pressure? [29]

Other organizations ask similar questions and may call the process an autopsy or postmortem. The U.S. Army follows an After-Action Review (AAR) model, which has been adopted by other organizations (Figure 2.4).

Figure 2.4   After-Action Review encourages self-reflection

The After-Action Review (AAR)
• Is a dynamic, candid, professional discussion • Focuses on results of an event/task/activity • Identifies how to sustain what was done well • Identifies recommendations on how to improve shortfalls • Requires everyone's participation to help identify and correct deficiencies or maintain strengths
The AAR Is Not
• A critique or complaint session (everyone learns from each other) • A full-scale evaluation (or evaluation report) • A cure-all for all problems
The AAR Is Effective When
• Leaders support it • It is done immediately—by the team, for the team • Participants agree to be honest

Source: "After-Action Review: Technical Guidance," USAID From the American People, http://pdf.usaid.gov/pdf_docs/PNADF360.pdf, accessed June 4, 2017.

Post-event reviews evaluate successes as well as failures. The process can be formal, with a facilitator, or informal, and answers four questions:

- What was expected to happen?
- What actually occurred?
- What went well, and why?
- What can be improved, and how?[30]

Johari Window

In addition to these organizational processes, we can follow a model called the Johari Window. This classic model is one way to learn about ourselves and our relationships with others.

The grid shows how we assess ourselves and how others perceive us (Figure 2.5). Columns represent the individual (what you know or don't know about yourself), and rows represent a group (what others know or don't know about you). The four quadrants—or panes—illustrate the following:

- Arena: what is known to you and known to others
- Blind spot: what is unknown to you but known to others

Figure 2.5   The Johari Window is one tool for self-awareness

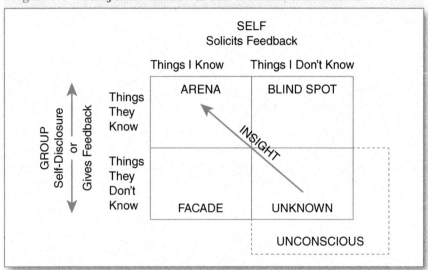

Source: Joseph Luft, "The Johari Window: A Graphic Model of Awareness in Interpersonal Relations," reproduced in National Training Laboratory, 1982, http://www.convivendo.net/wp-content/uploads/2009/05/johari-window-articolo-originale.pdf, accessed August 7, 2017.

- Facade: what is known to you but not known to others
- Unknown: what is unknown to you and unknown to others

Conceptually, the model is a way of thinking about how well we know ourselves in relation to how others know us. We develop over time by increasing our arena, so we know ourselves as we are known to others. By reducing our blind spots, we come to understand what others know about us. By reducing our facade, we are more open with others about what we know about ourselves.

Practically, the model can be used by selecting adjectives that describe you and asking others to do the same. Resources at the end of the chapter walk you through the process.

We can use simpler methods for self-reflection. Col. Eric Kail, an Army field artillery officer who directs a military leadership course at West Point, suggests simple questions for reflection, preferably asked by a mentor—for example, "What could you have done better, and why?" and, "Did you do anything wrong?"[31] When asked with a focus on learning and without blame, these simple questions work well.

Enlisting help from a mentor, trusted friend, or colleague is a good idea. Others help us learn from mistakes without being too hard on ourselves. We'll revisit the importance of being open to feedback throughout the book. Openness is relevant to many character dimensions; for example, it takes vulnerability to risk emotional exposure and humility to hear perceptions that conflict with your own.

Time for Reflection

The intellectual self-reflection process is essential to learning and requires time, but not too much time. A study at a global IT firm compared workers who participated in technical training with and without time for reflection. During just 15 minutes at the end of each day, workers thought about and wrote down lessons they learned. At the end of the training period, workers who had spent time reflecting performed 20% better on a test than staff who had worked through the time without reflection.[32]

The authors report similar results in other settings and organizations and recommend strategies for building downtime into work schedules. Taking vacation and taking breaks during the day, for example, have proven to increase productivity.[33] Many of us are overscheduled and fill our lives with busyness: meeting for no reason, obsessively checking email, constantly texting, signing up for activities we're not invested in, and overcommitting to social events. Scheduling downtime may be the best way to allow time for reflection and learning.

At the end of each chapter in this book are self-reflection questions and activities to develop each character dimension. These exercises focus on failures as well as successes.

Practicing Mindfulness Prepares Us Emotionally

To learn from failure and develop character, we must learn how to observe and hold on to emotionally painful experiences without indulging them. We must become self-aware, emotionally. This involves a measure of self-restraint. Emotional honesty requires slowing down the process of reacting. When we avoid reacting too quickly, we begin to observe and assess emotions in ourselves and others.

Failure and Emotions

As discussed, our first responses to failure are usually knee-jerk reactions: denial of our role in the experience or blaming and shaming ourselves or others. Once we start down the path of these reactions, the emotional consequences of failure can be severe. Our feelings may be hijacked by one sensitive, exposed nerve. Our minds may become fixated, unable to stop rehearsing what did or did not happen. Our bodies may become tense and crippled, unable to relax or sleep. To learn from failure requires that we learn to suffer through negative emotions without being overwhelmed by them.

We cannot avoid failure or loss; those experiences will find us. We cannot avoid emotional pain, except perhaps through addiction, which obviously isn't a good choice.

Instead, once we are aware of failure and sense a knee-jerk reaction emerging, the first step toward emotional honesty is to accept what has happened as simply a fact of life. We can't always control what happened, but we may be able to control our reactions. Being self-aware in these situations means observing ourselves to more accurately recognize our emotional state and that of others.

Health care professionals and psychologists use images of faces to help people identify pain and emotion. You may have seen the posters, "How are you feeling today?" that show different facial expressions. This simple tool is one way to slow down our reactions. We take this step before trying to manage our emotions too quickly, for example, by suppressing them or by being undone by them. Next, we'll see how practicing mindfulness is another approach to honoring emotion without indulging it.

The Value of Mindfulness

When asked how people can develop self-awareness, Daniel Goleman suggested practicing mindfulness:

> Self-awareness means the ability to monitor our inner world—our thoughts and feelings. Mindfulness is one method for enhancing this essential capacity—it trains our attention to notice subtle, but important signals, and to see thoughts as they arise rather than just being swept away by them.[34]

Plenty of research demonstrates the value of meditation and mindfulness for reducing stress and work conflicts and increasing satisfaction and resilience.[35] In one study, university students who experienced anxiety about academic evaluation (for example, taking tests) participated in a mindfulness-based stress reduction program. After eight weeks, the students experienced positive results in these areas: "(1) finding an inner source of calm, (2) sharing a human struggle, (3) staying focused in learning situations, (4) moving from fear to curiosity in academic learning, and (5) feeling more self-acceptance when facing difficult situations."[36]

Because of the positive results of mindfulness, several companies have encouraged employees to engage in the practice. Deutsche Bank, BASF, Monsanto,[37] Target, General Mills,[38] Capital One Finance, and the NHS Mental Health Trust[39] are some of the companies that see the benefits of mindfulness at work.

Google Example

Google, for example, offers mindfulness training called Search Inside Yourself, which thousands of employees have taken since 2007.[40] The leader of the program, Chade-Meng Tan, says his practice made him a kinder person:

> If you don't have the foundation of peace, joy, and kindness, it is very hard, day to day, to always do the right thing. If somebody says something negative, your first thought is "that guy is an a_____,"[41] and you want to defeat that guy. So it takes a certain amount of practice to say "Wait a minute, that guy's just doing his job. He's a good person, and so I have to work with him by understanding why he's doing that, and then help him succeed."[42]

Meng describes three aspects of Search Inside Yourself:

- *Attention training:* At any time, whatever is happening to you—whether you're under stress, you're being shouted at, or anything else—you have the skill to bring the mind to a place that's calm and clear. If you can do that, it lays the foundation for emotional intelligence.
- *Self-knowledge:* Once your mind is calm and clear, you can create a quality of self-knowledge or self-awareness that improves over time, and it evolves into self-mastery. You know about yourself enough that you can master your emotions.
- *Creating mental habits:* For example, there is the mental habit of kindness, of looking at every human being you encounter and thinking to yourself, "I want this person to be happy." Once that becomes a habit, you don't have to think about it; it just comes naturally.[43]

We can see the benefits of mindfulness to building leadership character. Training our minds reduces stress and anxiety, which allows us to become more self-aware and able to learn from failure. Mindfulness builds emotional resilience and helps us be more compassionate, which is one of our character dimensions.

Compassion is important in how we interact with others, and being compassionate with ourselves is important too—particularly when we fail.

Taking Care of Our Bodies Prepares Us Physically

Practicing good physical self-care helps us manage our visceral or gut reactions. Although these reactions are part of our core being, they may work against us in developing leadership character.

Visceral Responses

Failure and other challenges often provoke physical as well as emotional reactions. In her book *Animals Make Us Human*, Temple Grandin, a high-functioning woman with autism, helps us appreciate how animals and humans share core emotional processes.[44] Our visceral, or "gut-level," responses help us identify, establish, and maintain the physical space we need. Our physical senses benefit us by keeping us safe and by giving us pleasure.

We're hardwired for positive and negative experiences. We're curious about the world around us, care for others, and seek pleasure through play and lust. We're also hardwired to be angry or frustrated when we're thwarted in our attempts to achieve our goals, and to react with fear or panic when we're threatened.

Both positive and negative biological processes can be problematic. Unrestrained curiosity, care, play, or lust can be disruptive or damaging. Although fear, panic, and rage may protect us, they can also completely stymie us and those around us. Focusing these visceral processes for our benefit, yet avoiding excess in either the positive or negative aspects, is a core issue in the development of character.

In addition, positive and negative experiences are not equal. We are far more sensitive to what is negative or threatening than we are to what is positive or an opportunity, which is important for our evolutionary protection. But often, our reactions are so immediate that we are unaware of why we did what we did.

Let's take an example of a manager yelling at you for making a mistake. Do you yell back? Do you quit? Are you in shock and do you not respond? These are biological "fight," "flight," and "freeze" reactions, and none is particularly helpful in this situation. In a moment of fear or panic, people will react differently; knowing and managing our reactions may help us "stay in the moment."

Exercise and Breathing

Without some control over our reactions, we will have a difficult time reducing our stress. Exercise, mindful breathing, and yoga can reduce blood pressure, anxiety, depression, and aggression—and increase optimism, pain management, and emotional and impulse control. Part of practicing mindfulness is focusing on the simplicity of breathing and limiting all other stimuli, especially stressful thoughts and emotions. Amy Cuddy's research at Harvard Business School explores using our bodies to manage fear and stress, and she notes these and other benefits from yoga.[45,46]

As we might expect, people under stress tend to reduce physical activity.[47] This is unfortunate because, as you probably know, in addition to mindful breathing, physical activity reduces stress.[48] Research shows that physical activity decreases perceptions of[49] and sensitivities to[50] stress, so it serves as a buffer and protects us. Physical activity can be as simple as walking, singing, or dancing. People who are more physically fit also have lesser physiological symptoms and recover more quickly when exposed to stress; they experience lower blood pressure spikes, and their pulse rate decreases faster.[51]

With the physical benefits of mindful breathing and exercise, we may reduce the physical and psychological impacts of failure so we can get on to the work of seeking new knowledge for self-improvement. With greater physical and emotional awareness, we can accept conflicting perspectives about what is real and helpful and maintain a clearer balance between ourselves and others. When we are in good physical shape, well rested, and nourished, our curiosity will run freer and operate with greater clarity. In other words, we will have an easier time adopting a learning orientation when failure inevitably strikes.

SUMMARY

Failures are a necessary part of success and are critical to innovation. We have to take risks in order to succeed, and by definition, some risks will not turn out as planned. Failure presents an opportunity for us to learn, and we do this by neither dismissing nor wallowing in our situation.

Although our tendency may be to deny failure or to blame ourselves or others, adopting a learning orientation ensures we take the lessons we need. Organizational cultures can foster learning, and some reward and celebrate failure.

Failure affects us intellectually, emotionally, and physically, and strategies that address all three are important for character development. We can manage through failure by engaging in self-reflection, mindfulness, and physical activity.

In the next chapter, we'll explore the first character dimension, vulnerability. Vulnerability helps us acknowledge and accept failure when it does happen.

Concept Review Questions

1. Why do people avoid failure?

2. What are typical, unhelpful, reactions to failure?

3. Describe the value of self-reflection to learning from failure.

4. What are some ways to manage through failure intellectually, emotionally, and physically?

Self-Reflection Questions

1. How do you view failure? Write down words you associate with failure.

2. How does your view of failure affect how you live your life? Do you tend to avoid failure, embrace it, or something else?

3. Think of a time you failed and learned a great lesson. What was the experience, and what did you learn? If you had to do it over, would you do anything differently?

4. When you do fail at something, how do you learn from it? Do you have a practice you follow?

5. Now think of a time when someone close to you failed and you helped the person reflect on what happened. How was the experience for you? What did you learn?

6. Describe a mistake you made—twice. Where did the learning fall short?

7. How do you typically react to failure and stress physically? What helps you cope? What physical activity could help you in the future?

Assessment

Use the Johari Window model in Figure 2.5 to identify how you perceive yourself and how others perceive you. Complete this activity with a team or a group of people who know you. First, place adjectives in each of the four quadrants for yourself; then ask others to do the same for you. You will find an online version with a list of adjectives at http://kevan.org/johari.cgi, or you can choose your own adjectives.

When you get the results, discuss what you learned with your team. What most surprised you about what others know or don't know about you? Which quadrant should get your attention? Do you want to reduce your blind spots, increase the arena, etc.? How will changing the windowpanes benefit you and the team?

Mini-Cases

Consider the following scenarios. On your own or with a partner, discuss the best course of action in each case. What would you do, and what factors into your decision?

Scenario 1

In the middle of a job interview, you hit the hiring manager's box of paper clips, which land all over the office.[52] You thought the interview was going well before that point. How will you handle the situation?

Scenario 2

You have been working on a team project for the past four months. You were excited about submitting the first deliverable, a recommendation report, to your manager. Unfortunately, your manager isn't happy with the results. The team received an email with pointed questions about your conclusions and how you got the results. How will you discuss the feedback and plan next steps with the team? You're disappointed, but you want to approach the situation as a learning opportunity.

Scenario 3

One of your coworkers returned from a sales call looking upset. She said sarcastically, "That went well." You ask, "What happened?" She says she doesn't want to talk about it. How can you help her in this situation?

Individual Activity

Ask yourself four questions to practice self-reflection:[53]

1. Who am I? What are my character strengths and deficiencies today?

2. Who am I becoming? What is my character today, and what is it likely to be tomorrow if I continue the way I'm doing things now?

3. Who do I want to be? What would I like to change about my character to achieve greater satisfaction and impact on others?

4. What am I going to do to become who I want to be? What actions will I take, by when, to develop my character? How will I assess my progress?

Team Activity

With a team you have worked with in the past, reflect on your experience. Use the After-Action Review process and discuss the four questions:

- What was expected to happen?
- What actually occurred?
- What went well, and why?
- What can be improved, and how?

After you respond to these questions, summarize your discussion. What did you learn about yourselves and about your work as a team? What will you do differently next time?

Paired Activity

With a partner, share your views on failure. Then discuss mindful meditation and prepare to practice.

Planning Questions

1. What are your views on failure? How has your attitude about failure changed over the years?

2. What are your views on mindfulness and meditation? What do you know about the topics in addition to what you have read in this chapter?

3. Have you tried meditation? Is it a regular practice for you?

4. How open are you to trying meditation?

Practice and Reflection

Take turns talking, and allow plenty of time after each person speaks to listen and ask clarifying questions.

Individual Activity

If mindful breathing isn't part of your daily practice, try it for at least five minutes a day for a week. Consider one of Thich Nhat Hanh's guided breathing meditations,[54] or follow instructions from The Greater Good Science Center at the University of California, Berkeley.[55] The video and website follow similar steps to walk you through the process: finding a comfortable position, relaxing your body, observing your breathing, and focusing your attention.

Reflection Questions

After one week, reflect on your experience and consider sharing your experience with a partner:

1. Overall, how was the experience for you?

2. How, if at all, did the experience change throughout the week?

3. How, if at all, did the experience change your view of meditation?

4. Will you continue the practice after the week? Why or why not?

3

Vulnerability

Risking Exposure

Chapter Overview

For our first major case, we'll see how Volkswagen leaders avoided vulnerability at a tremendous cost to the company. They deceived customers and regulators with a software device to mask emissions and then covered up their deceit for as long as possible. They didn't want to admit failure and risk exposure, which would have limited fines and damage to the brand. Leaders who demonstrate vulnerability are open emotionally and are willing to apologize when they're wrong. Vulnerability builds connection and fosters solidarity. Vulnerability is the act of opening ourselves up to other influences even when that connection may threaten us personally or professionally.

Volkswagen's "Clean Diesel" Dupes Customers

Volkswagen made headlines in 2015 when the company was questioned about emissions from its diesel vehicles. Nitrogen oxide (NOx) emissions were significantly lower in test situations than on the road. The U.S. Environmental Protection Agency accused the company of installing software, later called "defeat devices," to cheat emissions tests. Volkswagen eventually admitted that more than 11 million vehicles worldwide, including TDI diesel models of Jettas, Golfs, Beetles, Porsche Cayennes, Audis, Touareg SUVs, and Passats, had the device installed.[1]

In addition to the environmental impact and legal trouble, the company had an immediate public relations problem. VW had cheated the government as well as consumers. Volkswagen had advertised its new line of cars as using "Clean Diesel" technology, which sounds like an oxymoron—and now we know that it is (Figure 3.1).

With the slogan, "Diesel—It's No Longer a Dirty Word," Volkswagen launched an aggressive advertising campaign targeting customers who considered themselves "responsible," "progressive," and "environmentally conscious." The company's U.S. marketing department concluded that this group would "rationalize themselves out of their aspirations and justify buying lesser cars under the guise of being responsible."[2]

While reading the newspaper, scanning Facebook, or watching the Super Bowl, customers saw ads such as "Three Old Wives Talk Dirty." In one 30-second spot, three women debate "Old Wives Tale #6: Diesel Is Dirty" in a Volkswagen Golf TDI (Figure 3.2).

Customers were drawn to Volkswagen's claims that these cars had 95% fewer NOx emissions than gasoline cars. However, they didn't realize they were driving around town spewing up to 4,000% more than the legal limit. According to the Federal Trade Commission's filing, the company's "Clean Diesel" models "have contributed—and will continue to contribute—to environmental and human health harms including smog, acid rain, water quality deterioration, childhood asthma, adult respiratory ailments, and premature death."

Customers wanted to do the right thing for the environment, but they didn't get what VW promised: "fuel efficient, clean emissions vehicles that are also fun to drive."[3] VW leaders denied responsibility, which we'll discuss in Chapter 6, but our focus here is on their refusal to be vulnerable.

Vulnerability Means Risking Exposure

In the previous chapter, we discussed the tendency to deny failure. Allowing ourselves to be vulnerable is critical to facing failure and being

Figure 3.1   Volkswagen's diesel crisis unfolds

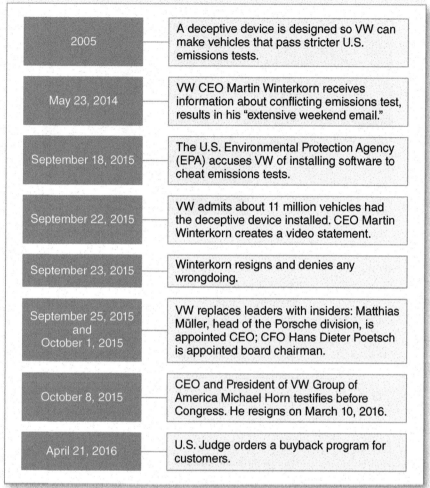

2005	A deceptive device is designed so VW can make vehicles that pass stricter U.S. emissions tests.
May 23, 2014	VW CEO Martin Winterkorn receives information about conflicting emissions test, results in his "extensive weekend email."
September 18, 2015	The U.S. Environmental Protection Agency (EPA) accuses VW of installing software to cheat emissions tests.
September 22, 2015	VW admits about 11 million vehicles had the deceptive device installed. CEO Martin Winterkorn creates a video statement.
September 23, 2015	Winterkorn resigns and denies any wrongdoing.
September 25, 2015 and October 1, 2015	VW replaces leaders with insiders: Matthias Müller, head of the Porsche division, is appointed CEO; CFO Hans Dieter Poetsch is appointed board chairman.
October 8, 2015	CEO and President of VW Group of America Michael Horn testifies before Congress. He resigns on March 10, 2016.
April 21, 2016	U.S. Judge orders a buyback program for customers.

Sources: "One Year Later: Timeline of Volkswagen Diesel Emission Scandal," *Chicago Tribune*, September 21, 2016, http://www.chicagotribune.com/classified/automotive/ct-timeline-volkswagen-diesel-emission-scandal-20160921-story.html, accessed June 14, 2017; "Timeline: Volkswagen's Long Road to a U.S. Dieselgate Settlement," *Reuters*, January 11, 2017, http://www.reuters.com/article/us-volkswagen-emissions-timeline-idUSKBN14V100, accessed June 14, 2017.

able to learn from it. Vulnerability means being open and willing to risk emotional exposure. Although a weakness in some circumstances, vulnerability is a strength in relationships.

Figure 3.2   VW commercial explains "Clean Diesel"

Woman 1:	How do you like my new car?
Woman 2:	Isn't diesel dirty?
Woman 3:	Ohhhh, just say it's beautiful for Christ's sake!
Woman 2:	I think it's beautiful, but aren't diesels dirty?
Woman 3:	Yeah, that's true.
Video Caption:	Old Wives' Tale #6: Diesel is Dirty
Woman 1:	Oh, that used to be dirty. This is 2015.
Woman 3:	No no no, no no no. Listen to me, Terry. Diesel in Latin means dirty.
Woman 1:	I'll prove it to you.
Woman 3:	You're going to ruin your scarf! Oh, look what she's doing!
Woman 1:	See how clean it is?
Woman 3:	It's not dirty, but you still have a dirty mind!
Woman 1:	I do not.

Source: "FTC Charges Volkswagen Deceived Consumers With Its 'Clean Diesel' Campaign," Federal Trade Commission, March 29, 2016, https://www.ftc.gov/news-events/press-releases/2016/03/ftc-charges-volkswagen-deceived-consumers-its-clean-diesel, accessed June 10, 2017.

Vulnerability Defined

Brené Brown at the University of Houston Graduate College of Social Work popularized the idea of vulnerability in her TED Talks, which have garnered millions of views. She defines vulnerability as accepting "uncertainty, risk, and emotional exposure"—what we face every day of our lives.[4]

From hundreds of interviews, Brown identified vulnerability as one way to ward against shame. She defines shame as "an intensely painful feeling or experience of believing we are flawed and therefore unworthy of acceptance and belonging." Shame leads to feeling trapped, isolated, and powerless.[5]

Perhaps paradoxically, vulnerability offers resilience from shame. By acknowledging negative events and feelings, we allow others to offer empathy. When others relate to us in this way, our feelings are normalized; in other words, we don't feel so alone. Then we can accept our feelings and begin to develop strategies for managing through them.[6]

We are vulnerable, for example, when we approach new situations and when we face failure. Let's take an example of starting a new job. You may feel excited, but you probably also feel uncertain about the job expectations and your ability to do well. Maybe you took a risk by changing jobs, and the responsibilities are a stretch for you. Or maybe you face emotional exposure with your coworkers when trying to build relationships and by revealing what you don't know by asking questions.

Most people approach a new job with vulnerability, and this is expected of new employees. Otherwise, you may be perceived as a know-it-all. Coworkers expect us to be a little awkward during lunch, to ask questions, and to make mistakes. In this example of a new job, we see vulnerability as a strength—a willingness to expose our weaknesses in order to form relationships and to learn.

We're also vulnerable when we inevitably fail. We feel rejected when our new coworkers go to lunch without inviting us. We're frustrated when we struggle to complete an assignment. And we're embarrassed when we make mistakes. But we face these setbacks rather than denying them, as we learned in the previous chapter.

Instead of spiraling into shame, we reach out and talk about what is troubling us. We take the risk and demonstrate vulnerability in an effort to form connections.

VW in Denial

Former CEO Martin Winterkorn and others wanted to protect themselves and the company, yet they put the company and themselves in a worse position. The Harris Poll 2016 Reputation Quotient showed Volkswagen last out of 100 automotive companies in February 2016, with an overall rating of "very poor."[7] In addition, the company paid $22 billion in restitution,[8] Audi paid an additional $1.2 billion,[9] and six VW leaders face criminal charges in the United States.[10]

We see two significant examples of VW leaders avoiding vulnerability. First, creating a cheating device allowed the company to pass EPA tests and to keep up with increasing competition for environmentally friendly vehicles. Without a competitive model, the company could have forfeited revenue and market share. Instead, they used deception to build loyalty to the brand.

Second, internally, the company spent years covering up the software manipulation. When it became clear that regulators knew about the device, employees "destroyed thousands of documents" and "generated reams of false or misleading data."[11] Only when the Environmental Protection Agency threatened not to approve upcoming diesel models did Volkswagen executives confess what they knew.[12]

Executives did whatever it took to avoid exposure—to avoid vulnerability—but only contributed to public anger. Given the global scope and level of deviance associated with the company, the emissions issue would have been a scandal regardless. But Volkswagen could have avoided the extent of "Dieselgate" if the leaders hadn't denied—for more than a year—that test discrepancies weren't just a technical aberration. Analysts say VW would have paid a fine of hundreds of millions of dollars, instead of the billions they spent, if they had been honest about inconsistent test results.[13] Leaders couldn't face the pain, which only compounded the problem.

Vulnerability as a Strength

Our focus is on relationships, but in some disciplines, vulnerability is a weakness. In computing, vulnerable data can be manipulated by hackers. In video games, invulnerability means being impervious, or protected.

When we think about people who are vulnerable, we may get images of people needing help and protection. Like vulnerable data, vulnerable people can be exploited or manipulated. In some ways, VW's customers were vulnerable; they wanted to do the right thing for the environment, and the company preyed on their weakness.[14]

But allowing ourselves to be vulnerable in relationship with others—to be open, to face fear and possible rejection—is more of a strength than a weakness. As leaders, we have a choice about how we present ourselves to others and how to respond to feedback. We can choose openness, or we can choose to protect ourselves. Protection is tempting, as Brown says:

> *Perfect* and *bulletproof* are seductive, but they don't exist in the human experience. We must walk into the arena, whatever it may be—a new relationship, an important meeting, our creative process, or a difficult family conversation—with courage and the willingness to engage. Rather than sitting on the sidelines and hurling judgment and advice, **we must dare to show up and let ourselves be seen**. This is vulnerability.[15]

If we chose protection, we are living out of fear and will face disconnection—exactly what VW got from customers, shareholders, and international governments.

Vulnerability Builds Connection

To be vulnerable is to be human, and humans are driven to connection. Those connections allow us to work together in common cause. Rather than wear a mask, leaders choose vulnerability because it builds relationships. We'll see how VW leaders distanced themselves and how Blue Bell Creameries' CEO faced its constituencies to build connection.

Hiding and Avoiding

Leaders who can't be vulnerable isolate themselves from others and put the organization at risk. Because they don't feel "good enough" (shame), they hide mistakes and avoid asking for help. As we see in the VW case, if leaders had admitted their failings to regulators, they would have limited the damage.

Volkswagen's first major public communication was an attempt by then CEO Martin Winterkorn to apologize. But Winterkorn is stiff—reading from a script and saying the words but not convincing us that he feels remorse. He blames the problem on "the terrible mistakes of a few people," which downplays the extent of the deception, and he fails to take full responsibility. Winterkorn protects himself. He refers to the issue as "irregularities" and says, "We are working very hard on the necessary technical solutions," as if a simple software change would fix the problem.[16]

Winterkorn resigned the next day, possibly at the request of the board of directors. In his resignation statement, Winterkorn said, "I am not aware of any wrongdoing on my part."[17] Skeptics wonder how the chief executive could not know, particularly given Volkswagen's top down organizational culture.[18] U.S. Attorney General Loretta Lynch said, "Volkswagen knew of these problems, and when regulators expressed concern, Volkswagen obfuscated, they denied, and they ultimately lied."[19]

Winterkorn's successor, Matthias Müller, also struggled with vulnerability.[20] Hired from within Volkswagen, he tried to reframe the issue during a 2016 NPR interview. Müller claimed they had misunderstood the American law and said, "We didn't lie. We didn't understand the question [at] first."[21] After much criticism, VW's communications department asked NPR for another interview, which NPR granted. Müller delivered a better apology but blamed the first interview on "all these colleagues of yours and everybody shouting." In other words, it was noisy.[22]

VW leaders also avoided customers' anger. By all accounts, customer communication and solutions were slow. VW failed to use classic crisis management approaches, such as sympathy and compensation.[23] Websites and social media accounts were silent when the scandal first broke, and VW initially offered customers the "Volkswagen TDI Goodwill Package" consisting of two $500 loyalty cards and three years of free roadside assistance.[24] Customers waited another five months for a buyback program the company wanted to avoid entirely.[25]

Taking Off the Mask

Leaders may overcompensate for feeling inadequate by wearing a mask of confidence and bravado. Good leaders aren't perfect, and no one expects them to be. But when we feel pressure to be invincible, we may wear a mask to *appear* perfect. Unfortunately, the facade pushes people away. In her teaching and writing, Brown discusses the idea of "wholehearted" living—approaching relationships with our whole selves, warts and all. By being overly guarded, we may be most at risk and have the most to lose.

The better choice, the more difficult choice, is choosing connection: admitting failure, asking for help, and showing what we don't know. Brown also says, "Vulnerability is the birthplace of innovation, creativity, and change."[26] When people are vulnerable, they are not afraid of offering a suggestion or presenting an idea and potentially looking foolish. They can take criticism without falling apart. Then people can work together to solve problems and to create something new.

Leaders also allow others to be vulnerable. When people share something personal—when they are vulnerable with you—how do you react? One way to build connection is to be vulnerable yourself. Admitting your own failings may put others at ease and allows for a more intimate, honest conversation.

We see some of the shell cracking in Michael Horn, the president and chief executive of Volkswagen Group of America. Like Winterkorn, Horn delivered a video apology on September 22, 2015. But he demonstrated a bit more emotion and used conversational language, such as, "We have totally screwed up." Although he admits, "Our company was dishonest,"[27] he, too, denies knowledge of wrongdoing.

During testimony before Congress in October 2015, Horn said, "These events are deeply troubling. I did not think that something like this was possible at the Volkswagen Group. We have broken the trust of our customers, dealerships, and employees, as well as the public and regulators."[28] When asked how it was possible that executives didn't know, Horn answered well (Figure 3.3).[29] We see a glimpse of vulnerability.

Figure 3.3   Michael Horn's testimony demonstrates some vulnerability

Mr. Barton:	Do you really believe, as good, as well run as Volkswagen has always been reported to be, that senior-level corporate managers/administrators had no knowledge for years and years?
Mr. Horn:	I agree it's very hard to believe.
Mr. Barton:	Yes.
Mr. Horn:	And personally, I struggle as well, yes.
Mr. Barton:	That is an honest answer. I appreciate that.

Source: "Volkswagen's Emissions Cheating Allegations: Initial Questions," U.S. House of Representatives Document Repository, October 8, 2015, http://docs.house.gov/meetings/IF/IF02/20151008/104046/HHRG-114-IF02-Transcript-20151008.pdf, accessed April 21, 2017.

Leaders don't need to be fearless, just open to imperfection. As David Brooks writes in his book, *The Road to Character,* "To be healed is to be broken open."[30] We live wholehearted lives when we are willing to be vulnerable.

Blue Bell Creameries Example

Blue Bell Creameries provides a better example of vulnerability to build connection. When Blue Bell Creameries stopped ice cream production because of an outbreak of Listeria, which causes food poisoning, President and CEO Paul Kruse said, "We are heartbroken about this situation and apologize to all of our loyal Blue Bell fans and customers."[31] A month later, he posted a video titled "An Agonizing Decision," with more bad news (Figure 3.4).

You can see the pain on Kruse's face and hear it in his voice. The pain is real and understandable: Blue Bell was founded in 1904 in Brenham, Texas, and has been owned by the Kruse family since 1919.

Although not everyone was pleased with the company's decisions, a YouTube comment summarizes Kruse's presentation and leadership character well (Figure 3.5). Rich Invents acknowledges Kruse's vulnerability and respects him for genuinely expressing emotion.

Again, vulnerability is a difficult choice. We face our shortcomings in order to build connection and stay whole. Kruse chose to expose himself and his company to strengthen customer loyalty. It took a while, but the company has changed procedures and introduced new flavors, and the product returned to store shelves two years later.[32]

Figure 3.4   Blue Bell CEO demonstrates vulnerability

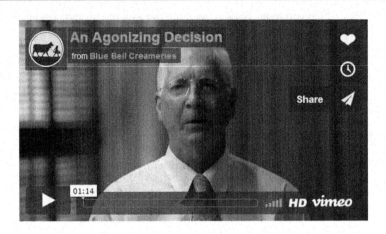

The most difficult decision I have had to deal with in my life is the incredibly tough decision to reduce pay and lay off some of our great people at Blue Bell. We're all part of one team, and we tried to keep everyone on the payroll for as long as possible. The whole process of getting ready to make our ice cream again and to get it right is taking longer than we anticipated. . . . This is a terribly sad day for all of us at the company and for me personally. We are needing to take this step to ensure a successful return and the possibility of a strong future for Blue Bell Creameries. But it still hurts—a lot.

Source: AL.com, "Blue Bell CEO Announces Layoffs and Salary Reductions," YouTube, May 15, 2014, https://www.youtube.com/watch?v=t63kCbQvjfI, accessed June 10, 2017.

Figure 3.5   YouTube response compliments vulnerability

 Rich Invents 1 year ago

Some people in his position are very good at giving such announcements and you can see they are simply reading words and care not of what they are saying. It is very clear in Mr. Kruse's case with this announcement that this is definitely NOT the case. He is genuinely struggling with the actions he needs to take to help save the company and making such decisions and the implementation of them as he is so painfully doing is what makes two things, a quality leader and an honorable man. I wish him and all at Blue Bell Creameries tremendous success and a secure and happy and prosperous future ahead!

Source: Rich Invents, "Some people in his position . . . ," comment on YouTube video, 2015, https://www.youtube.com/watch?v=t63kCbQvjfI, accessed April 22, 2017.

Apologizing Is Good for Business

One particularly challenging part of being vulnerable is the willingness to apologize. Leaders avoid apologizing because of the potential exposure, but apologies are useful for those aggrieved and for rebuilding an organization's image.

The Reluctance to Apologize

In addition to avoiding vulnerability, leaders may experience corporate pressure not to apologize. In his book *Crisis Communications*, Steven Fink blames lawyers partly for companies' reluctance to be more human. Lawyers are concerned primarily about litigation—and they should be. The adage "What you say can and will be held against you" is true.[33]

But that adage holds for public opinion too. The media, consumers, and social media trolls also will judge what you say—or don't say. Lawyers are overly cautious when they advise clients to avoid saying much at all. The public needs to hear from a company's leaders, particularly in cases of wrongdoing. Responding with "no comment" or blaming others, as VW did, only leads to more criticism.

From his 30 years of experience working with companies through crises, Fink says, "I've never seen a single instance where not saying 'we're sorry' ever staved off litigation."[34] Instead, he advises clients to apologize when appropriate and to let their emotions show, particularly in cases of fatalities: "It's normal to feel anguish. It's normal to internalize everything. . . . It means you have a heart. Let the world see it."[35]

Fink suggests telling the truth and doing so early for two reasons. First, an apology gives leaders "peace of mind and clear-headedness to face the situation head-on." He advises, "Take your lumps early and get it over with." Second, an apology helps to rebuild a leader's reputation and the company's reputation.[36] An apology is probably good for the soul (although this is a tough premise to research), and it's good for building future business relationships.

Medical Examples

Although lawyers worry that apologies fuel lawsuits, research shows that apologies have the opposite effect. Actor and author Alan Alda tells a story of his dentist cutting off his frenum. (You can feel yours by putting your tongue inside your upper lip and on top of your front teeth.) Unfortunately for Alda, his actor smile looked more like a sneer. When he complained, he received a letter from the doctor that he described as "formal and cold." Alda believed the purpose of the letter was to discourage a lawsuit, but he says, "Until I saw the tone of his letter, I hadn't even thought of suing (and I never did)—but if he wanted to avoid a suit, he was going about it in exactly the wrong way."[37]

Research confirms Fink's advice and Alda's experience that apologies reduce lawsuits, and the medical community is catching on. The University of Michigan Health System (UMHS) developed "The Michigan Model,"[38] which includes "full disclosure of medical errors."[39] On its website, UMHS summarizes its approach of disclosure—and apologizing:

> Apologize and learn when we're wrong, explain and vigorously defend when we're right, and view court as a last resort.
>
> We care deeply about our patients, and we take it very seriously when one of them is injured, concerned, or unhappy about the care we have provided. We also care deeply about our staff, and we want to support and protect them so they can continue to do great work. And, we want to create as safe an environment as possible for both patients and staff.[40]

The approach has resulted in fewer presuit claims and lawsuits and, when people do sue, less severe claims, faster settlement times, reduced legal fees, and reduced malpractice insurance premiums. Several other health care programs, including medical centers at Stanford University and the University of Illinois Medical Center, have adopted similar models and found similar positive results.[41,42]

Apologies as a Strength

Like medical practitioners, corporate leaders are beginning to understand the value of an apology. Investor and hedge fund manager William A. Ackman surprised reporters when he apologized for an investment in Valeant Pharmaceuticals that didn't turn out well. Ackman is known as a "brash activist" who won't apologize for anything.[43]

Valeant was in the news for drug price hikes; for example, the cost of a drug taken by AIDS patients was increased 5,500% in one day. The stock dropped from $257 to $12.11, leaving Ackman's firm with a $4 billion loss.[44] In a letter to shareholders, Ackman apologized and took responsibility for the decision:

My approach to mistakes is that I personally assume 100 percent of the responsibility on behalf of the firm while sharing the credit for our success. While I and the rest of the Pershing Square team have suffered significant losses from this failed investment as we are collectively the largest investors in the funds, it is much more painful to lose our shareholders' money, and for this I deeply and profoundly apologize.[45]

Public perception of apologies has shifted from a sign of weakness to one of strength. But apologies must be sincere, ideally demonstrating vulnerability. As a result, they are usually painful and involve asking probing questions about what really happened: "How did I get here, and how did I drift from the person I aspire to be?" They are not a way to get something from the other; instead, they encourage real feedback from those affected. Finally, a sincere apology means similar mistakes are not made in the future.[46]

Apologies express guilt, but they are not about shame, introduced earlier. Shame is different from guilt. Guilt is about our behavior—what we do. Guilt is, "I'm sorry, I made a mistake." Shame is, "I'm sorry, I am a mistake." Admitting a mistake is adaptive; feeling shame is damaging, correlated with addiction, depression, eating disorders, violence, and so on. Brené Brown says, "Shame drives too big tapes: never good enough, and if you can talk it out of that one, who do you think you are?"[47] With people on full display on social media, it's easy to feel as though we don't measure up by comparison.

VW compared themselves to competitors and to tougher EPA emissions standards and didn't measure up. They could not live up to expectations and, instead, hid behind consumers' vulnerabilities. That's the irony of vulnerability: we think of it as a weakness because, as Brown says, "we've confused *feeling* with *failing* and *emotions* with *liabilities*."[48] Expressing emotion is not a sign of failure or limitations—quite the opposite.

Rolling Stone Gets It Right

We see an example of vulnerability and a meaningful apology from the editor of *Rolling Stone* magazine. When the magazine published an article, "A Rape on Campus," about the University of Virginia, the editors probably felt as though they were doing a great service. The article reported a rape in a fraternity and blamed college administrators for not doing enough to address sexual assault on campus.

However, the scathing article was not well researched.[49] The reporter tried to protect a student, "Jackie," but important facts didn't line up, and people were unfairly accused. In litigation, the reporter and media company were found guilty of defaming a University of Virginia associate dean.[50]

But long before the lawsuits, *Rolling Stone* leaders faced their own failings. They asked the Columbia University Graduate School of Journalism to conduct an external review and promised to publish the results, which were damning. In a nearly 13,000-word report, researchers concluded, "*Rolling Stone*'s repudiation of the main narrative in 'A Rape on Campus' is a story of journalistic failure that was avoidable."[51] The report is published on *Rolling Stone*'s website under the title, "What Went Wrong?"[52] Preceding the report is "A Note from the Editor," in which he laid bare their flaws and acknowledged the pain caused (Figure 3.6).

The situation is particularly interesting because rape is underreported partly because victims feel shame. *Rolling Stone* wanted to give voice to those who cannot speak for themselves, yet as the editor says, they fell far short.

Connection Is Built or Destroyed on Social Media

Perhaps nowhere do leaders feel more vulnerable than on social media. When United Airlines denied boarding to two teenagers for wearing leggings, a passenger overheard, and you can predict the rest. Twitter users responded with 174,000 daily mentions. But people didn't realize the girls were traveling for free as relatives of a United employee. When the airline offers these free tickets, they have a dress code because travelers are considered representatives of the company.[53] People may disagree with the policy, but the reaction was disproportionate to the situation. Social media invites hasty reactions and, at times, cruelty.

Social media hurts, despite what Milo Yiannopoulos, the British public speaker and former senior editor for Breitbart News, says. On the HBO show *Real Time With Bill Maher*, Yiannopoulos was reflecting on his tweets about Leslie Jones's performance in *Ghostbusters*, including calling her "barely literate" and comparing her to an ape.[54] On the show, he was incredulous that he had hurt her feelings, concluding, "Mean words on the internet don't hurt anyone."[55]

We know that is simply not true. Bullying, harassment, hate speech, and otherwise tormenting people online have been linked directly to suicide attempts. A study of 2,000 middle schoolers found that those who had been "cyberbullied" were twice as likely to attempt suicide as students who hadn't experienced cyberbullying.[56] For his own behavior, Yiannopoulos got himself permanently banned from Twitter.[57]

Figure 3.6   *Rolling Stone* managing editor demonstrates vulnerability

A NOTE FROM THE EDITOR

Last November, we published a story, "A Rape on Campus" [RS 1223], that centered around a University of Virginia student's horrifying account of her alleged gang rape at a campus fraternity house. Within days, commentators started to question the veracity of our narrative. Then, when The Washington Post uncovered details suggesting that the assault could not have taken place the way we described it, the truth of the story became a subject of national controversy.

Uses appropriate emotional language.

Doesn't shy away from the explicit term "gang rape."

Admits the extent of the controversy.

As we asked ourselves how we could have gotten the story wrong, we decided the only responsible and credible thing to do was to ask someone from outside the magazine to investigate any lapses in reporting, editing and fact-checking behind the story.

Admits to potential failures.

We reached out to Steve Coll, dean of the Columbia School of Journalism, and a Pulitzer Prize–winning reporter himself, who accepted our offer. We agreed that we would cooperate fully, that he and his team could take as much time as they needed and write whatever they wanted. They would receive no payment, and we promised to publish their report in full. (A condensed version of the report will appear in the next issue of the magazine, out April 8th.)

Demonstrates impartiality and transparency.

Describes the personal impact.

This report was painful reading, to me personally and to all of us at Rolling Stone. It is also, in its own way, a fascinating document—a piece of journalism, as Coll describes it, about a failure of journalism. With its publication, we are officially retracting "A Rape on Campus." We are also committing ourselves to a series of recommendations about journalistic practices that are spelled out in the report. We would like to apologize to our readers and to all of those who were damaged by our story and the ensuing fallout, including members of the Phi Kappa Psi fraternity and UVA administrators and students. Sexual assault is a serious problem on college campuses, and it is important that rape victims feel comfortable stepping forward. It saddens us to think that their willingness to do so might be diminished by our failings.

Retracts the article, which no publisher wants to do.

Commits to real change.

Apologizes to specific groups and recognizes the "damage" caused.

Recognizes the far-reaching implications of their "failings."

Source: Sheila Coronel, Steve Coll, and Derek Kravitz, "Rolling Stone & UVA: Columbia School of Journalism's Report," *Rolling Stone*, April 5, 2015, www.rollingstone.com/culture/features/a-rape-on-campus-20141119, accessed April 21, 2017.

Volkswagen wasn't immune to the wrath of social media. Mocking memes and consumer Facebook groups called on Volkswagen to respond.

In the book introduction, we learned how important a CEO's reputation is to the company's reputation. Yet 61% of Fortune Global 500 leaders have no social media presence.[58] They are missing out on an opportunity—as VW did—to connect with customers because they see social networking as a distraction and a potential danger.[59] They fear emotional exposure—and as we know, this fear is real. But which is worse, hiding from the conversation or engaging in it?

Leaders can't hide from the public scrutiny, and ignoring a social media mob only fuels its fury. According to the report "In Reputation We Trust," "company wrongdoing overshadows many of the good deeds and community engagement that a company participates in. Consumers report that they are more likely to discuss corporate scandals and wrongdoing (43%) than corporate good deeds (37%), environmental protections (31%) and community services (29%). Companies have to consistently apply more muscle to communicating their societal and environmental contributions to overcome any negative news that can suddenly surface."[60]

In other words, much of the online conversation about companies is negative. Leaders do best by admitting failures and engaging detractors instead of ignoring or trying to squelch them. Public perception is more important than reality; it's best to stay in the conversation—and to be vulnerable.

SUMMARY

Volkswagen leaders avoided vulnerability and caused more trouble for the company. Instead of facing potential failure, they deceived customers and enforcement agencies and then denied doing so.

Since then, the company has recovered well. In 2017, VW replaced Toyota as the best-selling automaker worldwide.[61] Analysts say Müller has been easing the company's rigid decision-making process and focusing more on innovations, such as self-driving, electric vehicles.[62]

Volkswagen leaders have also demonstrated vulnerability. In 2017, VW and other German auto companies were in the news for colluding on technology affecting exhaust gases. Although BMW denied the accusation, VW leaders, perhaps learning a lesson from the past, admitted that five German companies met "several times a year" and had been "co-ordinating the development of their vehicles, costs, suppliers, and markets for many years, at least since the Nineties, to the present day."[63]

Vulnerability is a strength. By being vulnerable, we open ourselves up to connection with others. We admit mistakes and weaknesses to avoid shame and to allow others to know and to support us. By demonstrating vulnerability, we gain power and remove it from our critics.

In his book *Discover Your True North*, Bill George writes that vulnerability is essential to "feeling good in our own skin."[64] We'll explore this concept as part of authenticity next.

EXERCISES

Concept Review Questions

1. How would you describe vulnerability in relationships?
2. What is shame, and how does vulnerability help us avoid feeling it?
3. What is the value of apologizing?
4. Why should leaders have a social media presence?

Self-Reflection Questions

1. Think about a time when you avoided exposure. What did you fear? What did you do to avoid the risk?
2. When have you experienced shame? How did it affect you, and how did you react?
3. Have you been vulnerable in a situation and then regretted it? Maybe you felt comfortable with someone who took advantage of your openness. How did the situation affect you?
4. Think about your friendships. Are you more vulnerable with some friends than with others? Are some more vulnerable with you? Which do you consider to be the most meaningful friendships?
5. How do you answer that dreaded interview question, "What is your biggest weakness?" Do you say, "I work too hard" or "I'm too committed"? Hiring managers see through these responses. What could you say that really is a weakness and would demonstrate self-reflection?
6. Think about a missed opportunity to be vulnerable. Was there a time when someone needed your help and your bravado got in the way? What could you have done differently?
7. What examples can you find of people being vulnerable—or not—in entertainment (for example, movies, TV, podcasts)?

Assessment

Take a fresh look at the Johari Window exercise from the previous chapter. How do you think vulnerability might play a role in your results? For example, the arena pane is where you are open: what you know and what others know about you is the same. But your facade is known only to you. Why do others not know these things about you? What reasons do you have for hiding these parts of yourself? Similarly, your blind spots are known to others but not known to you. What reasons might you have for avoiding seeing these things about yourself that may be obvious to others? Is it possibly too painful to accept them?

Consider talking with others about your observations and asking them for ideas. With greater vulnerability, you can be more open and increase your arena, so that what you know about yourself and what others know about you is consistent.

Mini-Cases

Consider the following scenarios. On your own or with a partner, discuss the best course of action in each case. What would you do, and what factors into your decision?

Scenario 1

It's your first day on a new job, and you work with a team of seven people. You overhear them planning lunch together, and they're not including you. How do you feel, and what will you do?

Scenario 2

You manage a team of four employees, and one of them asks to meet with you. She is obviously nervous when she tells you that she is speaking on behalf of the team, and that they all feel overworked. You're very upset about this because you thought they enjoyed the work and chose to stay late to finish a project that's due at the end of the month. You feel awful that people feel this way and that you didn't notice. How will you handle this situation with this employee and with the rest of the team?

Scenario 3

You manage Brother International's Twitter feed, and you see this public mention of a laser printer the company sells: "I'll never buy another @Brother printer. The Toner Low light is on, and it won't print, but the last page was perfectly clear! #Ripoff." You know the company uses this strategy to get people to buy expensive replacement cartridges even though the old ones still have toner left. How will you respond?

Individual and Optional Video Activity

This is an opportunity to practice a sincere apology. Think about a time when you hurt someone or did something you regret. How could you apologize in a way that demonstrates your vulnerability?

Planning Questions

1. What comes to mind first?

2. What happened? Who was affected?

3. Why did it happen? How can you take responsibility for the situation without blaming others? At the same time, if others were involved, you can certainly explain their role and how it affected decisions you made.

4. How was the issue discovered? Did you admit it first, or were you called out for it?

5. How will you encourage the other person to participate in the conversation? What questions will you ask? How will you get feedback?

6. How will you avoid making a similar mistake in the future? How can you convince the other of your commitment?

7. Are these questions painful? Is it too painful for you to talk about? If so, what are other situations you could use for practice?

Practice and Reflection

Prepare saying the apology. Consider recording yourself and getting feedback from a classmate, colleague, or friend. Did you demonstrate vulnerability? How did you feel? What did you learn from the experience? You likely displayed other dimensions we'll cover later in the book as well.

Paired Activity

Schedule a quiet time and place to talk with a friend you know well. Think about something personal you would like to share and ask your friend to do the same. What troubles or worries you, what do you not like about yourself, or when have you felt like a failure? This will involve some risk, so be careful about the decision, but don't miss the opportunity to be vulnerable and to deepen the connection and your friendship. Perhaps you'll open the door to hear something in return—maybe something similar to how you feel or what you have experienced.

Planning Questions

1. What are you considering sharing with your friend? Why is this important to you? Why haven't you shared it in the past?

2. What reaction are you hoping to get? Be careful here—you may not get what you expect or hope for. What is the worst that can happen? Are you prepared to handle whatever reaction you get?

3. How will you set up the conversation?

4. How will you react to what your friend says? How will you remain open regardless of what is said?

5. If your friend has trouble offering something meaningful, how can you encourage him or her without being invasive or threatening?

Practice and Reflection

Take turns talking, and allow plenty of time to listen after each person speaks. You don't have to have answers. Just listen and appreciate the difficulty the person may have in sharing the information. If you can relate to the experience, talk about your own feelings, but be careful not to overshadow your partner's. For example, instead of, "You think *you* have problems!" try something like, "I often feel that way too."

Spend some time debriefing. How did it feel to talk in this way? What did you learn about each other?

4

Authenticity

Living as Yourself

Chapter Overview

General Motors delayed recalls and put CEO Mary Barra on the spot with regulators, customers, and the media. New to her role, Barra seemed to grow into it and become more sure of herself—more as she had been in previous roles. Authenticity is essential for emotional well-being. Despite criticism about authentic leadership, authentic leaders are neither rigid nor moral dictators. People who are authentic bring their whole selves to work and are happier and more engaged. Authentic leaders know themselves and feel comfortable with who they are for better or for worse.

General Motors Delays Recalls

By some estimates, General Motors management knew about a faulty ignition switch for more than a decade before recalling about 800,000 cars in 2014. Over the next few months, the recall number ballooned to about 29 million, some with steering and other issues. The defective switches were the most troublesome: the engine would shut off, power steering and brakes became disabled, and airbags would not inflate.[1]

Many deaths were linked to the faulty ignition switches. Although GM first argued the total was only 13, the company later admitted to likely causing 124 deaths.[2] They hadn't included, for example, a back seat passenger who died in a crash. At the time, the company was still trying to blame airbags for the trouble and said that only the driver was killed because the airbag didn't inflate. But the ignition cutoff caused the crash, which ultimately killed both teenaged girls when the car collided into trees.[3] In addition to deaths, the defect caused 275 injuries[4] (Figure 4.1).

In the end, the crisis cost GM more than $1 billion. The company paid $900 million in a settlement with the U.S. Department of Justice and $595 million to victims' families and shareholders.[5]

Like Volkswagen, the company took too long to admit failure and tried to avoid exposure, or vulnerability. But our focus in this chapter is on another character element, authenticity. At the beginning, CEO Mary Barra seemed to struggle, but she eventually showed us more of herself.

Authentic Leaders Are True to Themselves

Mary Barra's early communications during the recalls illustrate inauthenticity and may be a result of her new CEO role. Later, we see more of who Barra is as a person. Being authentic means being genuine—putting your whole self forward.

Inauthenticity Illustrated

As with many leadership character dimensions, we may have an easier time observing when authenticity is lacking. Early academic literature defined *inauthenticity* as "excessive plasticity" to comply with role expectations and being "overly compliant with stereotypes and demands" of the leader's role.[6]

Perhaps role compliance explains Mary Barra's initial response. What was it like to be the first female CEO of a major global automotive company? Perhaps she was just finding herself in her new position. Maybe Barra didn't have or didn't feel that she had the "authority"—the root of "authenticity"—to be more like herself?

Mary Barra was no stranger to the auto industry. Her father had worked at Pontiac, a former division of GM, for 39 years,[7] and she had started her career as a co-op student at the plant in 1980. After that, she moved up the ranks until she was appointed CEO on January 15, 2014, and was elected to the board of directors in January 2016.[8]

Figure 4.1   GM's recall crisis unfolds

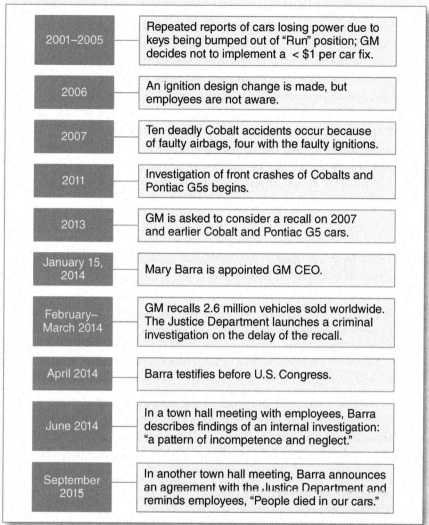

2001–2005	Repeated reports of cars losing power due to keys being bumped out of "Run" position; GM decides not to implement a < $1 per car fix.
2006	An ignition design change is made, but employees are not aware.
2007	Ten deadly Cobalt accidents occur because of faulty airbags, four with the faulty ignitions.
2011	Investigation of front crashes of Cobalts and Pontiac G5s begins.
2013	GM is asked to consider a recall on 2007 and earlier Cobalt and Pontiac G5 cars.
January 15, 2014	Mary Barra is appointed GM CEO.
February–March 2014	GM recalls 2.6 million vehicles sold worldwide. The Justice Department launches a criminal investigation on the delay of the recall.
April 2014	Barra testifies before U.S. Congress.
June 2014	In a town hall meeting with employees, Barra describes findings of an internal investigation: "a pattern of incompetence and neglect."
September 2015	In another town hall meeting, Barra announces an agreement with the Justice Department and reminds employees, "People died in our cars."

Sources: "General Motors' Corporate Culture Crisis: An Assessment of the Ignition Switch Recall," Arthur W. Page Society, January 16, 2015, http://www.awpagesociety.com/attachments/1edd5184509636aabbdc07ef0c3546e0facf5c0c/store/00f8d9b37cec4d725c881b7235467635ae ab21b4d2333398c819839d426b/General-Motors-Case-Study-2015.pdf, accessed May 8, 2017; Peter Valdes-Dapena and Tai Ellin, "GM: Steps to a Recall Nightmare," CNN: Money, May 21, 2014, http://money.cnn.com/infographic/pf/autos/gm-recall-timeline/, accessed June 11, 2017.

Less than a month into Barra's tenure, on February 7, 2014, the company began issuing recalls.[9] In her early communications, Barra was more defensive and guarded. During a congressional hearing—less than three months into the job—Barra was on the hot seat.[10]

Unfortunately, what she said and how she said it sounded insincere. In her testimony, she defended the company's process: "As soon as I learned about the problem, we acted without hesitation. We told the world we had a problem that needed to be fixed. We did so because whatever mistakes were made in the past, we will not shirk from our responsibilities now and in the future. Today's GM will do the right thing."[11]

She did apologize, saying, "I am deeply sorry." However, sitting in front of photos of loved ones who died in GM cars, families wanted to hear more. A victim's father said, "She's not doing anything except stonewalling."[12]

She came across as stiff, and it's hard to know whether she felt restrained by the setting, by the regulators, by the GM board of directors, by GM's crumbling culture, or by herself. Regardless, she did not come across as authentic.

Authenticity Defined

In his book *Discover Your True North*, Bill George gives us a clear, simple explanation of being an authentic leader:

> [B]eing an authentic leader is being who you are, being the genuine person. And people today know who is authentic and who is not, particularly the Millennials. There really is a turnoff for people [who] are faking it to make it. So I think you have to be true to what you believe in every day.[13,14]

In academic literature, authenticity is defined as "the unobstructed operation of one's true or core self in one's daily enterprise." We view people who are authentic as sincere and genuine. Social psychologists Michael Kernis and Brian Goldman divide the concept into four components:

- Awareness and knowledge of yourself
- Unbiased, objective processing
- Acting consistently with who you are
- Being genuine and not "fake" in relationship with others.[15]

We see the relevance of self-awareness discussed in Chapter 2 to becoming more authentic. Kernis and Goldman emphasize "*unbiased, objective* processing." From our discussion on judgment, we know this is difficult; we are prone to misinterpret information, particularly about ourselves. Honing our judgment helps us accurately process information from others and develop a better understanding of who we are. Then we can relate to others and be perceived by others as consistent and genuine.

In messages to GM employees, we see Mary Barra as more genuine. In one video, she says, "After all, something went wrong with our process in this instance and terrible things happened," and, "As a member of the GM family and as a mom with a family of my own, this really hits home for me."[16] In a town hall meeting with employees, Barra announces an agreement with the U.S. Attorney's Office and doesn't get far into her talk before reminding everyone of their responsibility:

> Before I talk about the settlement agreement, let's pause for a moment and remember that people were hurt, and people died in our cars. That's why we're here.
>
> I have said many times how sorry I am about what happened. On behalf of all of us, I have apologized to the families who lost love ones and to those who were injured. And I do so again today. We let those customers down in that situation. We didn't do our job.[17]

The news headlines read, "People Died in Our Cars." Perhaps Barra was showing more of her own values and those she hoped would represent "today's GM"—a phrase she repeated throughout her testimony and interviews.

The Personal Value of Authenticity

Research shows great value in living an authentic life. In psychology, authenticity is considered essential to well-being. Authentic living is correlated with relationship satisfaction, self-esteem, and happiness, while people who feel inauthentic, for example, feeling that their personality varies depending on their role, report more depression and anxiety.[18,19]

To be authentic, we recognize we're not perfect, and we present ourselves to others "warts and all." People who are authentic are willing to be vulnerable. They know their weaknesses and are open about them; they ask for and receive the help they need.

But being authentic doesn't mean we don't change, as we'll see next. Authentic people take responsibility for themselves and their choices over time. People who value authenticity recognize they are not the same people as they were yesterday or will be tomorrow. They strive to be better over time.

Becoming more authentic may involve changing old, negative images of ourselves.[20] We explore who we used to be and who we want to become. Later, we'll discuss how this process may take place, and we'll see the value of authenticity in organizations.

Authenticity Doesn't Mean
Being Rigid or Morally Correct

Although important to mental health, being authentic doesn't mean we're inflexible or that we're correct. We can be true to ourselves, yet we have to live among others.

Flexibility

Critics contend that authenticity, as a leadership concept, encourages people to be rigid: "I am who am I, and I don't have to change for anyone." As we saw in Chapter 1, Jeffrey Pfeffer at the Stanford Graduate School of Business argues that leaders aren't expected to be authentic; rather, they need to adapt to different situations.[21]

Pfeffer has a point, but more recent definitions of authenticity include flexibility. In her *Harvard Business Review* article, "The Authenticity Paradox," Herminia Ibarra at INSEAD argues that though a new role may stretch us in ways that make us feel fake, we may be uncomfortable just because the role is new.

For example, as leaders take on more responsibility in an organization, they will experiment with new approaches and communication styles.[22] This adaptation doesn't mean we're not "being real," but that we're trying to figure out what works, which may be outside our comfort zone. Ibarra emphasizes including external perspectives as we learn new ways of being in different situations with different people. New actions change us and how we interact with others.[23]

Authenticity isn't fixed because people are not fixed. We evolve over time, and self-acceptance is a lifelong journey. We can never be 100% authentic; we're complicated people at home and at work and won't be *exactly* the same everywhere we go. For example, a study of English, Russian, and American adults found that we are most authentic with partners, then with friends and parents, and then with work colleagues.[24] Further, although much of the literature has focused on authenticity as a trait—a stable characteristic—more recent research shows that authenticity is variable, with people feeling both authentic and inauthentic in certain situations.[25]

Although we see similarities in authenticity internationally, Ibarra presents the challenge of an "American" concept of authenticity. Leaders from other cultures may feel uncomfortable—inauthentic—if their organization values, for example, self-disclosure, such as personal stories that show how a leader overcame an obstacle. Such "storytelling" can feel like bragging to leaders from less individualist cultures.[26] We don't have a universal perspective of authenticity.

Different work situations may require different parts of you. You may be in an individual contributor role without people reporting to you, but you may have tremendous influence, which requires you to take "authority." Or you may be a senior-level manager and take a back seat to let others lead. In these situations, you are being true to yourself—and being an adaptable leader.

Not a Moral Dictator or Referee

Critics also say authentic leaders run the risk of thinking they are always right. In *The Road to Character*, David Brooks takes issue with Bill George's definition of authenticity. George writes, "If you want to be an authentic leader and have a meaningful life, you need to do the difficult inner work to develop yourself, have a strong moral compass based on your beliefs and values, and work on problems that matter to you."[27]

While George favors the inner voice, Brooks disavows this concept of authenticity as a "romantic idea that each of us has a Golden Figure in the core of our self. There is an innately good True Self, which can be trusted, consulted, and gotten in touch with. Your personal feelings are the best guide for what is right and wrong."[28] Brooks warns against losing touch with others and prefers the idea of an "external, objective good."[29]

We should strive for a balance. Brooks is right: we have to be careful not to confuse authenticity with being an authority of all things—particularly morality. People aren't inherently either moral or immoral, and being authentic doesn't mean you're moral. For example, in Chapter 1, we saw the former CEO of Countrywide Financial criticize customers in danger of losing their homes. He was authentic—true to himself and what he believed—but most people would question his morality. You can be 100% authentic and true to yourself *and* be dead wrong. Yet some might argue with Brooks's concept of an "external, objective good": is there one "right" answer in all situations?

Brooks is fighting against an evolving notion of character, as we learned in Chapter 1, that is increasingly about résumé-building and external success. He argues that some concepts of character, including "self-control, grit, resilience, and tenacity," may give us permission to be selfish.[30] But we define authenticity to include what is good for others. Being authentic certainly doesn't mean being selfish; we need to be adaptable, particularly at work.

Authentic Leaders Bring Their Whole Selves to Work

Being authentic at work has positive outcomes for individuals and for organizations. When we bring our whole selves to work and encourage others to do the same, we create an inclusive working environment.

Positive Outcomes

How authentic people feel with coworkers is partly influenced by external factors, such as where they work.[31] Employees who feel that their organization's culture is in sync, or congruent, with their core self report feeling more authentic at work. In addition, employees may feel more authentic at work when they have more autonomy. In other words, if we have more control over our work, we can be "ourselves."[32]

In addition to the personal benefits discussed earlier, studies have found many positive outcomes of authenticity in the workplace. Researchers validated a measure of authentic leadership and found it related to followers' positive feelings about an organization, group trust, and identification with a supervisor.[33] Another study confirms this relationship between authenticity and organizational commitment: "Leaders who remain true to the self in their behavior and are open and non-defensive in their interactions with others will be perceived as walking the talk, delivering on promises, and aligning words with deeds."[34]

More authentic employees have a better workplace experience. When people share more of who they are, they report greater job satisfaction, a stronger sense of community, lower job stress, and higher levels of engagement.[35,36] A field study and related experiment found that when employees were oriented into a new company, focusing on personal identities and what makes people unique instead of emphasizing company goals and conformity resulted in higher retention rates and better work quality.[37]

Employee engagement is particularly important to organizations. Gallup research shows that engagement has been consistently dismal since 2000. Only 13% of employees worldwide and 32% in the United States feel "involved in, enthusiastic about, and committed to their work and workplace."[38] What inspires engagement is complicated, but recognizing authenticity at work is an important component.

Whole Selves

PepsiCo chairman and CEO Indra K. Nooyi encourages employees to bring their "whole selves" to work. She wants people to be who they are instead of playing a fake role on the job:

> The only way we will hold on to the best and brightest is to grasp them emotionally. No one may feel excluded. It's our job to draw the best out of everyone. That means employees must be able to immerse their whole selves in a work environment in which they can develop their careers, families, and philanthropy, and truly believe they are cared for.[39]

Mary Barra echoes these themes in her own philosophy of work. Since the recall, she has talked openly about the importance of work/life balance—making time for her family. She told a CBS interviewer, "Family is important. My children are important, and there are key events in their life I want to be a part of."[40] During another *Fortune* interview, she said it's important "to help people through the different phases of their life—when they start a family, when they find themselves in a situation when they're caring for aging parents." She joked, based on her own experience, "When you're 8½-months pregnant, it's probably not the best time to have career development discussions."[41]

To foster authenticity, Barra focused on supporting women to avoid "converting from a career to a job" because of family choices. For example, she implemented a program to help women who have been out of the workforce come back to the company.[42]

Bringing our whole selves to work may take time. In one study, employees who said they were authentic reported taking a few months or more than a year to "share their true selves at work." Most of this group—60%—felt authentic within three months, 22% took nine months, 9% took 10 to 12 months, and another 9% took more than a year.[43] Sometimes, people need time to feel comfortable, and they may want to prove themselves and their ability to do the job first.

Fitting In

Being authentic at work may be easier said than done. We face a delicate, difficult balance between being authentic and fitting in at work.

We have to get along in the world. Companies put a premium on "organizational fit."[44] A business suit may not feel right for you, but you'll have a hard time finding a company that will hire you wearing only underwear if that represents your authentic self. We don't have to like everyone, but disruptive behavior is another story. Leaders have to decide for themselves whether an organization is the right place for them—and sometimes, whether the people within the organization are in the right place.

In the *Breaking Bad* spinoff *Better Call Saul*, Jimmy wears colorful, mismatched clothes and plays bagpipes at the office. He is being his authentic self, but he also gets himself fired, which was the intent.

Social psychologist Mark Snyder identified the concept of "self-monitoring" as a way to assess the extent to which people change their behavior based on social situations. He argued that high self-monitors respond to social cues and context, adjusting how they behave to impress others, while low self-monitors are less willing to adapt, sticking with their perceptions of themselves.[45] At extremes, high self-monitors may be seen as inauthentic chameleons, while low self-monitors may be stubborn and socially awkward.[46]

The model is useful to consider how well we adapt, but it presents a false dichotomy. The question isn't whether we adapt or don't, but how skillfully we adapt in different roles and contexts without losing ourselves in the process. This causes tension in creating and participating in an inclusive work environment.

Inclusion

Brené Brown asked eighth-graders the difference between fitting in and belonging. Here are some of their responses:

- Belonging is being somewhere where you want to be, and they want you. Fitting in is being somewhere where you really want to be, but they don't care one way or the other.
- I get to be me if I belong. I have to be like you to fit in.[47]

Eighth-graders can be quite wise. To be ourselves, to have the opportunity to lead, and to do our best work, we need to be in a place where we belong. We need to feel included. The key to an inclusive group is being able to share openly what we find offensive or questionable about others without challenging their right to be in the group.

When we know each other, we work better together. Revealing ourselves requires us to be vulnerable as well as awkward at times.

Although it may be difficult to share who we are and to ask for what's important to us, this kind of openness—both revealing ourselves and appreciating what we learn about others—is essential to an inclusive work environment.[48]

People are drawn to real people. One study found that 75% of employees want their colleagues to share more of themselves.[49] Brooks writes, "C. S. Lewis observed that if you enter a party consciously trying to make a good impression, you probably won't end up making one. . . . If you begin an art project by trying to be original, you probably won't be original."[50]

But a Deloitte study of 3,129 employees found that 61% "cover" or hide something about themselves in order to seem more "mainstream." People may cover their affiliations, advocacy, appearance, and/or associations (Figure 4.2).

One example of affiliation is how open we are at work about religious practice. An article in the *Telegraph* describes the challenges of being openly

Figure 4.2   Sixty-one percent of employees "cover" one or more aspects of themselves

Source: Kenji Yoshino and Christie Smith, "Uncovering Talent: A New Model of Inclusion," Deloitte University, December 6, 2013, https://www2.deloitte.com/content/dam/Deloitte/us/Documents/about-deloitte/us-inclusion-uncovering-talent-paper.pdf, accessed June 11, 2017.

Christian in some workplaces. When asked about weekend plans, for example, employees don't mention church or Bible study. The author tells about a friend who "'came out' of the Christian closet." In response, someone asked, "You go to church? What, like, every Sunday?"[51] Employees at Christian companies, such as Hobby Lobby, Chick-fil-A, and In-n-Out Burger likely have an easier time, and more companies are making space, literally and figuratively, for employees to pray at work.[52]

Another example is openness about sexual orientation. In the book *Passion and Purpose*, Josh Bronstein talks about his decision to "come out"—to be openly gay at work:

> The energy required to hide my identity from those who I assumed wouldn't like it distracted me from the work I was being paid to do. Since then, being openly gay has only helped me professionally—I've benefited from a stronger sense of community and a professional network that spans functional silos, more confidence when speaking with senior leaders, and the comfort of always being able to use accurate pronouns.[53]

As it turns out, "Don't ask, don't tell" is not a great strategy.

Apple Example

Leaders can encourage authenticity by being authentic themselves. To model authenticity and pave the way for others, Apple CEO Tim Cook wrote, "I'm proud to be gay," in an open letter in *Bloomberg* (Figure 4.3).

The letter continues, and Cook explains why he decided to sacrifice his privacy: "So if hearing that the CEO of Apple is gay can help someone struggling to come to terms with who he or she is, or bring comfort to anyone who feels alone, or inspire people to insist on their equality, then it's worth the trade-off with my own privacy." He emphasizes the importance of belonging and his responsibility as a corporate leader, and we hear part of his process of self-discovery. We'll explore some approaches to becoming more authentic next.

Self-Awareness and Self-Acceptance Help Us Feel Comfortable in Our Own Skin

To be true to ourselves, we must know ourselves. In Chapter 2, we discussed self-reflection as an essential component of developing leadership character. Reflection, self-awareness, and self-acceptance are also critical to becoming more authentic. An authenticity scale shows where we are today, and a process helps us evolve and considers our personal identity.

Figure 4.3   Apple CEO Tim Cook writes about being gay

Tim Cook Speaks Up

By Timothy Donald Cook

Throughout my professional life, I've tried to maintain a basic level of privacy. I come from humble roots, and I don't seek to draw attention to myself. Apple is already one of the most closely watched companies in the world, and I like keeping the focus on our products and the incredible things our customers achieve with them.

> Provides context: why he has been reluctant to come out publicly before.

At the same time, I believe deeply in the words of Dr. Martin Luther King, who said: "Life's most persistent and urgent question is, 'What are you doing for others?'" I often challenge myself with that question, and I've come to realize that my desire for personal privacy has been holding me back from doing something more important. That's what has led me to today.

> Explains part of his rationale: that his coming out might help others.

For years, I've been open with many people about my sexual orientation. Plenty of colleagues at Apple know I'm gay, and it doesn't seem to make a difference in the way they treat me. Of course, I've had the good fortune to work at a company that loves creativity and innovation and knows it can only flourish when you embrace people's differences. Not everyone is so lucky.

> Acknowledges his good fortune and ability to be himself at work.

While I have never denied my sexuality, I haven't publicly acknowledged it either, until now. So let me be clear: I'm proud to be gay, and I consider being gay among the greatest gifts God has given me.

> Shares his identity clearly.

Being gay has given me a deeper understanding of what it means to be in the minority and provided a window into the challenges that people in other minority groups deal with every day. It's made me more empathetic, which has led to a richer life. It's been tough and uncomfortable at times, but it has given me the confidence to be myself, to follow my own path, and to rise above adversity and bigotry. It's also given me the skin of a rhinoceros, which comes in handy when you're the CEO of Apple. . . .

> Talks about his being gay as a strength.

Source: Timothy Donald Cook, "Tim Cook Speaks Up," *Bloomberg*, October 20, 2014, https://www.bloomberg.com/news/articles/2014-10-30/tim-cook-speaks-up, accessed May 8, 2017.

Authenticity Scale

To be authentic, we need clarity about our core values, goals, emotions, and identity.[54] As one measure, psychologists developed a 12-question authenticity scale (Figure 4.4). Items represent three components of authenticity:

- Authentic living involves being true to oneself in most situations and living in accordance with one's values and beliefs.
- Accepting external influence is the extent to which one accepts the influence of other people and the belief that one has to conform to the expectations of others.
- Self-alienation refers to the inevitable mismatch between conscious awareness and actual experience (the true self).[55]

Figure 4.4   An authenticity scale offers a tool for self-reflection

	Statement	Rate each item on a scale from 1 = *does not describe me at all* to 7 = *describes me very well*
1.	"I think it is better to be yourself than to be popular."	
2.	"I don't know how I really feel inside."	
3.	"I am strongly influenced by the opinions of others."	
4.	"I usually do what other people tell me to do."	
5.	"I always feel I need to do what others expect me to do."	
6.	"Other people influence me greatly."	
7.	"I feel as if I don't know myself very well."	
8.	"I always stand by what I believe in."	
9.	"I am true to myself in most situations."	
10.	"I feel out of touch with the 'real me.'"	
11.	"I live in accordance with my values and beliefs."	
12.	"I feel alienated from myself."	

Scoring Instructions

- Total Items 1, 8, 9, and 11 for Authentic Living
- Total Items 3, 4, 5, and 6 for Accepting External Influence
- Total Items 2, 7, 10, and 12 for Self-Alienation

Source: Alex Wood, Alex Linley, John Maltby, Michael Baliousis, and Joseph Stephen, "The Authentic Personality: A Theoretical and Empirical Conceptualization and the Development of the Authenticity Scale," *Journal of Counseling Psychology*, Vol. 55, No. 3 (2008), pp. 385–399.

Responses give you a snapshot of where you are today and present opportunities for development. Consider where you are now and ways to become more authentic.

Becoming More Authentic

Authentic leaders aren't perfect; their focus is on understanding themselves to become more authentic over time. Bill George offers one process for doing so, using the analogy of peeling back an onion[56] (Figure 4.5).

The outer layers of the onion are first. Strip away how you express yourself: your hair, clothes, body language, and whatever you consider to be your leadership style. These are external representations but offer little depth about who you really are.

Next, consider your needs, desires, strengths, and weaknesses. Whether you enjoy ballet or reggae, are good at tennis or bad at bowling—these are not the core of who you are as a person.

Now you're getting closer and can consider your motivations and capabilities. What drives you? External motivations include, for example, money, job titles, recognition, status, and winning. As you mature, you'll find more internal motivations, such as personal growth, internal job satisfaction, and helping and impacting others. What are your strengths? What distinguishes you from others at work? For what type of work are you best suited?[57] In other words, what are you good at, and what do you enjoy?

Finally, you're at the core: your shadow sides, vulnerabilities, life story, and blind spots. The tools discussed in Chapter 2 will help with this lifelong

Figure 4.5   Peel back the layers of an onion to find the authentic self

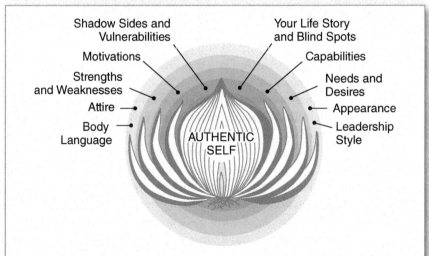

process. Self-awareness and self-reflection are critical, and you will likely involve others for feedback. Completing the Johari Window and authenticity assessment are useful ways to begin.

Peeling back the onion involves thinking about ourselves and our history in new ways. George suggests examining our "life story" and experiences to understand and reframe where we've been to find congruence with who we are today and who we want to become.[58] This process could involve revealing some deep, dark muck from our past, for example, abuse or neglect, and may require professional help to plod through. But without this work, negative stories and beliefs about ourselves may keep us stuck. Doing the work leads to self-acceptance and a more meaningful, connected life. Knowing ourselves and accepting our story allows us to relate well to others who may have experienced something similar.

Brené Brown argues that "wholehearted" people, as we discussed in Chapter 3, are "willing to let go of who they should be in order to be who they are."[59] Becoming an authentic leader requires introspection, feedback, support, self-compassion, and self-acceptance. It also requires rigor—commitment and diligence. Introverts may find this process easier than extroverts do.

Our self-discovery also may take our entire lives. We're constantly sorting out who we are, and we may be ambivalent about who we want to be. In addition, people come and go in our lives, which shapes how we define ourselves as well as how we're perceived by others.

Identity

Much of the authentic leadership literature focuses on living our values, beliefs, and desires. But how we self-identify—not just what we believe and do but who we are—is important too. In addition to the questions in the authenticity scale, you might ask questions about your identity. How do you define yourself? With what groups do you affiliate? How would you describe what's most important to you? Are you comfortable with who you are? Are you comfortable "in your own skin"?

We can imagine that one way Mary Barra self-identifies is as a woman, and this may distinguish her communication and way of managing through a crisis. In 2016, she was number one on *Fortune*'s U.S. Most Powerful Women in Business list.[60] We know that women and men—not each one of us, of course, but as a group—have different communication styles. Women's communication tends to focus on relationships and making connections, while men's communication focuses on gaining respect and status.[61]

A study in *Public Relations Review* compared GM's communications to those of Toyota, which faced a recall crisis in 2010. Researchers found that

Barra's communications conveyed a sense of urgency in fixing problems and expressions of apology. In contrast, CEO Akio Toyoda's[62] messages focused on defending the company, including shifting blame, explaining why the company's response was slow, and describing future actions the company planned to take, with an emphasis on quality instead of safety. The researchers concluded, "GM, whose crisis communication response was female-specific, received more positive [media] coverage than Toyota, whose crisis communication[63] was male-specific."

Maybe after Mary Barra felt more comfortable in the job—without the scrutiny she endured during the recalls, hearings, and investigations— she could be more of who she really is. Before she was CEO, she was the executive vice president of global product development and global purchasing and supply chain. In an interview with *Fortune*, she said, "The simple thing I say to [the team] is, 'no more crappy cars,' and that resonates." She's a straight-shooter. (She also said, "I like cars that go fast.")[64]

Maybe her team needed to be "freed up," as Barra says, to get back to their *own* values and make better decisions. She said, "Sometimes there were so many boundaries put on them, we didn't give them a recipe for success."[65] In Chapter 1, we learned that too many rules and procedures may, paradoxically, prevent people from making better ethical choices. Unlike the VW situation, which involved intentional deceit, Barra blames the passive culture: "individuals seemingly looking for reasons not to act."[66] Observers call GM's culture "insular" and a "nod culture."[67] Barra asserts, "In the end, I'm not afraid of the truth."[68] With more freedom and authority, people can be more authentic.

We Want to Connect With Real People on Social Media

We see the importance of an authentic voice on social media. Progressive Insurance was criticized for "robo-tweets" when the company fought an insurance claim for a woman who died in a car accident. The Twitter account manager tweeted the same message several times (Figure 4.6). Contrast these tweets with those from DiGiorno Pizza. In this situation, the Twitter account manager didn't realize the hashtags #WhyIStayed and #WhyILeft were used by people who had been in domestic violence situations. The DiGiorno representative wasn't afraid of being vulnerable—being exposed for making a dumb mistake—and he shows that he's a real person.

DiGiorno's strategy worked well for the brand. After two days of apologies and high social media activity, DiGiorno stopped tweeting for three

Figure 4.6

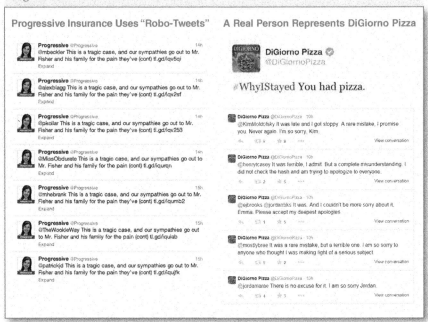

| Progressive Insurance Uses "Robo-Tweets" | A Real Person Represents DiGiorno Pizza |

Sources: Brian Patrick Eha, "Progressive Robo-tweets Spark Social Media Crisis," CNN Tech, August 16, 2012, http://money.cnn.com/2012/08/14/technology/progressive-tweets/index.html, accessed May 7, 2017; Laura Stampler, "DiGiorno Used a Hashtag About Domestic Violence to Sell Pizza," *Time*, September 9, 2014, "http://time.com/3308861/digiorno-social-media-pizza/, accessed May 7, 2017.

weeks. Negative comments ceased, giving the pizza company a fresh start. The Twitter account manager returned cautiously at first and eventually recovered his "edgy voice" until positive comments surpassed prescandal levels.[69] Progressive didn't apologize as DiGiorno did; instead, they just stopped the robo-responses and answered individual tweets.

A Gallup study found that few people are influenced by companies' social media presence alone. Instead of chasing fans and followers, companies should focus on building relationships with existing customers to convert them to brand advocates. To do this, Gallup suggests that companies be authentic and responsive.[70] When the American Airlines social media team brainstormed words for the company's Twitter responses, they generated "genuine," "authentic," "transparent," "savvy," "clear," "professional," and "warm"—never "scripted."[71]

Like corporations, political candidates get better responses for conversational tweets. When Bernie Sanders, former U.S. senator from Vermont, was running for president, he had a ghostwriter on Twitter, which is questionable for authenticity but good for followers. When Sanders was too busy campaigning, 27-year-old Hector Sigala learned that writing "We gotta" do something received more responses than "We have got to." As Sigala says, "That's because it sounds like Brooklyn Bernie."[72]

The "Brooklyn Bernie" strategy is supported by research in the public relations field. Studies have found that when companies use a conversational, "human" voice during a crisis, perception of interactivity increases, leading to improved reputation and willingness to buy company products.[73] We can see why DiGiorno Pizza was forgiven and Progressive's situation escalated.

SUMMARY

Authenticity is important to well-being and has many positive benefits for organizations. We can be authentic but not rigid; adaptability to different situations doesn't make us less authentic, because we are evolving over time and can never be 100% authentic in all roles.

When Mary Barra was new in her role, she faced congressional hearings and seemed stiff and insincere. Later, particularly when she is in front of employees, we see more of her genuine self. She advocates bringing our whole selves to work, and we see her demonstrate her own authenticity as she talks about the importance of her family.

Barra led GM out of the crisis and has fulfilled her commitment to create "today's GM." Auto industry analysts praise Barra for shifting the culture, particularly encouraging employees to raise issues early on. More comfortable in her role, Barra leads in her own way. As one analyst said, "We've never seen anybody run GM like this. She's breaking all the rules."[74]

Knowing ourselves and our limits helps us feel more comfortable with who we are. To create an inclusive working environment, we don't cover ourselves; our identity is inseparable from who we are at work. As we mature, others can know and rely on us.

Next, we'll see the relevance of authenticity to integrity. As we come to understand and accept ourselves, we are more consistent over time.

EXERCISES

Concept Review Questions

1. What does authenticity involve?

2. What is the value of living an authentic life to individuals and to organizations?

3. How do people "cover" themselves in organizations, and what is the downside?

4. What are some ways to become more authentic?

Self-Reflection Questions

1. Have you known someone you considered "fake"? How would you describe this person's behavior? How did you feel about the person?

2. How would you describe yourself? How, if at all, does this description depend on your audience—for example, a prospective romantic encounter, employer, or friend? What differences do you notice in your descriptions, and how would you explain them? Try to describe one unifying view of who you are.

3. How comfortable are you with who you are right now?[75]

4. What do you consider to be most unique about you? How do you feel about these aspects of yourself? For example, are you proud of them, embarrassed by them, or something else?

5. Think about a time when you used or were recognized for using one of your unique gifts. How did it feel?

6. Think about a time when you felt most comfortable "in your own skin." Visualize as many details as you can. What can you learn from the memory?

7. Think about a time when you didn't feel you belonged. What happened? Did you try too hard to "fit in" or hide an aspect of yourself? What, if anything, could have been avoided? What can you learn from the experience?

Self-Assessments

Consider three self-assessments related to authenticity:

1. *Self-Monitoring Scale.* Are you a high self-monitor or a low self-monitor? Take an assessment at http://bit.ly/2pKsH6z or http://sciof.us/2qJo6AN. What did you learn about yourself? Consider the criticisms of this construct discussed either—for example, the dichotomous nature of the scale—to keep the results in perspective.

2. *Authenticity Scale.* Respond to the items in Figure 4.4. Which of the three components—authentic living, accepting external influence, or self-alienation— needs more attention in your life? What about the results surprises or disappoints you?

3. *True North Mirror.* Take an online assessment based on Bill George's book *Discover Your Truth North* at http://truenorthmirror.discoveryourtruenorth .org/. Results will show in the following categories: self-awareness, values, integrated life, support team, sweet spot, and individual activity. Based on the results, on which areas would you like to focus?

Mini-Cases

Consider the following scenarios. On your own or with a partner, discuss the best course of action in each case. What would you do, and what factors into your decision?

Scenario 1

You're a candidate for a new job and ask to meet your prospective team. You're glad you did because no one on the team is like you; you are the only _____. (Fill in the blank.) What is this characteristic, and how important is it that you are different? Will you take the job?

Scenario 2

You're the hiring manager for an auditing position. You're interviewing a strong candidate, and the conversation is going well. Toward the end, he says, "I just want you to know that I'm a Muslim, and I use work breaks to pray five times during the day." What do you say?

Scenario 3

You're in a high-status job that pays well, but you don't enjoy the work. What factors into your decision about whether to stay? How does this decision relate to your authenticity?

Paired Activity

Review Figure 4.2, which shows four ways people may "cover" or hide something about themselves in order to fit in. First, share with a partner ways you have observed others covering themselves in each aspect. Next, talk about ways in which you have covered yourself in any or all of these aspects. Provide some context: Why did you choose to hide something about yourself in the situation? Under what circumstances do you usually hide this or other aspects of yourself?

Planning Questions

1. What are you considering sharing with this person? Why is this important to you?

2. What reaction are you hoping to get? Be careful here—you may not get what you expect or hope for. What is the worst that can happen? Are you prepared to handle whatever reaction you get?

3. How will you set up the conversation?

4. How will you react to what others say? How will you remain open to whatever they share? How can you be open to the other person regardless of what is said, yet react honestly in a way that reflects your true feelings?

Practice and Reflection

Take turns talking, and allow plenty of time to listen after each person speaks. Focus on reflecting what you hear and appreciating the difficulty the person may have in sharing the information. If you can relate to the experience, talk about your own feelings, but be careful not to overshadow theirs. For example, instead of, "You think *you* had a hard time!" try something like, "I have felt that way too."

Spend some time debriefing. How did it feel to talk about this situation? What did you learn about each other?

Paired Activity

Schedule a quiet time and place to talk with a partner. This activity will take some vulnerability as well as help you explore authenticity. Talk about a time when you made a decision that reflects who you really are. Consider a job opportunity you rejected, a relationship you ended, or an organization you left. Or consider the opposite: a job opportunity you accepted, a relationship you formed, or an organization you joined—or something else that might surprise people who don't know you well. Use the same planning and practice and reflection questions as above.

Role Play or Video Activity

Imagine that you are communicating your decision from the previous activity to the person affected: a prospective employer, a friend, an organization's director, etc.

Planning Questions

1. What is the situation you will use? If it's the same you used in the paired activity above, what did you learn from talking about your experience?

2. Who is the person affected by your decision? Analyze the other's perspective. How do you think he or she might feel and react to your decision? How does that affect how you'll deliver the message?

3. How will you begin the conversation? What will you say next?

4. How can you be clear about why this is an important decision for you?

5. How will you avoid blaming or criticizing the other person or organization for your decision? In other words, what about *you* influenced your decision?

Practice and Reflection

Role-play the situation. Consider recording yourself and getting feedback from a classmate, colleague, or friend. Did you demonstrate authenticity? Did you also demonstrate vulnerability? How did you feel? What did you learn from the experience?

5

Integrity

Being Consistent and Whole

Chapter Overview

FIFA officials were arrested for corruption, which observers say had been going on for years. By any measure, these leaders lacked integrity, which includes consistency and wholeness. Behavioral integrity measures one aspect of consistency, and organizational context gives a fuller picture of leaders who are moral and whole. As trust in institutions erodes, leaders must work harder to be truthful and transparent—putting a premium on integrity as a dimension of leadership character.

FIFA Leaders Disappoint Athletes and Fans Around the World

As the most popular sport in the world, association football ("soccer" to Americans) includes about 250 million players in more than 200 countries and billions of fans.[1] The sport culminates every four years in the World Cup, which is watched by more people than the Olympics[2] and is organized by The Fédération Internationale de Football Association (FIFA).

In 2015, 14 FIFA officials, including nine former executives, were charged with fraud, racketeering, and money laundering. Criminal investigations began to answer questions such as: Were votes bought and sold to award the 2010 World Cup to South Africa? How were 2018 and 2022 World Cups awarded to Russia and Qatar? Did officials get kickbacks from sports advertisers? Later, 16 more officials were charged and accused of taking $200 million in bribes in addition to other forms of corruption (see Figure 5.1).[3,4,5] FIFA president Seth Blatter denied knowledge of wrongdoing, but an Independent Ethics Committee banned him and another executive from football for eight years.

The arrests represented a long history of ethical questions. In 2008, a British reporter, Andrew Jennings, wrote a book titled *Foul! The Secret World of FIFA: Bribes, Vote Rigging and Ticket Scandals.* In 2011, a former player from Argentina said, "FIFA is a big museum. They are dinosaurs who do not want to relinquish power. It's always going to be the same."[6] In 2014,

Figure 5.1   FIFA corruption scandal unfolds

November 2008	Sports reporter Andrew Jennings writes *Foul! The Secret World of FIFA: Bribes, Vote Rigging and Ticket Scandals.*
October 2010	British newspaper *The Sunday Times* alleges a cash-for-votes process for the World Cup.
June 2011	FIFA official Mohamed bin Hammam is found guilty of bribery and banned from football for life.
March 2015	*The Telegraph* reveals millions paid to FIFA official Jack Warner from a Qatari firm; he is later banned for life.
May 2015	14 FIFA executives are detained and charged in Zurich.
June 2015	FIFA president Seth Blatter announces his resignation; he is later banned for eight years.

Sources: "FIFA Corruption Crisis: Key Questions Answered," *BBC News*, December 21, 2015, http://www.bbc.com/news/world-europe-32897066, accessed May 30, 2017; Leon Siciliano and Sophie Jamieson, "FIFA: A Timeline of Corruption—in 90 Seconds," *The Telegraph*, March 22, 2016, http://www.telegraph.co.uk/football/2016/03/22/fifa-a-timeline-of-corruption—in-90-seconds/, accessed June 20, 2017; Austin Knoblauch and Barry Stavro, "A Timeline on the FIFA Scandal," *Los Angeles Times*, June 2, 2015, http://www.latimes.com/sports/soccer/la-sp-fifa-scandal-timeline-20150603-story.html, accessed June 20, 2017.

Lord Triesman, the former chairman of the Football Association, said FIFA "behaves like a mafia family" and "has decades-long traditions of bribes, bungs, and corruption."[7]

Damning evidence includes emails discovered between Blatter and the president of South Africa discussing $10 million being awarded to the country prior to the games in 2010.[8] A spokesperson for the South African Football Association condemned the allegations:

> Those individuals that brought the World Cup to South Africa were men of high integrity—men like the late President Nelson Mandela and our former President Thabo Mbeki.[9]

To the contrary, FIFA officials and others involved in the scandal *lacked* integrity and violated the trust of fans and players around the world. As with all the cases in this book, these leaders lacked other character dimensions, such as vulnerability, humility, and accountability. But our focus here is on integrity—leaders who are consistent and whole.

Leaders of Integrity Are Consistent and Whole

Consistency is the hallmark of leading with integrity. A leader's integrity is judged based on personal consistency and alignment with greater goals. Ethics codes are useful but not enough to inspire integrity. After defining this leadership dimension, we'll see where FIFA leaders fell short.

Integrity Defined

We have all heard the clichés "Walk the talk" and "Practice what you preach." Both mean behaving consistently with what you say, and this is an important part of integrity as a leadership character dimension.

Mary Crossan and her colleagues identified integrity as a leadership character dimension with the following elements: *authentic, candid, transparent, principled,* and *consistent.* When integrity is present in organizations, we see trust, transparency, and effective communication.[10]

In this book, we distinguished authenticity as a character dimension to elevate the concept and to focus on how we self-identify—who we are as people. We'll see the relevance throughout this chapter too.

Behavioral and Moral Integrity Definitions

Tony Simons at the Cornell SC Johnson College of Business and author of the book *The Integrity Dividend* isolates *behavioral integrity* to focus specifically on what leaders say and do. He defines behavioral integrity as "the fit between words and actions, as seen by others. It means promise keeping and showing the values you profess."[11]

A strict focus on behavioral integrity is useful for measuring results in an organization, as we'll see later, but misses, by definition, a link to morality.[12] Integrity is about word and deed, but our actions are part of a coherent system that is judged externally. If FIFA officials had said, "When I accept this position, I'll take bribes," and then they did so, they would technically demonstrate behavioral integrity. But we certainly wouldn't call them leaders of integrity or good character.

We need measures broader than behavioral integrity, but we have to be careful not to define integrity so broadly that it loses meaning entirely or simply means being ethical or "good." Incorporating moral integrity into our definition is useful.

Authors of an article in the *Journal of Change Management* conclude, "[P]erceived leader integrity may be better defined and measured as a multidimensional construct capturing both perceptions that the leader holds moral values and professes and enacts those values with an exceedingly high degree of consistency."[13] In other words, leader integrity depends on followers' perceptions of consistency *and* perceived moral behavior.

Wholeness

In our definition, leaders of integrity are whole. When you consider other forms of the word—*integral, integrated*—you can see the importance of wholeness. *Integrity* is from the Latin word *integer*, which means "intact," or whole, complete, and unbroken.

Consistency is important, but a leader's words and actions must align with a greater whole, for example, an organization's values. Whether we believe someone to have integrity takes into account the leader's environment, or the organizational context. As an organization, FIFA promises impartiality and fairness, and officials didn't live up to those expectations. Although personally consistent, FIFA leaders cannot be considered whole.

Alignment between what we do and what our organization promises makes us predictable and trustworthy. We know that a firefighter will break a window to save a child because the larger mission—saving lives—is more important than maintaining property. Trustworthy leaders are perceived as having ability (skills and competence), benevolence (acting in the recipient's interests), and integrity (reliability or consistency).[14,15]

At the same time, company values may conflict with our own. Leaders of integrity live by high ethical standards, not only within the standards of the organization but from their own sense of purpose. When external values don't align with our view of morality, we face an issue of integrity. We may act consistently with the company's expectations, but if we don't feel right about them, we cannot be considered whole.

The Disconnection Between Codes and Behavior

Ideally, internal codes guide people's behavior, but they aren't enough to inspire integrity. Simons argues, "A statement of values that lives in a desk drawer does more ill than good."[16]

From FIFA's own documentation, we see a contradiction. On its website in 2017, FIFA had a 60-page code of ethics dated 2012. Officials are expected to live by this code—to uphold the principles of the organization. One section speaks specifically to the "integrity of matches and competitions" (Figure 5.2) and "having stakes." Other sections warn against "offering and accepting gifts and other benefits" and "bribery and corruption."[17]

Too often, there is inconsistency between corporate codes and reality. A study of 300 public companies found that most have a code of conduct but don't enforce anything beyond simple compliance.[18] According to a Deloitte study, almost 20% of managers and employees said their organization had a sense of purpose, but leaders "didn't live by that code of conduct and, as

Figure 5.2   FIFA describes integrity in the code of ethics

Subsection 4: Integrity of competitions

25 **Integrity of matches and competitions**

Persons bound by this Code shall be forbidden from taking part in, either directly or indirectly, or otherwise being associated with, betting, gambling, lotteries and similar events or transactions connected with football matches. They are forbidden from having stakes, either actively or passively, in companies, concerns, organisations, etc. that promote, broker, arrange or conduct such events or transactions.

| Connects officials' responsibilities to the organization. | Uses clear, strong language to define expectations. | Specifically mentions practices that FIFA officials engaged in. |

Source: FIFA, "FIFA Code of Ethics," 2012 edition, https://resources.fifa.com/mm/document/affederation/administration/50/02/82/codeofethics_v211015_e_neutral.pdf, accessed May 31, 2017.

a result, that didn't have the same positive impact."[19] Punit Renjen, chairman of the board, summarized the lesson:

> If you want to be successful over the long haul, you have to have a sense of purpose that is clearly articulated and embedded in your organization and processes, but you also have to live it. There can't be two sets of rules.[20]

Employees depend on each other to work within organizational values. If caring for customers, for example, is a company's stated commitment, employees prioritize customer needs and managers reward their doing so. In turn, employees expect leaders to prioritize customers as well.

Behavioral Integrity Is Good for Business

Although the definition of behavioral integrity is narrow, the concept is useful for conducting research. Studies of behavioral integrity report positive effects on employees and their organizations.

Impact on Employees

To help understand the connection between authenticity and behavioral integrity, Tony Simons and others looked at the effect on employee commitment and performance. As we might expect from the previous two chapters, leaders who are authentic and willing to be vulnerable are perceived as having high behavioral integrity—what they say and do are aligned. Because of their consistency and because they manage perceptions well, authentic leaders inspire employees to feel connected to the organization. Even during times of change, these leaders can be trusted, which translates to positive work role performance, such as flexibility and offering suggestions.[21]

Behavioral integrity research demonstrates additional benefits to employees. When a leader's words and actions are aligned, followers trust and are more satisfied working for the person, are more engaged in their work, are happier in their jobs, and plan to stay with the organization longer.[22]

Impact on Organizational Performance

Simons's research also links behavioral integrity to company profitability. Hotel employee responses to questions about behavioral integrity—for example, "My manager practices what he/she preaches" and "When my manager promises something, I can be certain that it will happen"— correlated with the hotel's profitability more than measures of trust, fairness, and satisfaction (Figure 5.3). Simons describes the results of high manager integrity ratings:

- Deeper employee commitment, leading to
- Lower employee turnover and
- Superior customer service; all leading to
- High profitability.[23]

We have heard companies say, "Employees are our greatest asset," and then lay off 10% of their staff. This may not be a contradiction if, for example, a company needs to eliminate an underperforming branch to save the rest of the company. But, at least publicly, the decision represents an

Figure 5.3   Behavioral integrity correlated most strongly with hotel profitability

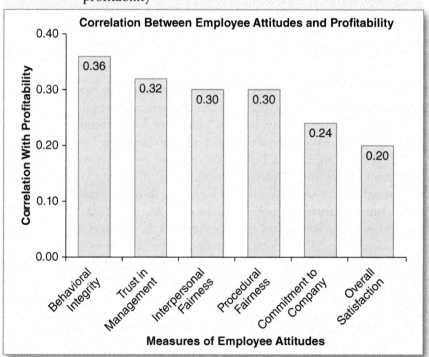

Source: Tony Simons, *The Integrity Dividend: Leading by the Power of Your Word* (San Francisco: Jossey-Bass, 2008), p. 10. Republished with permission of John Wiley & Sons, Inc.; conveyed through Copyright Clearance Center, Inc.

inconsistency with a promise, and we judge the leaders harshly, particularly because a layoff provokes fear.

A study of mergers highlights the importance of matching values and practices. The authors found that both overpromising and underpromising negatively affected employee productivity post-merger. But when organizational practices were consistent with espoused values, employee productivity was higher.[24]

We see many business benefits for leading with integrity. More important, as a dimension of leadership character, integrity inspires trust.

Trust in Organizations Is Eroding

The U.S. attorney general who investigated the FIFA case spoke of the impact on children who put their trust in the organization:

> When you're talking about sports, that's how we teach our kids about fair play and sportsmanship. We want them to look up to these sports figures. It's a character building exercise for them to play sports. . . . [The FIFA case] kills ideals—in young people, in people who look up to their figures and place their trust in organizations.[25]

Trust is an issue not only for FIFA but for companies and societies around the world. For 17 years, the Edelman Trust Barometer has evaluated people's views of trust and credibility. The 2017 survey of 33,000 people in 28 countries paints a dismal picture about our hope for the future: "only 15 percent of the general population believe the present system is working, while 53 percent do not and 32 percent are uncertain."[26]

Throughout the world, fear drives increasing distrust of governments, the media, nongovernmental organizations (NGOs), and business. Although business is faring better than governments and the media, CEO credibility has dropped to 37%, which is the lowest in the survey's history and 12 points lower than in 2016. Not surprisingly, people indicate they want more regulation of business and a slower rate of growth.[27]

In the United States, a Gallup poll of trust in institutions confirms Edelman's international findings (Figure 5.4). The only entity rated worse than big business is Congress.

Understandably, 58% of CEOs are somewhat or extremely concerned about eroding trust in business, according to a PricewaterhouseCoopers (PwC) report. PwC's global chairman describes how the definition of trust has expanded:

Figure 5.4   Confidence in U.S. institutions is low

Please tell me how much confidence you, yourself, have in each?		
	Great Deal	Quite a Lot
The Military	44%	28%
Small Business	33%	37%
The Police	31%	26%
The Church or Organized Religion	23%	18%
The U.S. Supreme Court	18%	22%
The Medical System	18%	19%
The Presidency	19%	13%
The Public Schools	18%	18%
Banks	14%	18%
Organized Labor	13%	15%
The Criminal Justice System	14%	13%
Television News	11%	13%
Newspapers	11%	16%
Big Business	9%	12%
Congress	6%	6%

Source: "Confidence in Institutions," *Gallup*, June 2016, http://www.gallup.com/poll/1597/confidence-institutions.aspx, accessed September 15, 2017.

Executive teams need to fully grasp the ethical and moral implications of their decisions, and communicate their actions with integrity. Trust must also be paramount between supervisors and employees.[28]

To increase trust in our institutions, leaders within organizations can cultivate it over time.

Leaders Who Model Integrity, Trust, and Transparency Cultivate Trust

Trust leads to better outcomes and is cultivated over time through our willingness to be vulnerable and through our transparency. We'll see an example from Chipotle to illustrate these concepts.

Better Work Outcomes

From his work applying neuroscience to people in organizations, Paul Zak confirmed the importance of trust. As employees worked, Zak measured oxytocin production in the brain and found that people are happier on the job when they're doing purpose-driven work with people they trust. He concluded that people at high-trust companies report the following compared to people at low-trust companies: 74% less stress, 106% more energy at work, 50% higher productivity, 13% fewer sick days, 76% more engagement, 29% more satisfaction with their lives, and 40% less burnout.[29]

Trust eases social interactions, so we can do more in relationship with each other. As Zak says, "Trust acts as an economic lubricant, reducing the frictions inherent in economic activity."[30]

Willingness to Be Vulnerable

When we offer our trust in others, we are willing to be vulnerable. Assuming you can't control a friend's actions, can you rely on him to do something that's important to you? Will you take the risk that he will come through and pick you up at the airport or help you move as he promised?

We are particularly vulnerable during times of change, when we live with uncertainty and more is at stake. After a corporate acquisition, will your manager protect your job? Research indicates one way people manage uncertainty is by judging leaders' actions as fair or unfair, which puts pressure on leaders, particularly during times of change.[31]

We are smart to approach relationships with "eyes wide open." We take calculated risks and know that trust isn't a guarantee. We choose to trust and engage others in good faith in order to have better relationships.[32] And trust is reciprocal: we model trust, and we are likely to receive it in return.

Evolving Trust Over Time

Trust changes over time and, depending on the people and circumstances, may be slow to grow. John Gottman, who studies trust in relationships, found that feelings of trust and betrayal are built in small ways, not, as we might think, by big events.[33] On the other hand, a big event—for example, a marital affair—can destroy trust quickly.

Gottman encourages us to view opportunities for connection positively. When we are tempted to avoid or turn away from others, we should choose connection instead.[34] Leaders have many chances to engage with employees and show concern for their welfare. A coworker looks upset at a staff meeting, comes to work looking tired, or is unusually quiet during a meeting. We would rather ignore it; after all, who wants to deal with someone else's problems? But Gottman tells us to ask what's going on. Opening up ways for people to talk with us tells them we care about them: "I've got your back" and, over time, "You can trust me."

Prioritizing connections over work is challenging. How do you balance a work deadline with an upset coworker? Gottman encourages us, when possible, to choose seemingly small emotional connections to cultivate trust.

Similarly, Tony Simons warns us to be careful about making even small commitments that we don't keep. Casual promises and loose language, such as "Be there in five minutes" when it's really 15, may leave people questioning our integrity.[35] Over time, our sloppiness may undermine trust. If you don't do the little things you say you'll do, will you do the big things?

Openness and Transparency

In addition to keeping their word, leaders with integrity are open to seeing their own role in compromising trust. When trust is broken, a leader of integrity asks, "Have I been trustworthy?" and "What responsibility do I have in this relationship?" When a team member doesn't follow through on a commitment, the leader asks herself, "Have I kept my *own* commitments?"

An article in the *Journal of Management* conveys the importance of transparency in cultivating trust. From a synthesis of the academic literature, the authors conclude that the concept of transparency exists in many domains at both the organizational and individual levels. They offer a blended definition: "Transparency is the perceived quality of intentionally shared information from a sender."[36]

Once again, we may see more easily when this aspect of character is weak. FIFA lacked transparency. The CEO of the public relations agency N6A had this advice for the organization:

> There's a completely transparent and objective system of checks and balances for the sporting part of all of FIFA's competitions that have been effective for decades. These same procedures should be applied to the business side of FIFA's dealings, and then the organization will slowly be able to regain the trust of their consumers by providing transparency and objectiveness into their critical business decisions that have been plagued by ambiguity for ages.[37]

Transparency typically includes disclosure, accuracy, and clarity,[38] which we might expect for leader integrity. You can openly share information, but if it's inaccurate or unclear, that won't bode well for how people perceive your integrity. People share—and overshare—all sorts of information on social media, but we know it's not all true.

Similarly, leaders share information, for example, in press releases and news statements, that is impossible to understand. When Time Inc. laid off 110 of its 7,200 employees, management communicated with jargon:

> Over the last couple of weeks, we have been realigning our organizational structure to better leverage our content creation, sales and marketing and brand development operations. Our primary objective has been to better position ourselves to operate with greater agility and optimize the growth areas of our operation. As a result, there will be some job eliminations. That is always painful but an unfortunate reality in today's business climate.[39]

In this case, Time is using persuasion tactics, such as downplaying and confusion,[40] to hide the truth: 1.5% of its workforce got canned.

Part of being transparent is making public statements. Boudewign de Bruin at the University of Groningen in the Netherlands explored how oaths serve as symbols of integrity. Researchers seem to agree that integrity involves keeping your promises, but de Bruin distinguishes between a mere promise and a promissory oath, which is public, often taken at a ceremony, and covers an indefinite period of time.[41]

The idea of making public statements is useful for leadership integrity. Robert Cialdini's research on persuasion teaches us that people will more likely follow through on their commitments if they are made public. Cialdini argues that people want "to be and to appear consistent with [their] actions, statements, and beliefs."[42] We can expect, then, when leaders promise year-end bonuses, employees are more likely to receive them, and when people sign up to complete a project, they will follow through.

Chipotle Example

Chipotle Mexican Grill is a controversial example of integrity and transparency. The company's "Food With Integrity" slogan promises, "We're committed to sourcing the very best ingredients we can find and preparing them by hand."[43] Although the company promotes food without genetically modified organisms (GMOs), critics counter that this doesn't equate to healthy food; they note scientific evidence supporting GMOs, the high caloric content of some menu items, and sweetened beverages.[44]

With more than 2,000 locations, Chipotle's business model is working, but the company hit a snag in 2015, when norovirus, *E. coli*, and *Salmonella* were reported in a few restaurants throughout the country. Founder and CEO Steve Ells has been front and center in fixing the issue and regaining consumer trust. When sales dropped 14.6% in one quarter, Ells admitted this was "the most challenging period in Chipotle's history."[45]

Focusing on food safety, the company has demonstrated transparency. On its website, a video shows actions taken with suppliers and farmers, new technology and procedures, and tracking systems. To train staff on new procedures, Chipotle closed all restaurants for four hours—and live tweeted the meetings.[46] Ells positioned Chipotle's changes as setting new industry standards for food safety.

Unfortunately, Chipotle had more trouble with foodborne illnesses in 2017. Despite the leader's transparency, whether the brand can recover fully remains to be seen.

Leaders With Integrity Tell the Truth

On a more fundamental level, leaders with integrity are honest. Although most people don't lie, some do. Those who mislead or omit important information do so to benefit themselves at the expense of others.

Why People Lie

Older research indicated that lying is a common practice, but newer studies tell a different story: most people tell the truth, and only a few of us are "prolific liars." Rather than looking at average numbers, researchers in the UK replicated a U.S. study. They argue that a small group of people needs to be isolated because they tell many more lies than the rest of us: 6.32 "white lies" and 2.86 "big lies" a day. The most frequent liars are young men with high occupational status.[47]

Why do people lie? Research suggests that frequent liars have psychopathic tendencies[48]—they don't see the emotional impact of their lies, or they don't believe lying is wrong. But most of us lie because of fear—the same reason we avoid failure. We're afraid or worried about something, so we protect ourselves or other people. We might lie to protect our status ("I didn't get the email") or to build relationships ("I like your sweater") or to belong ("I love football!"). People lie because they are insecure and can't accept the consequences of the truth: failing to measure up, losing a connection, or feeling left out.[49]

Of course, there are times when omitting information or not telling the "whole truth" may be appropriate. No good can come of criticizing a coworker's weight, and regulations may prevent us from giving certain information. But lying just to protect ourselves is a dangerous game. "Lies beget lies," meaning once you tell a lie, you may need four more to cover it up. People get hurt, and their trust in you diminishes over time.

Academic Institution Examples

Leaders who intentionally lie or omit important information may cause trouble for themselves and for their organization. For-profit schools have been criticized for providing misleading information to prospective students. ITT Technical Institute, for example, was closed after complaints of "deceptive marketing; strong-arm recruitment tactics; misleading information about costs, courses, graduation and job placement rates; inflated enrollment numbers; bait-and-switch schemes; subpar instruction; and more." The former dean of academic affairs had expressed concern about recruiting tactics, but he was fired.[50]

Several lawsuits have been brought against law schools for fudging job placement rates. A case against Thomas Jefferson School of Law was one of about 15 that made it to trial. The plaintiff, a graduate of the school, said she decided to enroll—and to accumulate more than $150,000 in debt—based on false information. The school counts part-time workers in nonlegal careers, for example, waitress or pool cleaner, as employed graduates. During the trial, the school's attorney told the jury, "I'm not here to tell you a law degree is a guarantee of career success, is a guarantee of riches. It's not. No degree is."[51]

The law school won the case, possibly because the jury thought the student should have known better and because they perceived her as arrogant.[52] Still, some believe law schools aren't delivering what they're promising either explicitly or implicitly.

American Spirit Cigarettes Example

As another example, when you look at packaging for American Spirit cigarettes, you might think they're healthier than they are (Figure 5.5). Critics cite the green design and labels, such as "natural," "additive free," and "organic," as deceiving to consumers. According to charges brought against Santa Fe Natural Tobacco Company and Reynolds American, these terms imply a safer cigarette and allow the company to charge a premium.[53,54] A tobacco researcher argues, "[Smokers] believe that their product is less harmful than other brands, but there is absolutely no evidence to support that belief."[55]

Figure 5.5   American Spirit promotes cigarettes as natural

Source: Brattain v. Santa Fe Natural Tobacco Company, Inc., Pacific Region, Northern District of California Civil Case No: 15-4705, https://www.truthinadvertising.org/wp-content/uploads/2015/10/Brattain-v-Santa-Fe-Natural-Tobacco-et-al-complaint.pdf, accessed May 31, 2017.

Company representatives said they didn't mean to imply the cigarette was less harmful; the intent was simply to develop a better choice for people who already smoked. A representative referred to the company as "the Ben & Jerry's of the tobacco industry." Robins Sommers, former CEO of Santa Fe Natural, claims, "The flavoring was from organic menthol crystals that were in the filter, not in the tobacco. It was pure mint."[56,57]

But the plaintiff's lead attorney argues that "organic"—how product components are grown—is irrelevant: "You're not ingesting tobacco, you're inhaling smoke. The smoke contains the smoke and the menthol, which is an additive, which is a deceit to tell anyone it contains no additives. It contains a tremendous additive—menthol."[58]

Under an agreement with the Food and Drug Administration, which Reynolds signed to avoid a class-action suit, the company can no longer call its product "natural" or "additive free." We might say that the Santa Fe Natural characters lack character. The lawsuits and settlement indicate that they lack integrity and misled consumers.

Alex Watkins, a certified-organic landowner who grows the Santa Fe tobacco, sums up the case:

> People just like that word [organic]. And they feel so much safer smoking. I mean, look, you're still sucking smoke in your lungs. Is it good for you? Hell no. But you ain't gonna stop people from smoking. They enjoy it. But I guess they got a sense of feeling that it's supposed to be better for you. Because, you know, it don't have any chemicals. Whatever eases your mind, I guess.[59]

This is behavioral integrity stripped raw: we might not like what Watkins has to say, but he tells the truth.[60]

Investors Seek and Demonstrate Integrity

Investment firms have a particular responsibility to act with integrity: they manage other people's money. Although some are bad actors, we see many positive examples in the financial industry.

Warren Buffett Example

Warren Buffett, chairman of Berkshire Hathaway, is known for his investment expertise and philanthropy; with Bill Gates and Facebook CEO Mark Zuckerberg, he started The Giving Pledge, a public commitment from billionaires to donate most of their wealth.

Buffett says his firm hires for three qualities: intelligence, initiative or energy, and integrity. He jokes, "And if they don't have the latter, the first two will kill you. Because if you're going to get someone without integrity, you want him lazy and dumb."[61] Buffett says part of having integrity is the willingness to say no—to avoid making promises you can't keep.[62]

Buffett also encourages people to buy low-cost index mutual funds instead of paying high fees to investors because, as he wrote in his popular annual shareholder letter in 2016, "[w]hen trillions of dollars are managed by Wall Streeters charging high fees, it will usually be the managers who reap outsized profits, not the clients."[63]

Betterment Example

Another example of integrity in investing is from Betterment, which *Business Insider* refers to as a "hot investing startup."[64] Betterment has no investment minimums, so the firm doesn't cater exclusively to wealthy people, and they follow Buffett's principles, such as charging low fees and investing in index funds.

CEO and founder Jon Stein also has been vocal about the Department of Labor's (DOL) fiduciary rule. The rule requires financial advisors to prioritize their clients' interests over their own. This sounds obvious, but financial investors sometimes have an inherent conflict: advisors can receive fees for investing in certain funds, and they might recommend funds that pay more than others, as Buffett warns. While some larger firms lobbied against the rule, Betterment took out full-page newspaper ads asking the public, "Do you trust your money manager? Maybe you shouldn't" (Figure 5.6).

Figure 5.6 Betterment promotes trust

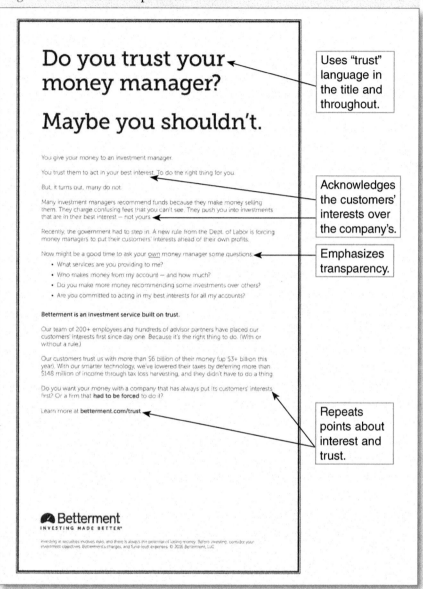

Source: Rachael Levy, "A Hot Investing Startup Wrote an Open Letter to Donald Trump, and Is Setting the Stage for a Battle on Wall Street," *Business Insider*, December 5, 2016, http://www.businessinsider.com/betterments-wall-street-journal-donald-trump-ad-on-fiduciary-rule-2016-12, accessed May 30, 2017.

With trust as an explicit commitment at the organizational level, Betterment sets clear expectations for their financial advisors. The company encourages clients to ask tough questions of their advisers, such as, "Do you make more money recommending some investments over others?" and "Are you committed to acting in my best interests for all my accounts?" At all levels of the organization, employees are expected to demonstrate integrity by being consistent and whole—upholding the company's commitment to act in clients' best interests.

SUMMARY

In June 2017, new chairpersons of the Independent Ethics Committee decided to publish full findings about the 2018/2022 FIFA World Cup bidding process. The organization claims this had been requested of previous chairpersons, but they refused.[65]

A FIFA statement ends, "For the sake of transparency, FIFA welcomes the news that this report has now been finally published." At the same time, the organization admits the report had been leaked to a German newspaper, so we might question whether the decision was meaningful at all.

Having leadership integrity means we are consistent and whole. For behavioral integrity, we do what we say we will do, aligning word and deed. Leaders with integrity also inspire trust because they act consistently with organizational values. People can count on them.

Without integrity, a leader's behavior is unpredictable, and we have a difficult time holding that person accountable, which we'll discuss in the next chapter. The FIFA report, totaling 434 pages, reviews World Cup decisions and recommends actions such as "enhanced reporting requirements." But as we'll explore next, rules and regulations may not be the best way to inspire accountability.

EXERCISES

Concept Review Questions

1. How would you define integrity in your own words?

2. More specifically, what is behavioral integrity? What are the limitations of this concept?

3. How does integrity benefit others and an organization?

4. What are some important considerations when cultivating trust?

5. What is the value of transparency?

Self-Reflection Questions

1. Think about a time when someone didn't follow through on a promise made to you. How did you feel? Try to understand the circumstances from the other person's point of view. Is it possible for you to understand their reasons?

2. Now think about a time when someone lied to you. Try the same questions above. Also, in retrospect, what did you miss about this person? Is there something you didn't see with "eyes wide open"?

3. Who is someone you trust? What makes this person trustworthy? No one's perfect; has this person ever disappointed you?

4. When have you not kept a promise or lied to someone else? Or when have you overcommitted and failed to follow through? Why do you think you failed? Was it out of fear or insecurity in some way? How have you grown since then?

5. Think about the biggest lie you have told. How were others affected by it? Have you apologized for it? Is there still time to do so?

6. Think about an organization to which you have belonged, for example, a workplace, school, club, or place of worship. Find the group's vision, values, or a similar statement on its website. To what extent do the organization's leaders follow what they profess, and where do they fall short?

7. What's an example of a decision that affected you negatively—for example, a rejection for a job, organization, or athletic team? In what ways was the decision transparent, and what other information would you have liked to know? If the decision had been more transparent, how, if at all, would it have affected how you feel about the results?

8. When have you made a decision that could have been more transparent to the people affected? Why wasn't the process more open? What value and downsides do you see of revealing more about how the decision was made?

Assessment

Think of a manager you worked for in the past. How would you answer these questions about this person's behavioral integrity on this scale?[66] For variations on this assessment, you can think of a friend, colleague, partner, or someone else in your life. You also can try answering the questions for yourself. You may have a difficult time being objective, but do your best.

Rating Scale:
1 = *strongly disagree*; 2 = *disagree*; 3 = *neither agree or disagree*; 4 = *agree*;
5 = *strongly agree*

Item		Rating
1.	There is a match between my manager's words and actions.	1 2 3 4 5
2	My manager delivers on promises.	1 2 3 4 5
3.	My manager practices what he/she preaches.	1 2 3 4 5
4.	My manager does what he/she says he/she will do.	1 2 3 4 5
5.	My manager conducts himself/herself by the same values he/she talks about.	1 2 3 4 5
6.	My manager shows the same priorities that he/she describes.	1 2 3 4 5
7.	When my manager promises something, I can be certain that it will happen.	1 2 3 4 5
8.	If my manager says he/she is going to do something, he/she will.	1 2 3 4 5

Mini-Cases

Consider the following scenarios. On your own or with a partner, discuss the best course of action in each case. What would you do, and what factors into your decision?

Scenario 1

When you met with your manager last month, you agreed to finish an important report by the end of the week. Today is Wednesday, and you're not confident you'll have it done. You have been waiting for information from someone in another department, and now you learned that she's on vacation until Monday. Let's assume this is an important report that your manager is expecting. How will you handle the situation?

Scenario 2

You're working as part of a new team, and the team leader doesn't seem to trust you. She gives you very small tasks and checks in several times a day. You would like more autonomy. What can you do to prove that you can be trusted to finish bigger parts of the project? In other words, how can you cultivate trust?

Scenario 3

One of your employees asks you if he can take off the rest of the week (three days) for a personal matter. This employee started with the company less than a month ago and has already called in sick twice. When you tell him that you can't approve his request, he cites a company statement in the employee handbook about valuing work/life balance and says he finds this inconsistent. How will you respond?

Individual Activity

Think about a decision you're planning to make. How can you make the decision-making process transparent? (If nothing comes to mind, consider a decision you made in the past or a decision others made that affected you.)

Planning Questions

1. What is the decision?

2. Who is affected and how?

3. How was the decision made? What criteria were used that are both explicit and implicit? What is not known to the person or people affected?

4. What information would be most useful for the person to receive? For example, could the information serve as feedback to help the person develop personally or professionally?

5. What is difficult about revealing the information? Do you fear hurting the person's feelings or damaging your relationship? Does giving information put your status in jeopardy in some way? In other words, what are the arguments against disclosing the information?

6. Given your analysis, what information will you share about the decision-making process, and what might you avoid saying and why?

Paired Activity

Prepare to explain the decision-making process described above. With a partner, role-play telling the person or people impacted about the decision and how it was made. Optional: Video-record yourself so you can review it after.

Planning Questions

1. What did you learn from analyzing the situation above?

2. Analyze the other perspective. What do you think the person wants to hear? You may disappoint the person.

3. How will you begin the discussion? What will you say next?

4. How will you balance being truthful and being hurtful?

5. How can you describe the situation in a way that is helpful and transparent?

Practice and Reflection

In what ways did you demonstrate integrity? Did you also demonstrate vulnerability? How did you feel? What did you learn from the experience? You likely displayed other dimensions we'll cover later in the book as well.

6

Accountability

Responding to Others

Chapter Overview

To learn about accountability, we'll see how Wells Fargo denied senior management's role and blamed employees for creating more than 2 million fake bank accounts. Companies and governments set incentives and regulations to guide behavior, but they are insufficient and may not be the best approach. Instead, organizations create a culture that encourages good ethical decision making. Leaders allow employees enough authority to use their judgment while giving them feedback along the way to prevent small mistakes from becoming serious mistakes.

Wells Fargo Sets Unrealistic Sales Goals for Employees

On the face of it, Wells Fargo's cross-selling strategy is simply smart business. Every bank does it. Companies spend far less selling additional products to existing customers—for example, a car loan to a mortgage holder or a credit card to a checking account owner—than trying to attract a new customer. In its 2015 annual report, Wells Fargo boasts building generations of loyal customers: "Earning lifelong relationships, one customer at a time, is fundamental to achieving our vision."[1]

But what does it take to meet the company's vision of lifelong relationships? Internally, former CEO John Stumpf used the slogan "Eight is great," referring to the goal of selling eight products to each Wells Fargo customer.[2] According to employee complaints, Wells Fargo's goals were unreasonable:

> Wells Fargo has strict quotas regulating the number of daily "solutions" that its bankers must reach; these "solutions" include the opening of all new banking and credit card accounts. Managers constantly hound, berate, demean, and threaten employees to meet these unreachable quotas. Managers often tell employees to do whatever it takes to reach their quotas. Employees who do not reach their quotas are often required to work hours beyond their typical work schedule without being compensated for that extra work time, and/or are threatened with termination.[3]

To try to reach their goals, bank employees got creative and opened about 2 million fake accounts over several years. Employees used one strategy, called "bundling," or telling customers they couldn't open an account without another being attached. Employees also moved funds from customers' current accounts to start new ones, created bogus email addresses for online banking services, and submitted applications for 565,443 credit card accounts without authorization. Customers paid overdraft and other fees for accounts they didn't open and didn't realize they owned (Figure 6.1).[4, 5, 6]

We might say Wells Fargo leaders and employees lacked integrity, but our focus here is on accountability. Wells Fargo may have satisfied shareholders, but the company has other stakeholders to which it needs to be accountable, including customers and employees.

Responsibility and Accountability Definitions Are Complementary

Although defined differently, responsibility and accountability are related, and both are relevant to leadership character.

Dictionary, Corporate, and Academic Definitions

The dictionary gives us traditional definitions of *responsible* and *accountable*:

> **Responsible:** answerable or accountable for something within one's power, control, or management.[7]

Figure 6.1   Wells Fargo fake bank account crisis unfolds

2011–2016	More than 2 million bank accounts and credit cards are opened without customer knowledge.
2011–2016	Wells Fargo terminates 5,300 employees for creating fake accounts.
September 8, 2016	Wells Fargo pays $185 million in fines.
September 20 and 29, 2016	CEO John Stumpf answers tough questions from U.S. representatives on Capitol Hill.
October 12, 2016	CEO Stumpf retires and forfeits some compensation.
October 12, 2016	Tim Sloan becomes CEO and promises, "Immediate and highest priority is to restore trust."
October 19, 2016	Criminal investigation is launched.
October 24, 2016	Wells Fargo begins running ads to restore consumer trust in the company.

Sources: Matt Levine, "Wells Fargo Opened a Couple Million Fake Accounts," *Bloomberg*, September 9, 2016, https://www.bloomberg.com/view/articles/2016-09-09/wells-fargo-opened-a-couple-million-fake-accounts, accessed June 13, 2016; Paul Blake, "Timeline of the Wells Fargo Accounts Scandal," *ABC News*, November 3, 2016, http://abcnews.go.com/Business/timeline-wells-fargo-accounts-scandal/story?id=42231128, accessed June 22, 2017; "The Wells Fargo Fake Account Scandal: A Timeline," *Forbes*, https://www.forbes.com/pictures/fkmm45eegei/eight-is-great/#45ca29963d6b, accessed June 22, 2017.

Accountable: subject to the obligation to report, explain, or justify something; responsible; answerable.[8]

From these definitions, we see accountability in rules and regulations and responsibility as more of a choice. We can demand accountability—an account or accounting—for a leader's actions. This differs from integrity, which is perceived by others but cannot be demanded of a leader.

Corporate consultants claim opposite definitions and emphasize accountability. The best-selling book *The Oz Principle: Getting Results Through*

Individual and Organizational Accountability set the foundation for company leaders to focus on the topic. Using this groundwork, one consulting and training company defines accountability as "making a personal choice to rise above one's circumstances and demonstrate the ownership necessary for achieving desired results." According to this definition, accountability is proactive and something you do yourself.[9]

In the leadership character research, accountability and responsibility sound comparable. Mary Crossan and her colleagues chose accountability as a leadership character dimension, while Fred Kiel chose responsibility as one of four "moral habits" of strong character leaders.[10] According to Crossan, accountable leaders accept consequences, are conscientious and responsible, and take ownership.[11] According to Kiel, responsible leaders take responsibility for personal choices, admit mistakes and failures, and embrace responsibility for serving others to "leave the world a better place."[12]

All elements discussed so far are relevant to leadership character. We're using *accountability* here to recognize the term more commonly used in organizations.

Wells Fargo's Promise

In Wells Fargo's 19-page "Vision and Values Brochure," the company promises accountability (Figure 6.2). As we learned in Chapter 5, we know the statement isn't enough to ensure ethical behavior, but it is useful to illustrate our definitions.

Leaders Avoid Accountability by Shifting Blame

Although Wells Fargo leaders said they were accountable for the fake accounts, their actions said otherwise. Instead, they blamed employees, which was particularly painful because of the pressure employees endured.

Blaming and Downplaying

Wells Fargo leaders knew about the fake accounts and warned employees to stop. At a two-day ethics workshop in 2014—two years before the story broke—employees were told not to open accounts without customers' knowledge and agreement. Management also terminated employees who engaged in such behavior.[13]

But the behavior continued. Why? The sales quotas didn't change and were still unattainable, and employees needed to keep their jobs. As the Los Angeles city attorney said, "Clearly the necessity to fire 5,300 employees shows that there is something that needs to change with Wells' internal oversight and with its practices generally."[14]

Figure 6.2   Wells Fargo promises accountability

Ethics

We strive to be recognized by our stakeholders as setting the standard among the world's great companies for integrity and principled performance. This is more than just doing the right thing. We also have to do it in the right way. Honesty, trust, and integrity are essential for meeting the highest standards of corporate governance. Our ethics are the sum of all the decisions each of us makes every day. Everything we do is built on trust. It doesn't happen with one transaction, in one day on the job, or in one quarter. It's earned relationship by relationship. We want our customers to trust us as their financial resource. . . . **We have to earn that trust every day by behaving ethically; rewarding open, honest, two-way communication; and holding ourselves accountable for the decisions we make and the actions we take. That's more important now than ever.**

| Identifies an external measurement system. |

| Extends beyond a minimum standard. |

| Implies judgment. |

| Emphasizes serving others. |

| Hints at accepting consequences. |

Source: Wells Fargo, "The Vision & Values of Wells Fargo," March 2017, https://www08 .wellsfargomedia.com/assets/pdf/about/corporate/vision-and-values.pdf, accessed June 13, 2017.

When the news became public, Stumpf immediately blamed employees for "misinterpreting" sales goals.[15] On Jim Cramer's *Mad Money*, Stumpf focused on employees who "didn't get it right."[16] During a later investigation, an email from Stumpf was discovered:

> Nothing could be further from the truth on forcing products on customers. In any case, right will win, and we are right. Did some do things wrong—you bet and that is called life. This is not systemic.[17]

Stumpf also tried to downplay the number of terminated employees by referring to them in percentage terms: about 1% of all employees. This percentage is deceptive because it included headquarters and other employees who had no direct customer responsibility—and it's still a big number of terminations. One customer put it well: "When 5,300-plus employees lose their jobs, it's not just them—they're the scapegoats."[18]

Effects on Employees

The blame stings, particularly when we hear stories of employees so afraid of losing their jobs that they suffered anxiety attacks, felt terrible guilt, and lost sleep. One drank hand sanitizer to manage her anxiety and another hid in the bathroom to cry. Many, of course, lost their jobs.[19]

Stumpf still refused to acknowledge the systemic nature of the problem. Although he said, "I'm responsible. I'm accountable. Anybody else—you know, in the

Photo 6.1   Senator Elizabeth Warren tells Stumpf, "You should resign."

Source: Getty Images.

company, we all feel when we fall short of that plan; we feel accountable and responsible,"[20] he didn't admit that sales targets were unrealistic, and no senior-level managers had been held accountable.

During a Senate Banking Committee meeting, Senator Elizabeth Warren from Massachusetts summed up the issue of accountability when questioning Stumpf:

> You have said, quote, "I am accountable." But what have you already done to hold yourself accountable? . . . . It's about responsibility. . . . So you haven't resigned, you haven't returned a single nickel of your personal earnings, you haven't fired a single senior executive. Instead, evidently, your definition of accountable is to push the blame to your low-level employees who don't have the money for a fancy PR firm to defend themselves. It's gutless leadership.[21]

What Warren calls "gutless," we might call poor judgment. Next, we'll see how incentives and regulations can only go so far in ensuring ethical behavior.

Incentives and Regulations Ensure *Some* Accountability

Of course, incentives are useful, and we need some regulations to hold people accountable. Yet these often fail because they are short-term, encourage the bear minimum, and rely on regulators, who also may fall short.

Incentives

We face a dilemma in designing incentive systems to reward behavior. In the first chapter, we saw how short-term rewards inspire short-term, undesirable behavior. Wells Fargo's compensation program rewarded what they got—more accounts—but employees lost sight of what was most important.

Longer-term incentives with an eye on ethical outcomes would have better success. But long-term rewards, particularly when people don't stay long in an organization and when shareholders demand short-term returns, may be difficult to implement.

Rather than aspiring to be rewarded by external incentives, leaders with strong character decide which external measures are most important to themselves, to others, and to the organization as a whole.

Limitations of Regulations

Also discussed in the first chapter, we have to be careful about trying to regulate ethical behavior. Stephen Cohen at the University of New South Wales argues that accountability systems ensure compliance—an "accounting"—but don't necessarily encourage ethical behavior and may discourage good judgment.[22] Sociologist William Bruce Cameron said, "Not everything that can be counted counts, and not everything that counts can be counted."[23] People in organizations from CEO John Stumpf to bank employees have to make their own ethical decisions.

Like incentives, accountability measures are often short-term—even if we want good long-term outcomes—and they cannot inspire excellence.[24] The seat belt buzzer in your car will get you to put on your seat belt, but it won't make you a better driver. We can force people to behave consistently—to demonstrate behavioral integrity—but we can't force them to be people of integrity.

In this sense, being accountable is simply meeting expectations; Cohen says measures may be most useful for identifying slackers and "free-loaders."[25] But he advocates a more proactive approach: assigning responsibility and expecting people to act "responsibly." With delegation comes authority to use good judgment and responsibility to justify it.[26]

Minimum Compliance

Although insufficient, regulations do encourage corporations to meet minimum standards. Trouble ensues when leaders deliberately skirt imposed requirements, and the regulations themselves may invite deception and discourage common sense. Corporate leaders become willful teenagers, staying out after a strict curfew and drinking behind the bleachers.

An article in the *Journal of Business Ethics* explores accountability for socially responsible investing (SRI)—for example, investing in companies focused on environmental sustainability or social justice, or avoiding companies that sell harmful substances. The author, William S. Laufer at the Wharton School at the University of Pennsylvania, identifies problems with both corporate compliance and reporting about these investment funds.[27] "Greenwashing" is one way companies skew information about their social responsibility. Laufer argues that corporations use a variety of techniques and get help from public relations firms to falsify or exaggerate claims and shirk responsibility. Confusion, posturing, and fronting (for example, scapegoating employees, as Wells Fargo did) shield management from liability through tacit acceptance of wrongdoing.[28]

The Role and Failures of Regulators

In these cases, it's up to regulators to find the culprits. But many U.S. government agencies aren't up to the task. For example, the U.S. National Highway Traffic Safety Administration (NHTSA) encourages people to "file a vehicle safety complaint," but reports criticize the agency's response. Referring to the GM ignition recall situation, a *New York Times* article begins, "Even as evidence poured into the nation's top auto safety agency pointing to dangerous defects in millions of vehicles, regulators repeatedly failed for years to root out problems and hold carmakers accountable." According to the *Times* article, a Transportation Department report identified "weak management, undertrained staff, and insufficient processes in place to properly review safety data."[29] Accountability failures abound.

Leaders Foster a Culture of Accountability

More effective than external measures is creating a culture of accountability. According to an American Management Association survey, managers say, on average, about 25% of employees "pass the buck"—don't accept accountability.[30] It takes leaders at all levels to change this. In organizations, senior leaders serve as role models with the goal of employees becoming more self-accountable. With regular feedback and guidance from managers, employees know when they're off course and can self-correct. Accountability becomes a conversation.

Organizational Context

Researchers at the University of Maryland explored the complexity of "accountability webs," which include individuals as well as workgroups. Individuals, for example, are accountable to their manager, to their workgroup, and to themselves. Accountability webs depend on cultural components, such as organization structure (hierarchy) and the strength of connections.[31]

Here's where we see the importance of organizational context in ethical decision making, discussed in the first chapter. "Everybody does it" is a common rationale for misbehavior. We look to our leaders and peers—our coworkers—for cues about what's right and wrong. If others shoplift, why can't we?

Fighting against the status quo is one of the greatest challenges of a leader, but an individual's resolve, as we'll explore more in the next chapter, can bring about change. In addition, other leaders in the organization play an important role. Leaders encourage accountability among workgroups by serving as role models and then guiding employees in making good choices.

Leaders as Role Models and Guides

Research demonstrates the importance of a leader's role in shifting the organizational context and encouraging followers' ethical judgment. When leaders serve as role models and hold their employees accountable, followers make better decisions. The tone is set at the top, but the emphasis is on self-leadership: employees managing their own behavior to align with goals they define.[32]

Reporting structure matters, particularly to gain compliance to rules, but relationships matter more in inspiring good behavior. A writer for the Society of Human Resources Management sums up the leader's role:

> Leaders who struggle with others' accountability view their job as mandating compliance. Those who get accountability right know that most people want to do great work. They view their job as creating an environment where commitment and self-discipline are volunteered.[33]

GM CEO Mary Barra said, "You can't fake culture." To encourage employees to report concerns about safety, GM created the "Speak Up for Safety" program. More than 3,000 issues were raised within a year. When Barra led human resources for the company, she replaced a 10-page dress code policy with two words: "Dress appropriately."[34] This allows employees to make good decisions and puts some responsibility on managers to help.

Giving Regular Feedback

Part of a culture of accountability is giving employees regular feedback; otherwise, they may not know when they're off track, which inevitably happens. Companies have traditionally required annual performance reviews between managers and employees. At their worst, this is the only time a manager sits down with an employee to talk about performance and goals. The process feels punitive.

Many leaders give feedback throughout the year, and some companies have moved away from the traditional performance review entirely. Smaller, more frequent assessments and feedback from direct reports and peers give a more complete picture and tell people where they stand on a regular basis. At PricewaterhouseCoopers, long performance reviews were changed to "snapshots" that employees can request anytime they want feedback, for example, after completing a project.[35] Companies such as Goldman Sachs separate feedback meetings from compensation decisions to focus on recognizing and improving performance.[36]

Goal-setting and progress reports keep people accountable for their work. Frequent meetings mean fewer surprises and more opportunities for people to get help for roadblocks and conflicts as they encounter them. With more regular coaching, small issues are less likely to turn into big problems and employees may be less inclined to hide problems and blame others. The key is to give feedback about behaviors as they happen instead of waiting until it's too late, which may cause a leader to be more critical than supportive.[37]

Our earlier definitions included the word *answerable*. A leader encourages employees—and accountable employees take the initiative—to talk through challenges of the job. Accounting becomes a conversation, a narrative about how an employee is doing and what can be improved. Ideally, rather than following a strict hierarchy, people in organizations answer to each other.

Accountable Leaders
Admit and Forgive Mistakes

As we discussed in Chapter 2, mistakes are essential for personal and professional development. In an accountability culture, people hold themselves accountable; they admit mistakes and take responsibility for solving problems. When they do, their leaders handle mistakes with grace and offer forgiveness.

Holding Yourself Accountable

Accountability means having high standards and holding yourself to them as you do others. Figure 6.3 shows a continuum of responses leaders may choose to hold others and themselves accountable. On the left side are ways leaders hold others accountable before and after an event—or something negative—happens. We see that responding *before* an event (in the second column) is only slightly better than *after* an event (in the first column).

On the right side of the chart, we see more proactive ways to avoid problems. By holding ourselves accountable, we set expectations before problems occur (the third column). We assign tasks and provide checklists, which is better than not doing so and is important in teaching and evaluating performance. But this orientation may encourage only a minimum level of performance, in

Figure 6.3   A continuum illustrates choices for holding others and ourselves accountable

	Less Accountability		More Accountability	
	Hold Others Accountable		**Hold Ourselves Accountable**	
	React to Events After They Happen	React to Behaviors Before They Lead to Events	Set Expectations Before Having to React to Behavior	Develop Skills at Holding Ourselves Accountable
Examples	Discipline people for poor performance or work habits	Criticize, for example, lack of attention to detail	Assign and schedule tasks; provide checklists	Specify results, measure progress regularly, and provide coaching
Typical Focus	Punishing and blaming	Babysitting and correcting	Teaching and evaluating	Owning results and problem solving
Likely Outcomes for Employees	Feeling dependent, fearful, and victimized	Feeling micromanaged	Feeling devalued; doing the minimum	Feeling valued, self-reliant, and focused on development

Source: Adapted from Craig Redding, "Increasing Accountability," *Organization Development Journal*, Vol. 22, No. 1 (2004), p. 65.

the same way rules and regulations are intended to guide ethical behavior and often fall short.

Ideally, leaders develop more skills in holding themselves accountable (the last column). We focus on results instead of specific tasks, so employees have more control over their own performance. With trust and regular feedback, employees take ownership of their work. In the end, they feel valued and are self-reliant. The goal is for employees to develop a sense of self-accountability and a focus on self-development.[38]

Admitting Mistakes and Solving Problems

In Chapter 3, we learned the importance of admitting mistakes and apologizing. Although we may feel exposed, when we go off track, we admit mistakes so we can help solve them. The admission becomes part of the solution. Rather than stuffing the unpaid invoice in a drawer, we hold our head high and ask for and offer help. An adage from managers in many organizations is, "Don't tell me a problem without a solution."

People may be more accepting of bad news than we realize. Researchers at the University of Michigan and Stanford University found that companies that admitted internal and controllable causes for negative events benefited from higher stock prices the following year. The authors believe that disclosing the real reasons—taking responsibility—for issues led to better outcomes because company leaders "appear more in control."[39]

We discussed the relevance of transparency to leading with integrity and cultivating trust. Transparency is also important in showing constituencies that we are accountable for our mistakes. Being accountable is more than keeping an accounting, or keeping good records. Accountable leaders share their records.

We can use lessons from studying integrity to practice transparency. We learned that transparency involves disclosure, accuracy, and clarity.[40] When we make mistakes, we can be open about them, give all the necessary information, and be clear about what happened and why.

Whether they caused the problem or not, accountable leaders step up to make things right. They take control. At one nonprofit organization, an employee's manager resigned, and she immediately asked for a meeting with the next level up (Figure 6.4).

Amber is taking responsibility to solve a problem, and Mabel would likely appreciate her initiative. Of course, Amber is also ambitious: taking on more work may put her in line for a promotion when the time comes.

Figure 6.4   An employee steps up

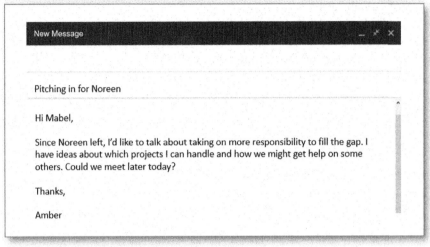

Source: Adapted from an email received August 18, 2017.

Forgiving Mistakes

Despite the best feedback and coaching, mistakes happen. When people go off course, how do leaders respond? Are employees punished, or are they treated as adults who can make good decisions but need some guidance?

A culture of accountability must include forgiveness. Fred Kiel identifies forgiveness as one of the four moral habits of strong character leaders. According to Kiel, forgiveness involves the following:

- Letting go of one's mistakes
- Letting go of others' mistakes
- Focusing on what's right versus what's wrong[41]

In their book *Communicating Forgiveness*, Vincent Waldron and Douglas Kelly define elements of forgiveness. The process involves a relationship between people where one has been harmed, and the act of forgiveness may involve a renegotiation of the relationship. The hope is that one or both parties feels more positively after forgiving or being forgiven.[42]

Forgiveness involves an internal emotional state as well as an interpersonal act, but both are not required. Crime victims, for example, can forgive an assailant without the person's knowledge.[43]

Forgiveness is associated with positive outcomes. For individuals, forgiveness has been linked to heart health, mental health, and happiness, while failing to forgive may lead to anger and resentment and has been linked to health issues.[44] In organizations, research shows that forgiveness after layoffs may decrease hurt feelings, allowing people to view the organization more positively and to move on.[45]

When leaders offer forgiveness for mistakes, positive feelings replace anger and bitterness. "How could you?" in an accusatory tone becomes "What do you think happened?" in an empathic tone. The leader genuinely cares about the person and is curious about the error, focusing on problem solving and learning: "How can we prevent this from happening in the future, and what can we learn from the experience?"[46]

Of course, leaders must discern between mistakes and willful violations. In the latter case, a leader can still forgive, but trust is damaged, and the employee may face other consequences.

Holding yourself accountable means being open to criticism yourself, a topic we'll cover with the character dimension humility. Holding yourself accountable also requires vulnerability and authenticity—risking exposure and being true to who you really are and can be. These are tough choices, but they are our choices.

External Leaders Step in When Boards Fail

When regulators, leaders, and boards fail to hold people accountable, external constituencies, such as shareholders, advertisers, clients, and the media, often step in.

The Wells Fargo Board's Failing Accountability

CEOs of publicly traded companies and executive directors of not-for-profit organizations report to a board of directors who should hold them accountable. But that doesn't always happen; boards need to be accountable as well.

After John Stumpf gave his testimony and failed to change public perception of the company, the board did take action. When he resigned, which the board may have forced, they didn't award severance pay and did "claw back" (withdraw) $79 million (and later, another $28 million)[47] that he could have received. Still, critics scoff at his payout: about $133 million in stock, deferred compensation, and pension funds.[48] To most of us, he made out well.

Why didn't the board of directors catch the 2 million fake accounts earlier? Why didn't they question how the retail division did exceedingly well? In any corporate scandal situation, people want to know what the board knew when—and if they didn't know, why not?

Some shareholders had these and other questions. They tried to effect change during Wells Fargo's annual shareholder meeting, which Reuters called "unruly."[49] Three protestors were particularly forceful and were removed from the meeting.[50]

Still, all 15 directors of the board were reelected, although some by a narrow margin.[51] Board turnover will happen eventually. Some directors are nearing the mandatory retirement age, and others may be forced out next year. But many were disappointed by the vote. As a professor at Columbia Law School said, "If we're serious about board accountability in this country, it's hard to understand the case for keeping these directors."[52]

Holding Board Members Accountable

Unfortunately, more annual shareholder meetings are being held online nowadays. Scott M. Stringer, comptroller of New York City, warns against this trend:

> [C]ompanies are using technological tools to whittle away at investors' rights and hide from accountability. If boards shirk this responsibility, share owners should join us in holding them accountable.[53]

In a *Harvard Business Review* article, Jeffrey Sonnenfeld at the Yale University School of Management argues for new ways to evaluate boards. Older thinking looks at simple measures, such as meeting attendance and stock ownership, but today's corporations require more board engagement. Sonnenfeld places high importance on the "social system" or "human element," including, for example, trust, respect, open dissent, individual accountability, and performance evaluation.[54,55] Here again, we see messier, qualitative measures instead of items that can be easily checked off. Such measures complicate how we measure accountability but, in the end, provide better guidance for organizational leaders.

Technology Company Examples

Other companies give us better examples. At first, Google took too long to respond to criticism about offensive and violent content, particularly on YouTube. Coca-Cola, Walmart, General Motors, AT&T, Johnson & Johnson, and others pulled YouTube ads to protect their own brands. Having a company's ad appear next to or on top of, for example, a neo-Nazi video, may not be best for these renowned businesses.

The companies' concerns are justified: an *Adweek*-commissioned survey found that 41% of consumers who see an ad next to offensive content feel worse about the brand and 36% believe the company is endorsing the content.[56] Google seemed to ignore complaints, but they couldn't ignore the loss of $1 billion in digital advertising revenue in one year.[57]

Although it took external pressure, Google has promised action. Philipp Schindler, Google's chief business officer, said, "While we recognize that no system will be 100% perfect, we believe these major steps will further safeguard our advertisers' brands, and we are committed to being vigilant and continuing to improve over time." The company added manual time to review and remove videos,[58] developed new technology to find videos, and prevented monetization and endorsements of "inflammatory religious or supremacist content."[59]

Similarly, Facebook was criticized for violent videos, such as suicides and a murder, and for "fake news," including "clickbait," which are ads disguised as news stories. The company's original concept was to connect people around the world, but CEO and founder Mark Zuckerberg has admitted, "There are questions about whether we can make a global community that works for everyone."[60] After initial resistance, Zuckerberg is demonstrating more accountability.

When videos showing a man planning and carrying out a murder went viral, Zuckerberg took personal action. At a developer conference, he apologized and promised to do more:

> We have a lot more to do here. We're reminded of this this week by the tragedy in Cleveland. Our hearts go out to the family and friends of Robert Godwin Sr. We have a lot of work, and we will keep doing all we can to prevent tragedies like this from happening.[61]

Soon after, Facebook announced hiring 3,000 people, for a total of 7,500, to respond to reports of inappropriate or offensive content. COO Sheryl Sandberg commented on Zuckerberg's post: "Keeping people safe is our top priority. We won't stop until we get it right."[62]

Although not quite admitting mistakes in the past, Google and Facebook are stepping up and will be accountable in the future if content on their sites isn't properly managed.

Whistleblowers Demand Accountability

When regulators, boards, shareholders, and senior leaders fail to keep people accountable, whistleblowers—often employees who expose illegal or unethical action—may be our only hope.

Whistleblowers at Wells Fargo

Wells Fargo management failed to listen to its own employees. The company had a confidential ethics hotline, but employees who called were discredited and fired. For example, five years before the scandal broke, Claudia Ponce de Leon reported that employees at her branch in Pomona, California, were creating false accounts. She realized that many accounts had the same address—that of the Los Angeles County Department of Public Social Services (Figure 6.5). She was terminated, and the company said it was because of her excessive drinking and other inappropriate behavior.[63]

OSHA's Role

Employees have recourse under whistleblower protection programs. Wells Fargo was ordered to pay $5.4 million and rehire a former wealth manager in Los Angeles, who had also reported bogus accounts. This is the biggest whistleblower award in the Occupational Safety and Health Administration's (OSHA) history.

But OSHA, like NHTSA discussed earlier, has come under scrutiny for ignoring complaints from Wells Fargo employees.[64] Over time, OSHA awarded merit in less than 2% of whistleblower cases, meaning few employees were eligible for back pay and/or getting rehired. Government reports from 1988 and 2010 cite OSHA for responding too slowly and for unfairly investigating complaints.[65]

This has become a recognized issue within the agency. OSHA issued a statement that it "has been working diligently to streamline investigative processes to ensure that whistleblower complaints are resolved quickly and

Figure 6.5   Wells Fargo employee questions customer addresses

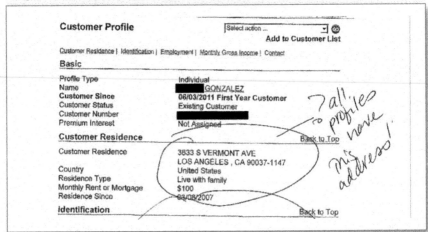

Source: Ann Marsh, "Wells May Be Forced to Welcome Back Another Whistleblower," *American Banker*, April 5, 2017, https://www.americanbanker.com/news/feds-may-order-wells-fargo-to-rehire-a-second-whistleblower, accessed June 15, 2017.

fairly."[66] Perhaps the Wells Fargo case is an example of the agency's turn-around, but change has been slow.[67]

The Whistleblower's Dilemma

Being a whistleblower takes a lot of courage—a character dimension we'll discuss next—and the process can be painful. A 26-year employee of Hyundai reported failures in proper engine checks, which could have prevented accidents. Kim Gwang-ho said, "I will be the first and last whistleblower in South Korea's auto industry. There are just too many things to lose." He also said, "I had a normal life and was better off, but now I'm fighting against a big conglomerate."[68]

Eventually, Kim was rehired with back pay, but for a while, his family was living off loans. His wife didn't want him to fight, but he persuaded her. Being a whistleblower is rarely a pleasant experience, and Kim is a terrific example of leading from any level of an organization for a positive result.

Leaders of high character cannot ignore unethical or illegal activity. Although their lives may be uprooted, they see coming forward not as a choice but as a moral necessity. This isn't an enviable position, but whistleblowers' goals transcend their personal needs. They do what they know is right.

Companies Improve Their Accountability

We see progress at Wells Fargo and at United Airlines. Their later communications illustrate many aspects of accountability we discussed in this chapter.

More Accountability at Wells Fargo

Over time, Wells Fargo has accepted more accountability for sales practices, and we have seen more transparency about their change process. The new CEO, Tim Sloan, speaks far more candidly about management's role in the scandal.

Excerpts from a video, "Board Report 'Offers Lessons That Will Influence How We Continue to Build a Better Wells Fargo,'" are included in Figure 6.6. The script illustrates ways to convey accountability to the people we serve.

The bank made other moves toward accountability. They terminated more senior leaders, cancelled cash bonuses totaling $32 million, and centralized some oversight functions.[69]

Still, Wells Fargo has a long way to go. Gretchen Morgenson wrote a column, "Fair Game," described as "examining the world of finance and its

Figure 6.6   New Wells Fargo CEO demonstrates accountability in a video (excerpts)

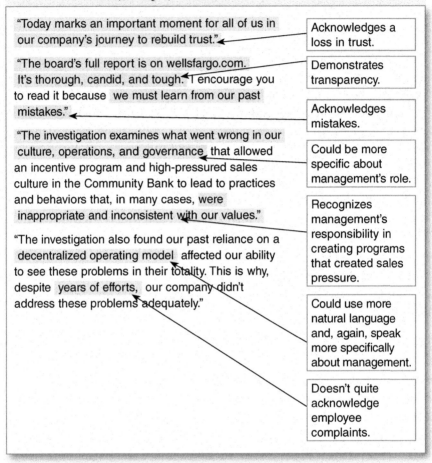

Source: Wells Fargo, "Board Report 'Offers Lessons That Will Influence How We Continue to Build a Better Wells Fargo,'" YouTube, April 10, 2017, https://www.youtube.com/watch?v= WKWKxYgXQ34&feature=youtube, accessed June 15, 2017.

impact on investors, workers, and families." In an article about Wells Fargo, she asks, "Is Mr. Sloan, an almost 30-year veteran of Wells Fargo and a seasoned insider, the best executive to lead the bank out of crisis?"[70] This remains to be seen.

Accountability at United Airlines

United's CEO Oscar Munoz fared better after the situation of dragging a passenger off the plane, mentioned in the Introduction and Chapter 2. He failed at first, blaming the passenger, but he later took full responsibility. In a TV interview, a video, a website statement, social media messages, and an email to Mileage Plus members (Figure 6.7), Munoz's accountability is clear.

Figure 6.7   United CEO Demonstrates Accountability in Email (Excerpts)

UNITED

MileagePlus # XXXXX620

Dear Ms Newman,

Each flight you take with us represents an important promise we make to you, our customer. It's not simply that we make sure you reach your destination safely and on time, but also that you will be treated with the highest level of service and the deepest sense of dignity and respect.

> Describes accountability up front.

Earlier this month, we broke that trust when a passenger was forcibly removed from one of our planes. We can never say we are sorry enough for what occurred, but we also know meaningful actions will speak louder than words.

> Is specific about what happened.

> Uses conversational, natural language.

For the past several weeks, we have been urgently working to answer two questions: How did this happen, and how can we do our best to ensure this never happens again?

It happened because our corporate policies were placed ahead of our shared values. Our procedures got in the way of our employees doing what they know is right.

> Admits the core, systemic problem.

Fixing that problem starts now with changing how we fly, serve and respect our customers. This is a turning point for all of us here at United – and as CEO, it's my responsibility to make sure that we learn from this experience and redouble our efforts to put our customers at the center of everything we do. [. . .]

> Takes personal responsibility.

I believe we must go further in redefining what United's corporate citizenship looks like in our society. You can and ought to expect more from us, and we intend to live up to those higher expectations in the way we embody social responsibility and civic leadership everywhere we operate. I hope you will

> Considers broad impact on others.

see that pledge express itself in our actions going forward, of which these initial, though important, changes are merely a first step.

Our goal should be nothing less than to make you truly proud to say, "I fly United." [. . .]

With Great Gratitude,

Oscar

Oscar Munoz

CEO

United Airlines

Source: Oscar Munoz, "Actions Speak Louder Than Words," United Airlines email, April 27, 2017, http://bit.ly/2sW8jmV, accessed June 21, 2017.

The email gives us another example of how to demonstrate accountability in our communications.

United settled a lawsuit with the passenger, whose attorney complimented Munoz:

Mr. Munoz said he was going to do the right thing, and he has. In addition, United has taken full responsibility for what happened on Flight 3411, without attempting to blame others, including the City of Chicago. For this acceptance of corporate accountability, United is to be applauded.[71]

Although the incident dominated international news for about a week, United, with Munoz leading the charge, recovered well.

SUMMARY

Overall, Wells Fargo's CEO Tim Sloan certainly demonstrates more accountability than Stumpf did when he said, for example, that employees "misinterpreted" their sales goals. Critics might say Sloan could sound more conversational and authentic. We still get the sense that he's reading from a script his head of public relations give him, although this may change as the bank rebuilds its reputation and Sloan gets more comfortable in his role, as we saw Mary Barra do in her role at GM.

Wells Fargo has a new chair of the board, a sign of progress, yet the company was in the news again for more unauthorized bank accounts, for signing customers up for unwanted auto insurance, and for charging improper mortgage fees.[72] Sloan has more work to do to recover the brand.

Strong leaders hold themselves and others accountable. We don't shift blame, and we realize it takes more than incentives, regulations, and governing boards to build a culture of accountability in an organization. Employees need regular feedback, and they need to trust that they'll be forgiven when they inevitably make mistakes.

Accepting responsibility and holding others accountable—as we saw in the whistleblower cases—takes courage. We'll discuss courage as a leadership character dimension next.

EXERCISES

Concept Review Questions

1. What are the key elements of accountability?

2. What are the limitations of incentives and regulations in encouraging accountability?

3. What are some ways a leader can create a culture of accountability?

4. How should leaders respond to their own and to others' mistakes?

Self-Reflection

1. Think about a time when you avoided accountability. Why did you do it, and how did it turn out?

2. Think about a time when you blamed someone else for something that was partly your responsibility. What would have been a better approach?

3. For the first two questions, what were the consequences? How did your choices affect others?

4. When have you stepped in to take responsibility for something that wasn't going well? What did you learn from the experience?

5. How have you changed over time? Do you notice any difference in your willingness to take ownership?

6. What has been your experience with getting feedback, for example, from a manager or a coach? What was helpful, and where did it fall short in guiding you?

Assessment

Take the Individual Accountability Quiz from Partners in Leadership at http://bit .ly/2w1fuYU.[73] Some items reflect aspects of other character dimensions as we define them, but this is still a useful exercise.

Team Activity

Complete the Individual Accountability Quiz with members of a project, volunteer, sports, or other team. Print the results and share them with each other. Are the responses what you expected? Overall, did people assess themselves as others would assess them?

Use the Johari Window introduced in Chapter 2 to help each other identify areas for development. Using the Accountability Quiz items as a guide, have each person on the team complete the matrix. For example, let's say you rated yourself a 3 for the statement "I feel personally invested," but your teammates' average for you is an 8. You might put this item in the "Hidden" box: it's apparent to you but not to others. Then you can work on making your level of investment clearer to your teammates.

Mini-Cases

Consider the following scenarios. On your own or with a partner, discuss the best course of action in each case. What would you do, and what factors into your decision?

Scenario 1

You just started working on a new project with people you don't know well. What are some ways you can hold yourself and others accountable? What agreements are important at the start? Consider concepts from this chapter and other ideas you have from your team experiences.

Scenario 2

Your manager calls you into his office and asks for product information for a customer. He seems annoyed that you haven't already sent it to him, but this is the first you're hearing about it. He says that one of your coworkers said you were working on this last week. You remember your coworker talking about a customer needing more information and giving her ideas for finding it, but you don't remember committing to anything. How will you handle this situation? Consider responses for your manager and coworker and any action you might take.

Scenario 3

You manage a team of sales representatives. Every Friday at noon, reps give you a report listing accounts contacted, projected sales, and other information. You printed them before you went to lunch and left a pile on your desk. At about 1 p.m., as you are coming back to your office, you see one of your sales reps slip a piece of paper into the middle of the pile. What will you do?

Activity

Imagine that a hiring manager asks you about a time you made a mistake that had a big impact on others. What will you say?

Planning Questions

1. What comes to mind first?

2. What happened? How can you describe the situation with just enough background and detail yet not too much?

3. Why did it happen? How can you take responsibility for the mistake without blaming others? At the same time, if others were involved, you can certainly explain their role and how it affected decisions you made.

4. How was the mistake discovered? Did you admit it?

5. What people, processes, profits, and so on were affected by the mistake?

6. How did others react? How did you respond to their reactions?

7. Did you apologize? How? What else did you do to fix the problems caused?

8. How did you feel about the mistake then? How do you feel about it now?

9. Most important, what did you learn? What example—told briefly—could illustrate that you learned from the experience?

10. Are these questions painful? Is it too painful for you to talk about, or can you talk about it in a way that shows emotions but allows you to tell the story in a coherent way?

11. What other situations could you talk about?

Role Play Activity

Prepare to respond to the hiring manager's question above: "Tell me about a time you made a mistake that had a big impact on others." Role-play the situation so that one of you asks the question and responds appropriately. Consider video-recording the interaction so you can watch it later.

Planning Questions

1. Analyze the interviewer's perspective. What do you think this person wants to hear?

2. How will you begin the response? What will you say next?

3. How will you avoid blaming or criticizing others (although you certainly can talk about others' roles in the situation)?

4. How can you describe the situation in a way that shows what you have learned from the experience?

Practice and Reflection

Consider your own feedback and ask the "interviewer" for feedback. Did you demonstrate accountability? Did you also demonstrate vulnerability? How did you feel? What did you learn from doing the role play?

7

Courage

Standing Up

Chapter Overview

When customers reported Samsung phones were catching fire, the company implemented a recall, but the communication wasn't clear, and the replacement phones also caught on fire. Courageous leaders make unpopular decisions and stand up for worthy goals. They are confident and resilient and don't fear confrontation or difficult conversations. Being courageous means taking measured risks, yet keeping self-righteousness in check.

Samsung Botches a Recall

In September 2016, after reports of 35 Samsung Galaxy Note 7 phones catching fire, the company recalled 2.5 million products, calling it an "exchange program" and "replacement program." They had to do something; photos and videos of phones melted, charred, and in flames because of a battery cell malfunction were going viral.

Adding insult to injury, regulatory agencies banned the phones from airplanes.[1] A phone in a man's pocket caught fire on a Southwest plane, so the decision was necessary. But the embarrassment to Samsung continued because airlines announced the ban in airports and on flights before takeoff.

Samsung blamed a "minute flaw," but the recall was enormous, affecting phones in 10 countries.[2] And it came at a bad time, just as Samsung was trying to compete against Apple's iPhone and was trying to "humanize" the brand with friendly-looking people and celebrity sponsors like Lil Wayne.[3]

Offering replacements seemed like a good decision. Although some questioned why it took the company a few days to respond to reports, other analysts applauded the speed.[4]

Unfortunately, replacement phones also exploded. More people were injured, and some phones caused fires.[5] The company reported that 90% of users chose a replacement Note 7 instead of switching to another device, which was good news.[6] However, the decision turned out to be a hasty one—perhaps a sign of wanting the trouble to simply go away. The tougher decision was to stop production (Figure 7.1). After reports of replacement phones burning, Samsung finally stopped production of the Galaxy Note 7 (Figure 7.1).[7,8,9]

A *Fast Company* article, "How Did Samsung Botch the Galaxy Note 7 Crisis? It's a Failure of Leadership," puts responsibility at the top of the organization. The article argues that company leaders should have stopped production of the phone until they were sure the battery issue was fixed.[10] The article continues:

> Just yesterday, when the news was already out that Samsung had (temporarily) stopped production of the Note 7, the company sent out a statement saying it had "adjusted its production schedules." It's this sort of mealymouthed talk that gives the impression that the whole thing is more about spin and share price than the real needs—indeed the safety—of customers.[11]

Being called "mealymouthed," downplaying the problem, taking shortcuts—some might call this lacking courage. Samsung's actions illustrate the opposite of courage, as we define the character dimension next.

Figure 7.1   Samsung recall unfolds

August–September, 2016	Several Note 7 phones overheat and catch on fire.
September 2, 2016	Samsung offers replacements or refunds.
September 8, 2016	Airlines tell passengers to turn off Note 7 phones.
September 15, 2016	The U.S. Consumer Product Safety Commission issues a recall.
October 6, 2016	Replacement phone ignites on Southwest flight.
October 11, 2016	Samsung halts all sales and production, yet hides this information within a website link.
October 14, 2016	The Department of Transportation bans Note 7 phones from airplanes.
January 23, 2016	Samsung accepts responsibility for its role in poor battery and smartphone design.

Sources: "Galaxy Note 7: Timeline of Samsung's Phones Woes," *BBC News*, October 11, 2016, http://www.bbc.com/news/technology-37615496, accessed July 5, 2017; Arjun Kharpal, "Samsung Permanently Halts Production of Its Galaxy Note 7; $18 Billion Wiped Off Shares," *CNBC*, October 11, 2016, http://www.cnbc.com/2016/10/11/samsung-permanently-halts-production-of-its-galaxy-note-7-18-billion-wiped-off-shares.html, accessed June 16, 2017.

Courageous Leaders Fight for Worthy Goals

Leaders demonstrate courage when they overcome fear to pursue worthy goals. After defining courage, we'll see how this dimension is measured and how it relates to other aspects of character.

Courage Defined

As with trust, courage is demonstrated in any job and in small moves—less typically by war heroes or people running into a burning house to save a cat. An employee demonstrates courage by refusing to work overtime to attend a family event. A manager demonstrates courage by speaking out against an unfair policy. A client demonstrates courage by questioning an invoice because the product is defective.

In each of these situations, people "voluntarily pursue a worthy goal in the face of fear or risk," as courage is defined in the academic literature. Courageous acts include an expression of the *individual* (standing out) and *involvement* (for the collective).[12] Not everyone is willing or able to stand out, and not everyone is committed to team goals. Courageous leaders aren't afraid of confrontation that will bring about positive change for others.

For leadership character, we're focusing on moral courage instead of physical courage, such as facing physical pain. In his book *Moral Courage*, Rushworth Kidder identifies three elements of moral courage: "a commitment to moral *principles*, an awareness of the *danger* involved in supporting those principles, and a willing *endurance* of that danger."[13]

Mary Crossan and her colleagues define behaviors of the courageous leader: "Does the right thing even though it may be unpopular, actively discouraged, and/or result in a negative outcome for him/her. Shows an unrelenting determination, confidence, and perseverance in confronting difficult situations. Rebounds quickly from setbacks."[14] Descriptors include *brave*, *determined, tenacious, resilient*, and *confident*.[15]

Embedded in this definition is the concept of grit. Angela Duckworth and her colleagues found that grit—"perseverance and passion for long-term goals"—is one predictor of academic success. In their definition, we see courage: "Grit entails working strenuously toward challenges, maintaining effort and interest over years despite failure, adversity, and plateaus in progress."[16]

We also see courage in commonly used words. To *encourage* means to fill with courage, spirit, or confidence.[17] We get *discouraged* when we're deprived of these qualities.[18] One question on Duckworth's Grit Scale is "Setbacks don't discourage me."[19] It takes courage to plow through when we feel discouraged and when someone else is actively discouraging us. The opposite of courage is cowardice—the cowardly lion in *The Wizard of Oz* who is afraid of his own shadow.

Courage Scale

Researchers have developed a scale for measuring "professional moral courage" as a managerial competency (Figure 7.2). The items are useful for showing us what courage involves in organizations. To compare results by theme, add scores for each (three questions) and divide by three. For an overall score, add all scores and divide by 15.

Figure 7.2   Professional Moral Courage Scale illustrates aspects of courage

	Theme 1: Moral Agency	
	A predisposition toward moral behavior and possessing a persistence of will to engage as a moral agent.	
1	I am the type of person who is unfailing when it comes to doing the right thing at work.	1 2 3 4 5 6 7 Never True Always True
2	When I do my job, I regularly take additional measures to ensure my actions reduce harms to others.	1 2 3 4 5 6 7 Never True Always True
3	My work associates would describe me as someone who is always working to achieve ethical performance, making every effort to be honorable in all my actions.	1 2 3 4 5 6 7 Never True Always True
	Theme 2: Multiple Values	
	The ability to draw on multiple value sets in moral decision making and to effectively sort out and determine what needs to be exercised, and to hold firm to beliefs despite external concerns or demands.	
4	I am the type of person who uses a guiding set of principles from the organization when I make ethical decisions on the job.	1 2 3 4 5 6 7 Never True Always True
5	No matter what, I consider how both my organization's values and my personal values apply to the situation before making decisions.	1 2 3 4 5 6 7 Never True Always True
6	When making decisions, I often consider how my role in the organization, my command, and my upbringing must be applied to any final action.	1 2 3 4 5 6 7 Never True Always True
	Theme 3: Endurance of Threats	
	Facing ethical or moral difficulty, whether a perceived or real danger or threat, with endurance.	
7	When I encounter an ethical challenge, I take it on with moral action, regardless of how it may pose a negative impact on how others see me.	1 2 3 4 5 6 7 Never True Always True
8	I hold my ground on moral matters, even if there are opposing social pressures.	1 2 3 4 5 6 7 Never True Always True

9	I act morally even if it puts me in an uncomfortable position with my supervisors.	1 2 3 4 5 6 7 Never True Always True

Theme 4: Going Beyond Compliance

Not only considering the rules but reflecting on their purpose going beyond compliance-based measures to consider what is right, just, and appropriate.

10	My coworkers would say that when I do my job, I do more than follow the regulations; I do everything I can to ensure my actions are morally sound.	1 2 3 4 5 6 7 Never True Always True
11	When I go about my daily tasks, I make sure to comply with the rules but also look to understand their intent to ensure that this is being accomplished as well.	1 2 3 4 5 6 7 Never True Always True
12	It is important that we go beyond the legal requirements but seek to accomplish our tasks with ethical action as well.	1 2 3 4 5 6 7 Never True Always True

Theme 5: Moral Goals

A drive for task accomplishment that includes the use of virtues (e.g., prudence, honesty, and justice) throughout the decision-making process to achieve a virtuous outcome.

13	It is important for me to use prudential judgment in making decisions at work.	1 2 3 4 5 6 7 Never True Always True
14	I think about my motives when achieving the mission to ensure they are based upon moral ends.	1 2 3 4 5 6 7 Never True Always True
15	I act morally because it is the right thing to do.	1 2 3 4 5 6 7 Never True Always True

Source: Adapted from Leslie E. Sekerka, Richard P. Bagozzi, and Richard Charnigo, "Facing Ethical Challenges in the Workplace: Conceptualizing and Measuring Professional Moral Courage," *Journal of Business Ethics*, Vol. 89, No. 4 (2009), pp. 565–579. Some items were updated to avoid reverse scoring (see https://www.signup4.net/Upload/KAIS13A/PHYE332E/ PMC%20Instrument%20Sekerka%20Bagozzi%20Charnigo%201-13.pdf).

Courage includes resisting the temptation to compromise or carry out unethical acts. This can be challenging, given the organizational context for ethical decisions discussed earlier. When everyone is cheating or stealing, we want the same benefit or result. But the courageous leader doesn't take shortcuts and is willing to call others out for doing so. We saw examples of whistleblowers demonstrating courage when they went against their company to report wrongdoing.

Courage and Other Aspects of Character

Courage has connections to other character dimensions discussed so far. In a study of military soldiers during a training program, researchers found that what links authentic leadership to followers' ethical and prosocial behavior is moral courage. In other words, leaders who demonstrate a moral perspective and are open, transparent, and self-aware may promote moral courage in their followers. These leaders inspired others to demonstrate moral reasoning and to put the group's interests above their own.[20]

Another study explored the relationship between behavioral integrity and moral courage. The authors concluded, "One way to manage behavioral courage ['the perceived consistency of action under adverse conditions'] is by managing behavioral integrity." Particularly in tough times, when leaders emphasize how they are living their values and following through on promises, they are seen as more courageous, and their performance is viewed more positively.[21]

Taking Measured Risks Improves Outcomes

When leaders demonstrate moral courage, they take risks, but they aren't foolish. Accurately assessing risk helps ensure a good outcome, and a government model serves as one guide. Yet people aren't "brave" for just being who they are.

Assessing Risk

Leaders at all levels in an organization make decisions by assessing risk. Without some measure of risk, courage is excessive. Jumping off a bridge or driving your car into a wall will likely get you killed. Creating a product without doing market research is a bold move—and it's probably foolish. A daredevil may be courageous, or he may be reckless.[22]

Rushworth Kidder suggests assessing potential risks in demonstrating moral courage. First, we must be willing to face ambiguity and confusion. Situations that require courage are rarely straightforward. Can we handle conflicting, complex points of view without having one "right" answer? Second, are we willing to face exposure? By taking action, we make ourselves vulnerable. Are we ready for the leadership role that's required? Third, can we accept the loss? We may lose our reputation, our relationships, or our job.[23]

In his book *Exit, Voice, and Loyalty*, Albert O. Hirschman discusses the tradeoffs between voicing complaints and leaving an organization. For example, an employee decides whether to complain about poor management practices or leave for a new job. Hirschman argues that exiting continues the cycle and may lead to further decline.[24]

This quandary raises the ultimate question when deciding whether to take action: Is it worth it? Do the benefits of demonstrating courage outweigh the risks? Who will be hurt, and are the casualties worth the positive outcomes for the greater good? These are some of the difficult questions a leader asks before choosing a courageous path. Whatever we choose, having people in your life to help weigh options and to support your decision is important.

A Government Model

The U.S. government gives us a useful risk assessment model we can apply to business situations such as Samsung (Figure 7.3). The first hazards are fire and explosion—clearly serious issues to avoid. The first assets at risk listed are people and property—also relevant to the Samsung situation. Relevant impacts are property damage, business interruption, loss of customers, financial loss, and loss of confidence. Given Samsung's communications, we might assume it placed business interests ahead of people and property. Perhaps, out of fear, the leaders underestimated the risk of battery issues in the replacement phones and the potential damage to people, property, and the brand.[25]

House of Cards Example

Another good example of risk assessment is actress Robin Wright fighting Netflix for equal pay for her role in the TV show *House of Cards*. On the show, she plays an executive of a nonprofit organization, and her husband and costar is a politician, played by Kevin Spacey.[26] In an interview, Wright said women get paid about 82% of what men do, and she wanted to be paid the same as her costar:

> I was looking at statistics, and Claire Underwood [Wright's character] . . . was more popular than [Spacey's character] for a period of time in a season, so I capitalized on that moment. And I was like, you'd better pay me, or I'm gonna go public.[27]

Figure 7.3 A risk assessment model applies to the Samsung situation

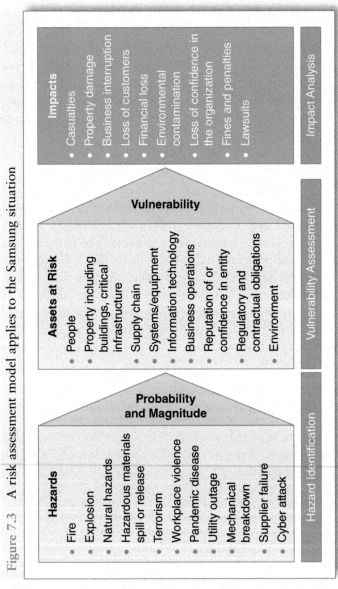

Source: Department of Homeland Security, "Risk Assessment," Homeland Security website, https://www.ready.gov/risk-assessment, accessed June 21, 2017.

Wright took a measured risk and acted at the right moment—when her character's ratings were high.[28] She stood up for what she thought was right but was no fool: she waited until she had the upper hand to ask for what she thought she deserved. The network responded, and she got her pay raise.

When Risk Isn't Involved

Courage must involve taking risks. In a moving TED Talk, "I'm not your inspiration, thank you very much," Stella Young, a comedian and journalist who uses a wheelchair, says she tires of strangers telling her she's so brave. Although she knows people mean it as a compliment, Young says we've been "told this lie that disability makes you exceptional." She also says the label is objectifying, as are images of people with disabilities on posters with motivational slogans. They benefit people without disabilities—to think "things aren't so bad for you, to put your worries into perspective."[29]

Young tells us she takes no extraordinary risks—she just lives her life as the rest of us do. Sure, she has physical challenges, but she says our expectations are far too low. Instead, we should reward real achievement.[30] Why do we call people with physical limitations an "inspiration"? Perhaps it's about our own fear. What if we were in a wheelchair? How well would we manage our lives?

Courage Means Facing Our Fears

To take risks, we must face our fears. Vulnerability is essential to courage, and we see an example in a common anxiety: public speaking.

Managing Fear and Panic

Fear is useful; without it, human beings would not survive. Fear warns us of physical danger to our lives and livelihood. Panic warns us of emotional danger of losing key relationships.[31] Both help us protect ourselves.

But our fears can stymie us. You have probably heard the expression "analysis paralysis." Sometimes people in organizations get stuck—they can't make a decision because they want it to be perfect, or they choose analysis over action because it's safe. They dread a negative outcome. If a decision doesn't turn out well, particularly in risk-averse organizations, senior management looks around for someone to blame. That dread causes people to get stuck, and it takes courage to manage through it.

Courage and Vulnerability

In addition to authenticity and integrity, courage and vulnerability are closely related. Courage is the ability to manage our anxiety even in difficult and potentially dangerous situations.

According to Brené Brown, "vulnerability is our most accurate measure of courage."[32] When we discussed integrity, we saw the link between small acts of kindness and strengthening trust. These small acts require courage—the courage to face another's emotions and to face our own vulnerability. We tend to avoid situations that make us uncomfortable, but we can choose to sit with discomfort and work through it instead. Brown suggests we make more courageous choices:

> Rather than deny our vulnerability, we lean into both the beauty and agony of our shared humanity. Choosing courage does not mean that we're unafraid; it means that we are brave enough to love despite the fear and uncertainty.[33]

In Chapter 2, we talked about TV mogul Shonda Rhimes. It took courage to manage her anxiety, but she chose hope over fear in order to have a better, more fulfilling life.

Anxiety About Public Speaking as an Example

Let's consider another example: speech anxiety. People in organizations give many types of formal and informal presentations, and all require some level of confidence and courage.

Speech anxiety is common but can be overcome, just like anything we dread. The anxiety manifests differently in each of us: some people experience a quivering voice, sweat profusely, or turn red, while others experience such intense anxiety that they feel paralyzed. A tool for managing anxiety offers 22 research-based strategies to try before, during, and after a presentation based on what works for each of us (Figure 7.4). Online, each strategy includes references and explanations.[34]

Many of these strategies are helpful for mustering courage for other leadership challenges. One way to change your thinking (a cognitive strategy) is to write out all your fears, identify which are irrational, and write a coping mechanism for each.[35] A behavioral, or physical, strategy is to practice mindful breathing, which we discussed as a strategy to manage failure. An affective, or emotional, strategy is to allow yourself to experience the feelings of anxiety and to reframe them as excitement. Your body reacts similarly to anxiety and excitement, so try to focus on the positive emotion instead of telling yourself to calm down or relax, which probably won't work.[36]

Figure 7.4   Speech anxiety can be overcome with strategies before, during, and after a presentation

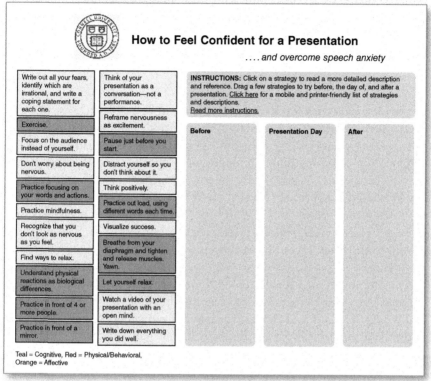

How to Feel Confident for a Presentation

.... and overcome speech anxiety

Write out all your fears, identify which are irrational, and write a coping statement for each one.	Think of your presentation as a conversation—not a performance.	INSTRUCTIONS: Click on a strategy to read a more detailed description and reference. Drag a few strategies to try before, the day of, and after a presentation. Click here for a mobile and printer-friendly list of strategies and descriptions. Read more instructions.
Exercise.	Reframe nervousness as excitement.	
Focus on the audience instead of yourself.	Pause just before you start.	Before Presentation Day After
Don't worry about being nervous.	Distract yourself so you don't think about it.	
Practice focusing on your words and actions.	Think positively.	
Practice mindfulness.	Practice out load, using different words each time.	
Recognize that you don't look as nervous as you feel.	Visualize success.	
Find ways to relax.	Breathe from your diaphragm and tighten and release muscles. Yawn.	
Understand physical reactions as biological differences.	Let yourself relax.	
Practice in front of 4 or more people.	Watch a video of your presentation with an open mind.	
Practice in front of a mirror.	Write down everything you did well.	

Teal = Cognitive, Red = Physical/Behavioral, Orange = Affective

Source: Amy Newman, "How to Feel Confident for a Presentation . . . and Overcome Speech Anxiety," speaking.amynewman.com.

Public, Unpopular Decisions Take Courage

Courage means taking the tougher road and doing so publicly. Although Samsung fell short, we see better examples, including one from Facebook.

Difficult Decisions

Samsung's leaders wanted to fix things quickly and took what seemed like the easy way out. Recalling phones without offering replacements would have angered customers and may have turned them toward Apple or other competitors. Halting production may have angered shareholders, who would resent the loss in revenue. Samsung tried to avoid both.

We have better examples of courageous leaders who make unpopular decisions and do so publicly. In the book introduction, we learned about Chesley "Sully" Sullenberger, who disobeyed instructions and risked

155 lives by landing a US Airways plane in the Hudson River. He then spoke out about failings in the airline industry.

In Chapter 6, we learned about Kim Gwang-ho, the longtime employee of Hyundai, who spoke publicly about safety issues. He defied his employer—and his wife—to do the right thing.

Facebook Example

Facebook CEO Mark Zuckerberg took a stand in a "Black Lives Matter" controversy. Someone at Facebook's Menlo Park, California, office wrote "Black Lives Matter" on the company's graffiti wall—a large, open space for employees to write anything. The expression typically stands for the activist movement against violence and racism toward Black people. Some Facebook employees didn't appreciate the sentiment; more than once, they crossed out the writing and replaced it with "All Lives Matter." The slogan suggests that other people, such as police officers, also matter, but it is considered an affront to the Black Lives Matter movement.

At Facebook, particularly, this is a touchy subject: only 2% of the company's employees are Black, and 4% are Hispanic.[37] Zuckerberg condemned the word change in a message to all employees (Figure 7.5). He could have stayed out of the fray. Instead, he jumped into the controversy and talked publicly about his disappointment. He also used strong language, calling the acts "disrespectful," "malicious," "deeply hurtful," and "tiresome."[38]

After Zuckerberg sent his message, dozens of Facebook employees showed their support, sitting or standing together at the company headquarters and holding "Black Lives Matter" signs.[39]

Courageous Leaders Tackle Difficult Conversations

Although it's tempting to hide during tough times, courageous leaders don't shy away from difficult conversations. Again, Samsung's communication failures show us what to avoid, and better examples show us how to stand up to others.

Samsung's Passivity

Samsung missed the chance to communicate more actively and directly. Critics call the response "passive" and point to recall announcements

Figure 7.5   Facebook CEO Mark Zuckerberg condemns changing "Black Lives Matter"

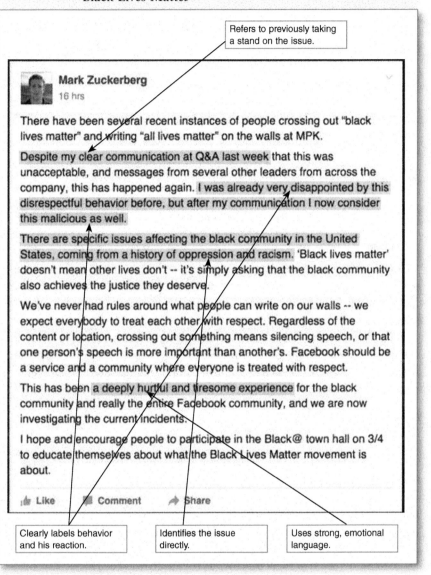

Source: Michael Nunez, "Mark Zuckerberg Asks Racist Facebook Employees to Stop Crossing Out Black Lives Matter Slogans," *Gizmodo*, February 25, 2016, http://gizmodo .com/mark-zuckerberg-asks-racist-facebook-employees-to-stop-1761272768, accessed June 21, 2017.

hidden on the website. For a defect that, as one brand consultant said, "can literally catch fire and burn your house down with you in it," communications fell short.[40]

Not until October 13—more than a week following reports of the *replacement* phones catching fire—did we hear from any company leader. At that point, Dong-jin Koh, president of mobile communications business for Samsung, gave the company's first apology.[41] (Another apology came a month later from Samsung president and CEO Gregory Lee—two months after the first recall.[42])

Communication experts also criticize Samsung leaders for their silence on social media:

> After you press send, tweet, and share your first media statement with your community, don't curl up under your desk and hope the issue will go away. It's vital that you keep your community updated on what is happening on a regular basis and keep the engagement live.[43]

Samsung's lack of communication shows us the importance of being actively public, particularly during harsh criticism. Samsung's first "replacement" announcement misses the opportunity for courageous communication (Figure 7.6).

In January 2017, Samsung announced the results of an investigation (Figure 7.7). We can see how using passive voice makes the response sound weak. The company's messages are ironic: Samsung products are intended to enable communication—not muddy it.

Tackling Tough Conversations

Few of us enjoy difficult conversations. Ending a relationship, firing an employee, quitting a job—many of us would rather send a text message. Unfortunately, these types of situations end up on social media and in the news. Authorities who took over a General Motors plant in Venezuela, leaving 2,700 employees out of work, communicated by text:

> GM informs you that social benefits will be transferred to employees' accounts due to the termination of your contracts.[44]

Although people prefer to give bad news later in a discussion—to ease into it—research tells us that receivers prefer to hear it first and get it over with.[45] Scholars have identified good reasons for delivering bad news in person, such as the ability to use and detect body language and to convey

Figure 7.6   Samsung's first replacement announcement lacks courage

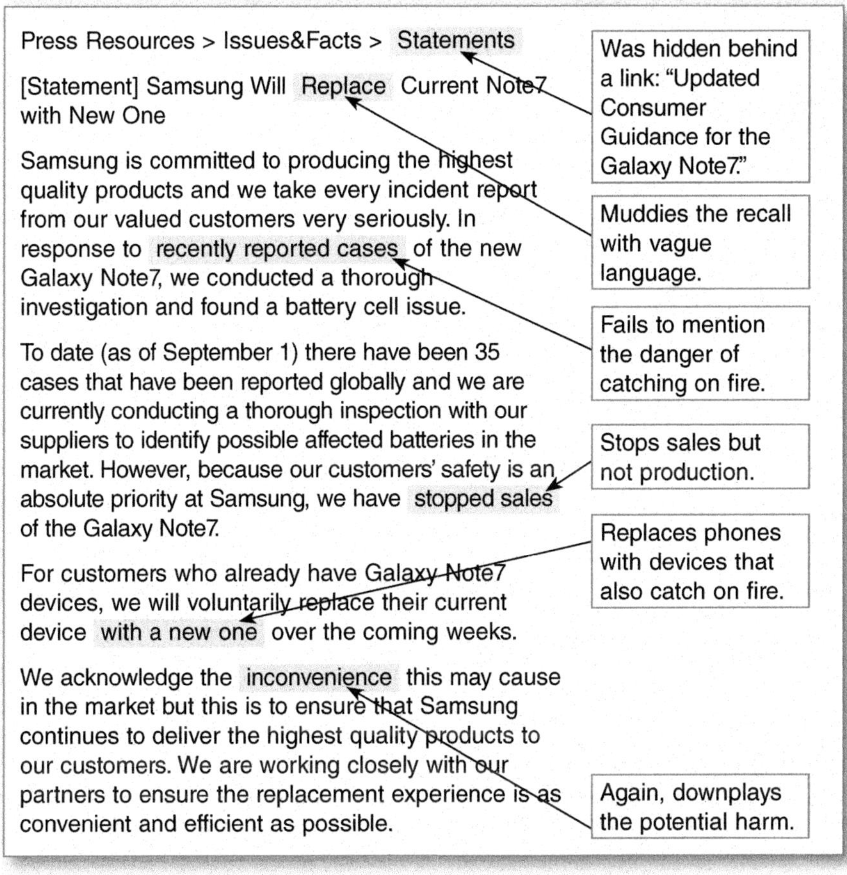

Press Resources > Issues&Facts > Statements

[Statement] Samsung Will Replace Current Note7 with New One

Samsung is committed to producing the highest quality products and we take every incident report from our valued customers very seriously. In response to recently reported cases of the new Galaxy Note7, we conducted a thorough investigation and found a battery cell issue.

To date (as of September 1) there have been 35 cases that have been reported globally and we are currently conducting a thorough inspection with our suppliers to identify possible affected batteries in the market. However, because our customers' safety is an absolute priority at Samsung, we have stopped sales of the Galaxy Note7.

For customers who already have Galaxy Note7 devices, we will voluntarily replace their current device with a new one over the coming weeks.

We acknowledge the inconvenience this may cause in the market but this is to ensure that Samsung continues to deliver the highest quality products to our customers. We are working closely with our partners to ensure the replacement experience is as convenient and efficient as possible.

- Was hidden behind a link: "Updated Consumer Guidance for the Galaxy Note7."
- Muddies the recall with vague language.
- Fails to mention the danger of catching on fire.
- Stops sales but not production.
- Replaces phones with devices that also catch on fire.
- Again, downplays the potential harm.

Source: Samsung, "Samsung Will Replace Current Note7 With New One," Samsung website, September 2, 2016, https://news.samsung.com/global/statement-on-galaxy-note7, accessed June 22, 2017.

respect and sensitivity.[46] At the same time, research shows some advantages of communicating bad news via email, for example, delivering a clear, consistent message to multiple employees at the same time.[47]

Communication researchers at Griffith University in Queensland identified more ways to tackle difficult conversations. They argue that these discussions typically involve "disagreement, defensiveness, and resistance," which can be mitigated with supportive behaviors, such as "empathy, equality, and description."[48] Demonstrating our understanding, relating to people as equals, and explaining issues clearly and objectively helps smooth these tough talks.

Figure 7.7   Samsung uses passive voice to announce obvious
              investigation results

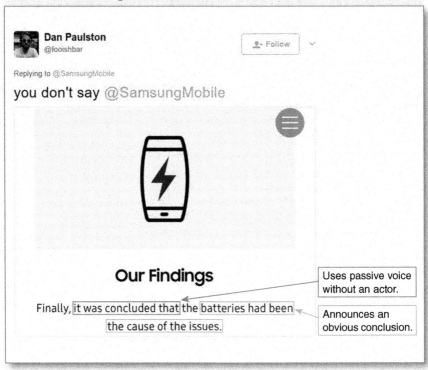

Source: Dan Paulston (@fooishbar), "You Don't Say @SamsungMobile," Twitter, January 23, 2017, https://twitter.com/fooishbar/status/823452930791575552, accessed November 8, 2017.

In their book *Crucial Conversations*, Kerry Patterson and her coauthors also stress the importance of handling difficult discussions well. They define crucial conversations as "a discussion between two or more people where (1) the stakes are high, (2) opinions vary, and (3) emotions run strong." According to the authors, people tend to handle these situations either with silence (sarcasm, sugarcoating, avoiding, or withdrawing) or with violence (controlling, labeling, or attacking).[49]

Indian Bank and Xerox Examples

Courageous leaders have difficult conversations without going to either extreme—silence or violence. When Ranjana Kumar took over as Indian

Bank's chair and managing director, she inherited bad loans, many from political and corrupt sources. Kumar tackled the situation head on, fighting what she called "fear psychosis" among the staff. She replaced staff and went after delinquent customers.[50] A former colleague describes her courage:

> As much as she cared about communicating with all members of her staff, she was not afraid to challenge the high and mighty defaulter customers, even in their own backyards. Her willingness to confront when warranted made her highly effective. In fact, her ability to call a spade a spade was what earned her the most respect.[51]

The Economist called her "India's turn-round queen." After a three-year restructuring plan, the bank added 800,000 new customers and turned an operating profit of 2.6 billion rupees.[52]

Former Xerox CEO Ursula Burns serves as another good example of courageous communication. In a CNN interview, Burns described growing up in a housing project in Brooklyn, New York:

> New York is a tough place. You have to speak up. You have to be a little gritty. . . . People would sleep under the stairs. You know, drug addicts or bums . . . it smelt like urine out in the hallway. It was definitely not safe.[53]

Burns described attending a company event 20 years before she become CEO. She recalled a comment from a coworker: "He didn't say 'Black people,' he said, 'Why are we hiring all these different types of people and women?'" She wasn't happy with the executive's comment, according to the CNN report:

> She stood up in front of everyone and chided him for displaying a lack of passion and principles. Her comments led to an "unfriendly" exchange between the two. Burns said, "I thought I was going to be fired. And my $29,004 would go 'poof' into the wind."[54]

The executive counseled Burns on her "inappropriate tone" but later hired her into a job that was instrumental to her career progression to CEO.[55] Her courage paid off, and Burns illustrates vulnerability and authenticity.

Radical Candor and Radical Transparency Are Two Ways Leaders Demonstrate Courage

Radical candor and radical transparency are tools for addressing difficult situations head on and for practicing openness. Both require vulnerability and courage.

Radical Candor

A direct approach to difficult conversations is best and takes courage. We want to avoid discomfort, but the better strategy is to work through it. Being uncomfortable is a sign that we're engaged in something important and difficult. Discomfort can inspire us to forge ahead—to take the opportunity to improve a relationship, even if the conversation is difficult.

In her book *Radical Candor*, Kim Scott supports a direct approach. To practice radical candor, leaders—again, at any level of the organization—care personally and challenge directly. An example of responding to someone who sends an email and forgets the attachment is shown in Figure 7.8.[56]

Scott promotes bringing your whole self to work, as we discussed in Chapter 4. She advocates knowing each other well in the workplace to build caring, supportive relationships. Although people may be distant at work, Scott encourages people to connect more on a human level.

Figure 7.8 Radical candor includes caring personally and challenging directly

Care Personally		
Ruinous Empathy	**Radical Candor**	
Do nothing because you're worried about **his** feelings	Reply to sender: "I didn't receive the attachment."	**Challenge Directly**
Do nothing because you're worried about **your** feelings	Reply to all, "You forgot the attachment!"	
Manipulative Insincerity	**Obnoxious Aggression**	

Scott also says that people fear communicating directly—both initiating and receiving direct communication—but eventually work better together:

> The most surprising thing about Radical Candor may be that its results are often the opposite of what you fear. You fear people will become angry or vindictive; instead they are usually grateful for the chance to talk it through. And even when you do get the initial anger, resentment, or sullenness, those emotions prove to be fleeting when the person knows you really care. As the people who report to you become more Radically Candid with each other, you spend less time mediating. When Radical Candor is encouraged and supported by the boss, communication flows, resentments that have festered come to the surface and get resolved, and people begin to love not just their work but whom they work with and where they work.[57]

People get emotional at work, and that's not a reason to avoid tough conversations. Instead, Scott recommends acknowledging emotions instead of ignoring them and taking a break in the conversation if necessary.[58] You might also prepare to be engaged viscerally. It's okay to feel physically tense, and you may want to close the conversation with a handshake or hug.

GM CEO Mary Barra also takes a direct approach, particularly during crisis situations. When asked how she motivates people, she explained, "One is being honest. I think people are smart and they're going to sense if you're BS'ing them a mile away. Don't try to sugarcoat things."[59]

Courageous leaders *want* to be challenged and have the guts to challenge others. If our ideas are sound, we won't cower when questioned.

Radical Transparency

Another approach that takes courage is practicing radical transparency, which means "putting openness above all other competing values."[60] In his *Wired* article "The See-Through CEO," Clive Thompson calls radical transparency "[a] judo move. Your customers are going to poke around in your business anyway, and your workers are going to blab about internal info— so why not make it work *for* you by turning everyone into a partner in the process and inviting them to do so?" Companies like Zappos allow employees to vent on a companywide wiki and tell suppliers about profits. According to CEO Tony Hsieh, "The more they know about us, the more they'll like us."[61]

To some leaders, radical transparency means everyone in the organization knows everything, for example, performance data. At Qualtrics, which provides online survey tools, all employees know each other's quarterly objectives, weekly goals, career history, and performance reviews and ratings.

Proponents of radical transparency argue that such openness removes worry about mistakes and false comparisons to colleagues.[62]

Bridgewater investment management is one example of a firm that promotes "radical truth and radical transparency." The company describes the practice: "We require people to be extremely open, air disagreements, test each other's logic, and view discovering mistakes and weaknesses as a good thing that leads to improvement and innovation."[63] To some, Bridgewater feels like a harsh place to work; employees are expected to tell what we might call the brutal truth. The company also has been criticized for being secretive about investment decisions.[64] We might call this a question of integrity: Do the leaders demonstrate consistency and wholeness?

Self-Righteousness Needs to Be Controlled

We discussed the problem of excess courage in the form of recklessness. Other extremes of courage may be considered self-righteousness or terror, and both should be avoided. We need perspective to make sure we're helping others, not hurting them.

About Self-Righteousness

Courage has been called the "difficult virtue" because it involves confrontation and is potentially destructive.[65] Let's be clear: having courage doesn't mean you're right. Courageous leaders have to keep themselves in check with others around them, which we'll revisit when we discuss humility. Otherwise, they may be considered self-righteous—smug and moralistic—as though only their view is the "right" one, and others' views are wrong.

Where's the line between courage and self-righteousness? Gavin Long shot three law enforcement officers in Baton Rouge, Louisiana, and left a suicide note to, perhaps reluctantly, justify his actions. In this excerpt, he wrote that he respected and knew good cops yet hated what bad cops got away with:[66]

> [N]ow if the bad cops, law makers, & justice system leaders care about the welfare, families, & well-being of their fellow good cops, then they (bad cops) will quit committing criminal acts against melanated people & the people in general. If not, my people, & the people in general will continue to strike back against all cops until we see that bad cops are no longer protected and allowed to flourish. B/C until this happens, we the people cannot differentiate the good from the bad.[67]

At the end, he wrote: "Look up, get up, & don't ever give up!" This was a call to action to challenge what he perceived as a corrupt system. This sounds like courage, but most people would call Long misguided at best and a terrorist at worst. He missed the risk assessment discussed earlier and did more harm than good.

Courageous leaders have to watch how they use force. Courage doesn't mean coercion; it involves making an offer you *can* refuse. If leaders resort to using force, maybe they aren't as confident as they think they are, or maybe the idea or solution isn't the right one after all. Radical candor means caring for others, not steamrolling them.

Starbucks Example

When President Trump enacted a travel ban for people from predominantly Muslim countries, people were fiercely divided, and Starbucks CEO Howard Schultz took a stand. In a message on the company's website, "Living Our Values in Uncertain Times," Schultz announced plans to help employees and hire 10,000 refugees.[68] Some considered his statement self-righteous—perhaps an excess of courage.

His statement was criticized on social media and at a shareholder meeting. An investor pointed out Schultz's inconsistency: he questioned why Schultz "lacked the courage to speak out" during travel bans under the Obama and Clinton administrations.[69]

At the shareholder meeting, Schultz had to wait for heckling to stop before defending his plans. He said the company had a "moral obligation" and promised no additional costs to the company to vet refugee hires. Schultz also said, "I can unequivocally tell you that there's zero, absolutely no evidence whatsoever, that there's any dilution in the Starbucks brand, reputation, or core business as a result of being compassionate."[70]

This statement may be true, broadly, but we have evidence that the brand and business did suffer in this case. After Schultz announced his refugee plan, a survey of about 4,800 people showed a decline in how people viewed the brand.[71] After the announcement, #BoycottStarbucks also was trending on Twitter.[72] Despite the impact on the business—and perhaps Schultz was in denial about some of it—he made an unpopular decision and stuck to it.

The audience's lens matters, and reactions in such situations may depend on politics more than anything else. Still, as leaders, we should watch our own indignation. Is our view the only right one? Courage includes managing through ambiguity. A courageous leader considers nuance and can discern what's right from many perspectives. One test for self-righteousness may be to ask whether we can receive negative feedback without being defensive. Can we accurately assess feedback and—if it's accurate—change our stance? Or do we just keep pounding our fists?

Having the confidence to live and lead by our conviction is good, but not if we don't consider others and not if we use them to justify our courage: "I know I'm right, so I will continue down this path regardless of those left behind." Passion is good; fanaticism is not.

SUMMARY

Samsung missed an opportunity to face the product recall more courageously. With stronger language and more decisive action, the company may have fared better in the media. Eventually, Samsung recovered. By the summer of 2017, the Galaxy S8 was selling well and, for the first time, Samsung's operating profits had outpaced Apple's.[73] But the Note 7 crisis is remembered as an example of the company's weak leadership.

Courageous leaders don't fear confrontation when necessary to accomplish goals for others. Radical candor and radical transparency require courage and may foster better relationships at work. At the same time, leaders need to assess risk and keep self-righteousness in check so they can serve others.

Professional tennis player Arthur Ashe encourages us to act courageously—with humility:

> True heroism is remarkably sober, very undramatic. It is not the urge to surpass all others at whatever cost, but the urge to serve others at whatever cost.[74]

We'll discuss humility as a character dimension next.

EXERCISES

Concept Review Questions

1. What does courage involve? What does a leader do to demonstrate courage?
2. How can a leader assess risk to improve the chances of a good outcome?
3. What are radical candor and radical transparency? What are some examples of what radical candor is *not*?
4. What's the danger of self-righteousness?

Self-Reflection

1. Describe a time when you held a minority view about something important yet didn't contradict the majority. What was the goal? Why wasn't it worth fighting for, or what held you back? What can you learn from the experience?

2. Who in your life would you call courageous? What is this person able to accomplish? What about this person do you admire?

3. Think about a time when you challenged someone's opinion or idea. What about it was hard for you, and what was easy? What did you accomplish?

4. Think about a time when you encouraged others to follow your idea or recommendation. What did you do successfully? How did others respond?

5. Think about a time when you had courage but underestimated the risk. What was the result, and how might you act differently in the future?

6. Has there been a time in your life that you may have been self-righteous? What was the position you held strongly? What consequences did your position have? How did it affect your relationships?

7. How comfortable are you with the idea of radical candor? To what extent have you practiced it in the past?

8. Have you experienced being cared for personally and challenged directly by a leader? How did it feel? How did it affect your performance or productivity?

Mini-Cases

Consider the following scenarios. On your own or with a partner, discuss the best course of action in each case. What would you do, and what factors into your decision?

Scenario 1

One of your team members submitted her section of a report for a class project, but you suspect it's not her own work. In a footnote on the last page are someone else's name, the same course number, and last year's date. She submitted the work online, and your three team members also have access to the file. How will you handle this situation?

Scenario 2

One of your coworkers wants flexible work hours so the team can work at staggered times, for example, 8 a.m. to 4 p.m. or 10 a.m. to 6 p.m. You like the idea, but you're not willing to fight for it. On the other hand, this is very important to your coworker. She talks about it every day and tries to rally the rest of the team to support her. She has raised the suggestion three times during team meetings, and you and others usually redirect the conversation. How would you describe your coworker's behavior? What will you do in this situation?

Scenario 3

You support the idea of radical candor, but a teammate's behavior falls more into the "obnoxious aggression" category. Earlier in the day, you overheard him tell a customer, "You need to be more careful with the product. It's not a toy, and you'll be responsible if it breaks again." How will you handle this situation?

Self-Assessment

Take the Professional Moral Courage Assessment in Figure 7.2 to learn about your-self and how you demonstrate courage. Use a seven-point scale to rate each item, where 1 = *never*, 4 = *sometimes*, and 7 = *always*.

Add up your scores under each theme (three questions each). For each theme, divide by three to get one score. For an overall score, add all scores and divide by 15.

Paired Activity

With a partner, discuss your ratings on the Professional Moral Courage Assessment. You may use these questions as a guide:

- To what extent do your responses reflect how you view yourself? What, if any-thing, surprised you about the assessment and your responses? Provide examples to illustrate your points.
- What can you learn from this experience? What do you see as your strengths, and where can you develop moral courage?

Paired Activity

Scenario

Think about an upcoming situation that makes you fearful or anxious. Try to work through your feelings.

Planning Questions

1. What is the situation, and what is your goal?

2. How do you feel about it? Try to experience the emotion.

3. Why do you feel the way you do? For example, are you afraid of hurting some-one else's feelings? Are you afraid of being vulnerable or looking foolish?

4. Which of your feelings are real, and which might be imagined? Try to distin-guish each.

5. Identify the real risks. What is at stake?

6. What could be the positive results of your taking action in this situation? How will your actions help others?

7. How can you prepare to receive negative feedback or different points of view? You may reconsider your points—or you may choose not to let go.

Role Play Activity

Scenario

Role-play your part of the situation above to demonstrate courage. You may work with a partner to role-play the scenario together. You may video-record your part or role-play the scenario with another student to review it later.

Planning Questions

1. What did you learn from analyzing the situation above?

2. Analyze the other perspective: how might the other person or people react?

3. How will you begin your part? What will you say next?

4. How will you balance being courageous with sounding self-righteous or too forceful?

5. How can you describe the situation in a way that is helpful and transparent?

6. How will you acknowledge negative feedback or doubts?

Practice and Reflection

Did you demonstrate courage? Did you also demonstrate vulnerability? How did you feel? What did you learn from the role play?

8

Humility

Learning From Others

Chapter Overview

Ride-sharing company Uber has enjoyed tremendous success, but company lead-ers have made questionable decisions. Former CEO Travis Kalanick could have been more humble—open, willing to learn, and respectful to others. Humility involves knowing our limits, taking different perspectives, and being curious. Humble leaders make space for others to thrive.

Constituencies Question Uber's Ethics

In just eight years, Uber cofounder and former CEO Travis Kalanick built a successful ride-sharing company employing 12,000 employees[1] and more than 450,000 drivers in 75 countries,[2] but his leadership character and business practices have been questioned. A string of news headlines reflect Kalanick's motto, "Growth above all else."[3] An adviser to Kalanick's earlier company said, "The Travis Kalanick I came to know 17 years ago was relentless in pursuit of his goals at the expense of those who supported him along the way, deluded by his own embellished personal narrative, and a serial prevaricator."[4]

Stories show a company wanting to win as a priority, using what some consider unfair, potentially illegal practices and disregarding complaints from employees and drivers. In 2014, Emil Michael, Uber's senior vice president of business—later called Kalanick's "right-hand man"[5]— suggested paying $1 million to find personal information about members of the media that could be used against them. Michael's comments were directed primarily to a reporter who wrote about sexism and misogyny at Uber.[6] Michael resigned three years later with about a dozen other executives who left over a five-month period (Figure 8.1).

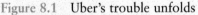

Figure 8.1   Uber's trouble unfolds

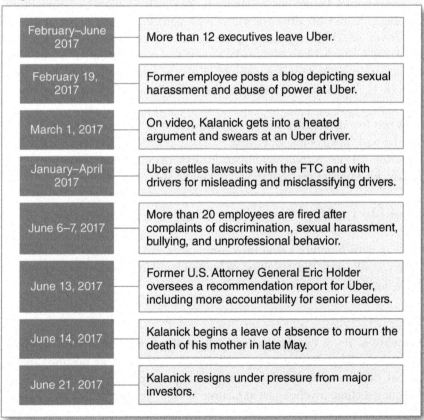

February–June 2017	More than 12 executives leave Uber.
February 19, 2017	Former employee posts a blog depicting sexual harassment and abuse of power at Uber.
March 1, 2017	On video, Kalanick gets into a heated argument and swears at an Uber driver.
January–April 2017	Uber settles lawsuits with the FTC and with drivers for misleading and misclassifying drivers.
June 6–7, 2017	More than 20 employees are fired after complaints of discrimination, sexual harassment, bullying, and unprofessional behavior.
June 13, 2017	Former U.S. Attorney General Eric Holder oversees a recommendation report for Uber, including more accountability for senior leaders.
June 14, 2017	Kalanick begins a leave of absence to mourn the death of his mother in late May.
June 21, 2017	Kalanick resigns under pressure from major investors.

Sources: Madeline Farber, "These Are All the Top Uber Executives Who've Left Since February," *Fortune*, April 12, 2017, http://fortune.com/2017/04/12/uber-execs-leaving-company/, accessed June 28, 2017; Alanna Petroff, "The Rise and Fall of Uber CEO Travis Kalanick," *CNN Tech*, June 21, 2017, http://money.cnn.com/2017/06/21/technology/uber-ceo-travis-kalanick-timeline/index.html, accessed June 28, 2017.

Uber also was in the news for capitalizing on local disasters with "surge pricing";[7] buying data from a service that accessed customers' emailed receipts from Uber's competitor, Lyft;[8] possibly stealing self-driving car technology from Waymo, a company owned by Google's parent, Alphabet;[9] and breaking Apple's rules by "fingerprinting" iPhones to track phones even after the Uber app was deleted. For this last offense, Apple CEO Tim Cook called Kalanick to his office to warn him in person.[10]

Uber also had disputes with drivers. Uber settled lawsuits with some drivers for classifying them as contractors instead of employees and promised to change some practices, for example, how it deactivated drivers.[11] A suit with the Federal Trade Commission cost Uber $28 million for Craigslist ads overstating drivers' potential income.[12]

Just months before his resignation, Kalanick embarrassed himself by arguing with an Uber driver on video. As Kalanick was getting out of the car, the driver asked him questions about decreasing pay and new services that he claimed affected him negatively. Kalanick shouted at him and ended the conversation with, "Some people don't like to take responsibility for their own sh__. They blame everything in their life on somebody else. Good luck!" He rated the driver with one star on the Uber app.[13]

When five major investors demanded Kalanick's resignation,[14] the board said he had "always put Uber first."[15] There is little dispute about that. The question for us is whether Uber leaders demonstrated humility.[16] Did Kalanick recognize his limitations and make space for others?

Humble Leaders Recognize Their Own Limitations

Leaders with humility know their limitations and seek improvement. Uber examples illustrate the definition of humility and how leaders lack this character dimension.

Humility Defined

Humility is about human limits: seeing and handling our own and others' limitations. Jorge L. A. Garcia, a philosophy professor at Boston College, argues that humility involves "being unimpressed with ourselves."[17] June Tangney, a clinic psychologist at George Mason, defines humility as follows:

> [T]rue humility is a rich, multifaceted construct that is characterized by an accurate assessment of one's characteristics, an ability to acknowledge limitations, and a "forgetting of the self."[18]

Humility is essential to cultivating character because it drives our self-awareness and willingness to learn. With humility, we come to understand ourselves and others and focus on personal growth and organizational learning.

Crossan and her colleagues included humility as a character dimension because of growing research and because they found it strongly predicted performance. Elements of humility include *self-aware, modest, reflective, continuous, learner, curious, respectful, grateful,* and *vulnerable.*[19]

We elevated vulnerability in this book to its own character dimension, and we can see the connection to humility. Like vulnerability, humility may be perceived as a weakness. Does it mean meek or subservient, being a "doormat"? It does not as we define it. In *Daring Greatly,* Brené Brown wrote about narcissism, contrasted with humility:

> [W]hen I look at narcissism through the vulnerability lens, I see the shame-based fear of being ordinary. I see the fear of never feeling extraordinary enough to be noticed, to be lovable, to belong, or to cultivate a sense of purpose.[20]

For some people, arrogance is an overcompensation for feeling inadequate. What seems like confidence is a mask for not feeling "good enough." In this sense, humility is paradoxical: it's about recognizing our limitations *and* having high self-esteem. In a study about dating, people who were more humble were more likely to garner romantic interest and were rated as more attractive than arrogant to potential dating partners.[21] We tend to see through arrogance and prefer to be around people who are more humble.

Humility can be observed by others. Bradley Owens at Brigham Young University and other researchers identified the following when humility is expressed:

- A focus on learning and personal growth
- An accurate perception of self, which is dependent on interactions with others
- Recognition of personal limitations and honest self-disclosure
- An appreciation of strengths and contributions of others[22]

Humility in Organizations

When humility is present in organizations, people are willing to discuss mistakes openly and focus on continuous learning. When humility is absent, we see arrogance and little commitment to improvement.[23]

In times of change, a realistic view of people and organizations helps leaders be nimble and manage uncertainty.[24] A humble leader asks, "How can we improve? What do others see that I also need to see?" Being humble allows us to learn from mistakes, which results in better performance over time.[25]

Studies show that humble leaders have a positive effect on team performance. When leaders demonstrated humility by admitting limitations, highlighting others' strengths, and being teachable, team members reported better task allocation and performance.[26] This includes disclosing what is relevant to the team and may not be seen by others. A humble leader is willing to say, "I don't have the experience working with this technology/product/client. Hiro, could you take the lead on this, given your experience?" Success then becomes more likely for the team.

Uber's Lack of Humility

At Uber, leaders failed to respond to criticism about its organizational culture. Perhaps the breaking point for Uber, and Kalanick's eventual resignation, was Susan Fowler's blog post. The former Uber engineer described sexual harassment as a common occurrence and referred to Uber as "an organization in complete, unrelenting chaos."[27] According to Fowler, bad behavior by good performers was tolerated, and her complaints to Human Resources went unanswered. In response, Kalanick wrote, "We seek to make Uber a just workplace, and there can be absolutely no place for this kind of behavior at Uber—and anyone who behaves this way or thinks this is OK will be fired."[28] Apparently, several employees did think it was okay; 20 people were terminated following an investigation into harassment claims.[29]

Fowler's post seemed to reflect a pattern. More than three years before her post went viral, Kalanick gave women advice for drinking and having sex at a company event;[30] he referred to women as "Boob-ers"; and the company advertised the French equivalent of Uber as offering "incredibly hot chicks" for a free 20-minute ride.[31]

Perhaps some of Uber's problems could have been avoided with a dose of humility. In 2014, when the reporter accused the company of misogyny, Emil Michael attacked back. But what if the leaders had listened to the feedback instead?

Another missed warning sign for Kalanick and for the board of directors is the parade of executive resignations within a few months. Even newcomers, such as Jeff Jones, hired as Uber's president from Target, lasted only six months. When Jones left, he said, "[T]he beliefs and approach to leadership that have guided my career are inconsistent with what I saw and experienced at Uber, and I can no longer continue as president of the ride sharing business."[32]

Kalanick gave us one example of self-reflection, in an apology statement, after he was caught on video with the driver. He writes, "The criticism we've received is a stark reminder that I must fundamentally change as a leader and grow up."[33] On the surface, it looks like a commitment to real change, but we might question his sincerity. He had little choice but to apologize when his behavior was on video.

Humility as a Management Strength

Leaders who demonstrate both personal and professional humility will inspire better performance in their organizations. In addition, CEOs with humility are rated more highly on important leadership skills.

Level 5 Leaders

From his 20 years studying organizations, Jim Collins identified humility as a distinguishing factor in taking companies from "Good to Great." Collins coined the term "Level 5" to describe the type of leader needed to transform an organization and sustain high levels of performance.[34,35]

Level 5 leaders "build enduring greatness through a paradoxical combination of personal humility plus professional will." They are a paradox because they demonstrate elements that we don't typically imagine as complementary. As Collins says, they "are a study in duality: modest and willful, shy and fearless." These leaders are likely to attribute their success to luck, yet they have high standards and "an unwavering resolve" for results[36] (Figure 8.2).

Again, we see the demise of the charismatic leader—the loud, boisterous glad-handler. In contrast, humble people demonstrate a "calm determination" that makes them powerful leaders.

Figure 8.2   Level 5 leaders demonstrate personal humility and professional will

Personal Humility	Professional Will
Demonstrates a compelling modesty, shunning public adulation; never boastful.	Creates superb results, a clear catalyst in the transition from good to great.
Acts with quiet, calm determination; to motivate, relies principally on inspired standards, not inspiring charisma.	Demonstrates an unwavering resolve to do whatever must be done to produce the best long-term results, no matter how difficult.
Channels ambition into the company, not the self; sets up successors for even more greatness in the next generation.	Sets the standard of building an enduring great company; will settle for nothing less.
Looks in the mirror, not out the window, to apportion responsibility for poor results, never blaming other people, external factors, or bad luck.	Looks out the window, not in the mirror, to apportion credit for the success of the company—to other people, external factors, and good luck.

The Humble CEO

From data collected about executives, KRC Research shows the importance of the "humble CEO." Executives who report to humble CEOs rate them more highly in internal and external communication, seeing these qualities as strengths rather than weaknesses (Figure 8.3).[37]

Humble Leaders Make Space for Others

Leaders with humility aren't the center of attention, yet they aren't beneath others either. In this section, we see more examples of arrogance and humility.

Grounded or "Down to Earth"

The root of the word *humility* is *humus*, which means "earth" or "ground." *Humilis* means, literally, "on the ground."[38] We can see how "down to earth" can describe someone humble.

Figure 8.3   Humble CEOs are better communicators

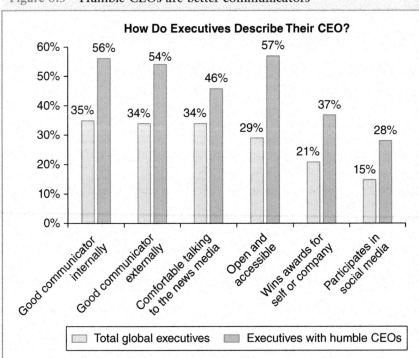

Source: Bradley Honan, "What Is CEO Reputation Premium, and Why Does It Matter for Your Organization?" KRC Research, http://www.krcresearch.com/what-is-ceo-reputation-premium-and-why-does-it-matter-for-your-organization/, accessed June 28, 2017.

But people confuse humility with humiliation, which is feeling shamed or degraded. We're not *shoved* to the ground. We are equal to others, neither inferior nor superior.

Eric Clay, a clinically trained chaplain, describes how to demonstrate humility through physical positioning when working with hospital patients:

> Chaplains and healthcare workers realize the power imbalance they have with patients. In order to challenge that and offer some real sense of equality, some of us have learned to sit so that our heads are at or below the level of the patients. The patient then speaks across on the level, or down to the professional who speaks up to the patient. When meeting with a family and staff, we would sit at the side of a table, off center—neither at the end of the table or in the middle of the side—to shift the dynamics of interacting.[39]

Through our positioning, we demonstrate that we are equal to others. A humble leader certainly would avoid standing over an employee's desk.

Not Flaunting

Humble leaders have high self-esteem, but they don't flaunt it. They let their accomplishments speak for themselves. Although not afraid to be seen, humble leaders make space for others, as a management coach explains:

> A well-developed sense of humility shines through in your behavior toward others. They feel affirmed, appreciated, encouraged, validated, and psychically nourished.[40]

The focus is on the other. As a team member, we demonstrate humility by making sure others feel valued. Coworkers welcome new employees by sharing their knowledge but never make them feel inferior. We offer our experience to be helpful, not demeaning.

David Brooks warns about the "broadcasting personality" encouraged on social media.[41] It may seem that Millennials, particularly, born between 1980 and 2000, are more concerned with themselves than with others. They do focus on individual academic achievement, but previous generations were criticized by their predecessors too. Baby Boomers, born in the 1940s until about 1964, were called the "Me Generation" until Millennials were similarly labeled. And Baby Boomers likely received that moniker because the previous generation suffered through the Great Depression and *really* had it bad.[42]

Humble leaders don't seek awards. They are more interested in seeing others shine.

Reese Witherspoon and Snap Examples

Although a stereotype, we see some celebrities struggling with humility. Police stopped Jim Toth for driving under the influence of alcohol (DUI) when his wife, actress Reese Witherspoon, was in the car. You may know her from the HBO show *Big Little Lies* or from the movies *Legally Blonde* and *Walk the Line*.

On video, we see Witherspoon protest: "I'm an American citizen. This is beyond. This is beyond. This is harassment. . . . I have to obey your orders? . . .You know my name, sir? You don't need to know my name? OK, you're about to find out who I am."[43] As Toth was getting arrested for the DUI, Witherspoon was arrested for disorderly conduct. Witherspoon apologized, but she showed us a bit of herself—as above others and above the law—and it wasn't flattering.

We see plenty of this arrogance in business leaders. TV host and money manager Jim Cramer criticized Snap Inc. CEO and cofounder Evan Spiegel for a remark about other technology companies. Spiegel was answering questions after Snap's first earnings report; the newly public company fell short of Wall Street's expectations. Someone asked whether he was afraid of Facebook, which had recently added some Snapchat-like features. Spiegel laughed and said, "People are going to copy your product if you build great stuff. Just because Yahoo has a search box doesn't make it Google." It sounds as though Spiegel is saying that Snapchat is superior to Facebook, and that the Snapchat app is like Google. Cramer said, "Humility is a fabulous thing":

> You've got to put him through some sort of gauntlet because this guy is so arrogant. He's so arrogant that I mean, honestly, Evan Spiegel, listen to me and listen to me good: you're going to introduce yourself next time, and then you're going to back off and let your CFO talk.[44]

On his show *Squawk on the Street*, Cramer also advised Spiegel: "You're going to say, 'You know what, I did not do the job I'd like to, but I'm going to work harder.'"[45]

Humble leaders can be competitive business people, but they don't deny others' success or bask in others' misfortunes. Let's contrast Uber and these examples with an example from Uber's competition, Lyft.

Lyft Example

As Uber was facing a host of bad news, John Zimmer, Lyft's president and cofounder, wrote an email to staff:

While we are proud of the values and actions that have always distinguished us, this is not a time to gloat, particularly when many of the events are rooted in personal pain for several individuals.[46]

In an interview after Kalanick's resignation, Zimmer said, "There's nothing to celebrate in this situation. But it does shine a light on the importance of values and ethics."[47] Of course, Zimmer has self-interests, but he modeled humility for his staff. He echoed the importance of humility in a later interview when he said, "If you're going to manage people or lead people, you have to be able to walk in their shoes and understand them."[48]

When we lead with humility, we recognize our interdependence with others. We see ourselves through our relationships with others—not in competition, but in relation with them. Bill George offers this advice for staying grounded: connecting with family and friends, being physically active, having a spiritual practice, doing volunteer work, and visiting places where we grew up.[49]

Assessments Teach Us About Humility

As with all leadership character dimensions, humility can be developed. With self-awareness and a willingness to change, leaders can become more humble. We see a definition in the HEXACO personality model, and attributes in a humility scale help us understand the concept further.

HEXACO Model

Measuring humility is an interesting quandary: Do humble leaders rate themselves as humble?[50] Do people with low humility inflate their self-ratings?[51] Humility is a major component of the HEXACO[52] model, proposed as an alternative to the traditional Big Five personality test. For this assessment, at least, research shows moderately consistent results between self-reports and observers' assessment of the individual.[53]

Honesty-Humility is one of six dimensions in the HEXACO assessment and is defined as follows:

Persons with very high scores on the Honesty-Humility scale avoid manipulating others for personal gain, feel little temptation to break rules, are uninterested in lavish wealth and luxuries, and feel no special entitlement to elevated social status. Conversely, persons with very low scores on this scale will flatter others to get what they want, are inclined to break rules for personal profit, are motivated by material gain, and feel a strong sense of self-importance.[54]

Research also shows a connection between the Honesty-Humility personality dimension and organizational politics. A study of employees found that, when organizational politics were high, those who scored low in Honesty-Humility were more likely to engage in counterproductive activity at work and more likely to worry about impression management.[55]

Humility Scale

In addition to the HEXACO assessment, researchers have identified scales specific for humility, such as the one in Figure 8.4. The questions tell us more about what humility involves.

From these statements, we see the emphasis on recognizing limitations, seeking feedback, and understanding effects on others.

Figure 8.4   Scale items tell us what humility involves

I seek out the truth about myself, even if it highlights my weaknesses.
I identify the contributions and inherent worth of others around me.
I view myself as a good partner to those I interact with (family members, coworkers, friends).
I am open to new information about myself.
I am aware that others have contributed to my accomplishments.
I view myself as a good member to a larger community (my local community, my workplace, other groups).
I do not react defensively toward criticism.
I appreciate the reality of being one person in a larger community.
What is important to me is working to improve the welfare of the community(ies) I value and/or belong to (my local community, my workplace, other groups).
I actively seek out information about my strengths.
My accomplishments don't make me more valuable than others.
I feel my fate is intertwined with the fate of those around me.
I actively seek out information about my weaknesses.
I feel connected to a purpose greater than myself.
I feel good when I cooperate with others.

Source: Adapted from Rob Nielsen, Jennifer A. Marrone, and Holly S. Ferraro, *Leading With Humility* (New York: Routledge, 2014), pp. 113–115. Republished with Permission of Taylor & Francis Group LLC Books; permission conveyed through Copyright Clearance Center, Inc

Leading With Humility Requires Perspective

Leaders need to keep themselves in perspective and understand the perspectives of others. Humble leaders know their view is not the only one. Managers and employees can learn from each other.

Not the Center of the Universe

Humble leaders recognize they are part of a much larger universe. We are just a small part of what happens in the world and in our organizations every day, and what matters most is the larger community.

As discussed earlier, business success may cause leaders to lose perspective. In an interview, Goldman Sachs CEO Lloyd Blankfein said the bank has a "social purpose":

> We're very important. We help companies to grow by helping them to raise capital. Companies that grow create wealth. This, in turn, allows people to have jobs that create more growth and more wealth. It's a virtuous cycle.

Then, at the end of the interview, when he may have thought the reporting was done,[56] he said they were just "doing God's work."[57] Particularly with Goldman's role in wealth generation, the comment overstated their work and sounded arrogant. The media repeated Blankfein's quote in news headlines.

Uber suffered a similar embarrassment when leaders used "God" language. The company developed a tool called "God View," which was sometimes used to track celebrities, politicians, and ex-partners of Uber employees. The employee who blew the whistle on the tool was fired.[58]

An employee at Goldman expressed concern about the culture in a public resignation letter in the *New York Times*, "Why I Am Leaving Goldman Sachs." He wrote that, when he had started as an intern, he'd felt "a spirit of humility" throughout the company. But 12 years later, the focus had shifted to prioritizing profits over doing what was right for clients.[59] In other words, the company had lost perspective.

Perspective taking is essential to learning. With humility, we come to know ourselves through others. In the academic literature, perspective taking means trying to understanding others' thoughts, feelings, and motivations.[60]

In addition to contributing to our personal development, the ability to take others' perspectives has positive organizational outcomes. Studies have found results such as communicating clearly, helping others more, focusing on ideas that will likely benefit others, and reducing stereotyping and prejudices.[61] Perspective taking also contributes to developing and repairing trust.[62]

Manager and Employee Perspectives

A booklet, "Walk Awhile in *My* Shoes," has two distinct sides: one from a manager's point of view and one from an employee's. Each begins with a letter to the other (Figure 8.5), and the interior pages identify challenges of

Figure 8.5   A manager writes to an employee

Dear Employee:

I am every manager. I'm known by many labels: owner, executive, department head, supervisor, team leader, boss . . . and sometimes a few less flattering ones I'd rather not mention but do know exist. — Admits limitations.

I am woman, and I am man. I'm every color, every belief, and every size. I'm old, young, and everything in between. I've worked here longer than you and not as long as you. I am a son. I am a daughter. I'm married and single, a parent and without children. I'm alone and I'm surrounded by people I care about deeply. — Presents self as equal to—not above—others.

Like you, I am a human being filled with joys, fears, frustrations, and hopes. Behind my "management façade," I feel, I laugh, and yes, I occasionally hurt. And, like you, I want to be understood, accepted, and appreciated.

The following pages are about opening up to you— about sharing my feelings on just a few of the many aspects of my job and how they affect me. Some of what you read may surprise you . . . some may bring a laugh or two. All of these pages, I hope, will encourage you to see me in a new and perhaps much different light. — Demonstrates openness. — Recognizes different perspectives.

I ask that you receive these messages with the same level of compassion and understanding that you wish from me as I read the flip side of this book. Chances are we're not as different as you may think. And just maybe you'll be more inclined to "meet me in the middle" where we can begin a new and better working relationship. — Makes space for others.

Hear me. Understand me. Walk awhile in my shoes.

Source: Manager letter in Eric Harvey and Steve Ventura, *Walk Awhile in My Shoes* (Dallas: Performance Systems Corporation, 1996).

the job. The manager pages describe having to *act* like a manager, being disliked, and grappling with "no-win" situations. The employee pages describe valuing recognition and performance feedback and wanting to understand why change happens.[63]

An effective leader can hold many perspectives at the same time. Opinions may overlap or contradict each other, but they are all worthy of consideration because the people who hold them are worthy.

Humble Leaders Seek Feedback

To gather other perspectives, leaders seek and accept feedback. Organizational feedback processes are common and useful. In addition, less formal approaches that leaders initiate demonstrate their openness to change and give leaders the information they need to improve.

360-Degree Feedback

One example of taking many perspectives is a 360-degree feedback process, which is common in many organizations.[64] Employees are evaluated by peers, people who report to them, and people to whom they report. Sometimes the process includes feedback from people outside the organization, for example, suppliers, partners, or clients. The process may be painful, particularly if leaders react to individual comments. But aggregating feedback from so many sources gives leaders a holistic view of their behaviors.

In some companies, employees will see the results of their manager's 360-degree feedback. Such an open process can be useful if the leader handles it well. We know that humility is about understanding one's limits. If a leader admits a weakness where employees are strong, the employees may be encouraged to step up. In this way, the leader provides coaching for the employees[65]—and may develop in the area as well. Also, when leaders ask for help, they increase trust and cooperation.[66]

Airbnb, Twitter, and SMRT Examples

Without a formal approach, senior executives may have trouble getting suggestions and honest feedback. At least three leaders have asked for input publicly during pivotal times. The first example is Brian Chesky, Airbnb's CEO. During the company's expansion and while facing some regulatory obstacles, Chesky tweeted, "If @Airbnb could launch anything in 2017, what would it be?" Chesky received more than 300 replies and responded to many of them personally on Christmas Day.[67,68]

Humble enough to imitate, Twitter CEO Jack Dorsey, a few days later, asked a similar question and acknowledged Chesky: "Following in the footsteps of Brian Chesky: what's the most important thing you want to see Twitter improve or create in 2017? #Twitter2017."[69]

Another CEO asked his staff, "What are you thinking?" Desmond Kuek had led SMRT, a transportation company based in Singapore, for four years before the company was sold and delisted from the stock market. During the shareholders meeting, a man stood up and publicly criticized Kuek, saying the previous CEO had done a better job.

Although he may have felt humiliated, Kuek didn't respond at the time. But two days later, he sent a long email to his staff about the change in ownership and to ask for their feedback, as he had done when he first started in the position.[70]

It takes strength and humility for a leader to ask for feedback in this way, and the responses weren't all positive. Some employees thought he was overpaid and should quit, although we'll never know what they said directly to Kuek. The company did change ownership, but Kuek is still the CEO and president today.

Reactions to Challenging Feedback

How open are you about hearing difficult feedback? Humble leaders ask for feedback and then have the courage to see multiple perspectives, which may conflict with their own.

Being open to constructive, or negative, feedback is sometimes easier said than done. We may say we're open to feedback, but hearing critical comments is almost always painful. We have to fight against what might be natural reactions to feedback. Rather than feeling shame, we use lessons learned about vulnerability to recognize that the feedback doesn't define us. Feedback represents someone else's view of one aspect of who we are. It's an opportunity for improvement—a chance to grow instead of a reason to hide.

Responding to the items in Figure 8.6 will give you an idea of how you typically respond to constructive feedback.

Curiosity Is Associated With Intellectual Humility

Intellectual humility is a type of humility that allows us to be open to changing our views. Leaders learn about different views by approaching issues with curiosity.

Intellectual Humility

Research about intellectual humility helps us understand more about how leaders can be open to different perspectives. A formal definition of intellectual

Figure 8.6   How do you react to challenging feedback?

1. Feel personally attacked. ("She doesn't like me." "We never got along.")	Never	Sometimes	Always
2. Think the worst. ("I'm going to get fired." "They're going to give this project to someone else.")	Never	Sometimes	Always
3. Blame yourself too harshly. ("I'm terrible at this." "This job is too hard for me.")	Never	Sometimes	Always
4. Blame others. ("Why is this *my* fault?" "Why isn't he talking to _____ about this?")	Never	Sometimes	Always
5. Argue with the feedback. ("That's not what happened." "She doesn't know the situation.")	Never	Sometimes	Always
6. Shut down. ("If he doesn't like my work, I won't continue on the project." "This is hopeless.")	Never	Sometimes	Always
7. Ignore the feedback. ("Too bad if they don't appreciate my work." "I'm not changing.")	Never	Sometimes	Always
8. Accept all feedback. ("I don't agree, but she must be right." "This doesn't align with my values, but I'll change anyway.")	Never	Sometimes	Always

Source: Adapted from Amy Newman, *Business Communication: In Person, In Print, Online,* 10th edition (Mason, OH: Cengage, 2017), p. 255.

humility is "recognizing that a particular personal belief may be fallible, accompanied by an appropriate attentiveness to limitations in the evidentiary basis of that belief and to one's own limitations in obtaining and evaluating relevant information." In other words, do you recognize that what you believe may be wrong, and are you willing to change your mind?[71]

Psychologists have developed a scale to measure intellectual humility. On a five-point scale with the endpoints "not at all like me" and "very much like me," participants rate themselves on the following items:

- I question my own opinions, positions, and viewpoints because they could be wrong.
- I reconsider my opinions when presented with new evidence.

- I recognize the value in opinions that are different from my own.
- I accept that my beliefs and attitudes may be wrong.
- In the face of conflicting evidence, I am open to changing my opinions.
- I like finding out new information that differs from what I already think is true.[72]

A Duke University study compared people they classified as intellectually humble and intellectually arrogant; the researchers described the category as those who rarely admitted to being wrong and were unwilling to change their minds. Given statements about controversial topics to read, including some "fake news," the humble group took longer to read and did a better job distinguishing what was fake. The arrogant group read quickly and didn't know the fake news was fake.[73]

This study supports another, which found that people with high intellectual humility did a better job of evaluating evidence in a persuasive argument. Because they knew their beliefs might be wrong, they more easily distinguished between strong and weak arguments.[74] We need to be vulnerable to be humble, and without humility, we cannot see what we have to learn.

Curiosity

As we might expect, studies show intellectual humility associated with qualities such as "openness, curiosity, tolerance of ambiguity, and low dogmatism."[75] Curiosity is defined "as a desire for knowledge and experience that motivates exploration." Researchers have identified two types of curiosity: specific and diversive. Specific curiosity is about finding a solution to a problem—for example, the best price for a product. Diversive curiosity is broader: the person seeks new information or new ways to synthesize what is already known.[76] Both are important for learning.

We don't always think of curiosity positively. The proverb "Curiosity killed the cat" warns us not to investigate too much, and the expression "idle curiosity" means we have too much time on our hands and may be apt to waste it in unproductive ways.

But, for leading with humility, curiosity is a powerful tool. We approach problems and questions with an open mind. We know we're not always right and want to hear other points of view.

In her TED Talk "Why You Think You're Right—Even If You're Wrong," Julia Galef distinguishes between soldier and scout mindsets. Soldiers want to beat the enemy, so they are motivated by proving they are right and the enemy is wrong. Scouts are interested in reality even if it contradicts their own thinking. Galef says the scout mindset consists of being open, curious, and grounded.[77] She's describing humility.

Two Chefs Illustrate Humility

Through two chefs' contrasting reactions to negative restaurant reviews, we see illustrations of arrogance and humility.

Negative Reviews

No chef wants a bad review of the restaurant, but it happens, and two examples show us how chefs respond with humility—or not. Both chefs have had tremendous restaurant success but received scathing reviews from Pete Wells, a critic for *The New York Times*.

Here are excerpts from Wells's review of David Chang's Momofuku Nishi:

> Too much of the cooking at Nishi is self-referential, inward looking and so concerned with technique that you can't help being conscious of it. In his early days, Mr. Chang served the kind of food chefs like to eat: intense, animalistic, O.K. with messiness, indifferent to prettiness. Nishi serves the kind of food chefs cook to impress one another.[78]

Wells's review of Thomas Keller's Per Se, where you'll pay $325 for a nine-course tasting menu, isn't much better:

> The kitchen could improve the bacon-wrapped cylinder of quail simply by not placing it on top of a dismal green pulp of cooked romaine lettuce, crunchy and mushy at once. Draining off the gluey, oily liquid would have helped a mushroom potpie from turning into a swampy mess. I don't know what could have saved limp, dispiriting yam dumplings, but it definitely wasn't a lukewarm matsutake mushroom bouillon as murky and appealing as bong water. . . .

> Servers sometimes give you the feeling that you work for them, and your job is to feel lucky to receive whatever you get.[79]

Chefs' Reactions

How did each chef react? In an interview with *The New Yorker*, Chang said ("F-words" omitted), "I can't ever read that review again—I'll get so ___ angry, I'll die. I made a lot of that food! I tasted it! It was delicious. And . . . ___! I believe in the ___ food we make in that restaurant, I believe it to be really delicious, I believe it to be innovative . . ."[80]

Six months after the review, in an interview in *Town and Country Magazine*, Thomas Keller said, "It was devastating." He noted what the magazine calls his "improbable trajectory" as a famous chef: "I barely finished high school." He also admitted, "Maybe we were complacent. I learned that, maybe, as a team, we were a little bit too arrogant, our egos too exposed."[81] In other words, he was humbled.

Two weeks after the review, Keller wrote a message "To Our Guests" on the Per Se website (Figure 8.7). In Keller's note, we see more examples of humility.

Figure 8.7   Thomas Keller demonstrates humility

To Our Guests:

At all of our restaurants, in our kitchens and dining rooms, we make every effort to provide you with the best possible experience. We consider it our professional responsibility to ensure that every one of you feels special and cared for. To us, it is imperative that we improve and evolve every day. We constantly examine ourselves, our menu, our service and our standards.

> Emphasizes continuous learning, a hallmark of humility.

Regretfully, there are times when we do not meet those standards. The fact that The New York Times restaurant critic Pete Wells' dining experiences at Per Se did not live up to his expectations and to ours is greatly disappointing to me and to my team. We pride ourselves on maintaining the highest standards, but we make mistakes along the way. We are sorry we let you down.

> Expresses emotion.

> Admits mistakes.

> Apologizes.

We are not content resting on what we did yesterday. We believe we can do better for ourselves, our profession and most importantly our guests. We have the opportunity, the tools, the self-motivation and the dedication to do so.

> Shows motivation to improve.

When we fall short, we work even harder. We are confident that the next time you visit Per Se or any of our other restaurants, our team will deliver a most memorable experience.

> Commits to doing better.

— Thomas Keller, Chef/Proprietor

Source: Thomas Keller, "To Our Guests," Thomas Keller website, https://www.thomaskeller.com/messagetoourguests, accessed July 1, 2017.

Both chefs continue to run successful restaurants. Another Momofuku is opening in New York City at the Seaport, and Per Se is still highly rated. Yet restaurantgoers and employees likely remember each chef's reaction to a disappointing review.

SUMMARY

Uber leaders lacked humility and created a less-than-desirable working environment for employees and drivers. As of this writing, Uber has hired a new CEO, yet the board and Kalanick are still at odds. What, if any, role Kalanick will have going forward is not yet resolved.

Although ambition drives success, arrogant leaders fail to see themselves in perspective; they see themselves as above others. Leaders with strong character prioritize good outcomes for more people.

Humility is a strength. John Zimmer illustrates the importance of knowing your limitations:

> The most important thing I've found is to know your weaknesses and hire people better than you. That takes a certain amount of confidence. I remember hiring folks with way more experience than me and feeling very unsure of my ability to lead them. The answer is to lead with values and vision.[82]

Humble leaders seek and learn from feedback. They are willing to be vulnerable and can resist the spiral into shame. They are also intellectually curious and willing to change their views.

Only when we see ourselves as equals and understand other perspectives can we offer compassion, a leadership character dimension we'll discuss next.

EXERCISES

Concept Review

1. What is humility, and how do we see it expressed?

2. How is humility a strength?

3. What is perspective taking, and what is the value?

4. What is intellectual humility?

Self-Reflection

1. Think about someone you consider humble. What examples of humility do you see?

2. Think about someone you consider arrogant. What elements of humility is this person lacking?

3. When have you asked for and avoided asking for help? When is this difficult for you?

4. When have you asked for and avoided asking for feedback? When is this difficult for you?

5. What is your typical approach to receiving feedback? Which of the items in Figure 8.6 show you ways to be more open to feedback?

6. Think about a time when you put others above yourself. What were the circumstances, and why do you think you took this approach? What could you have done differently to make space for others?

7. Think of a time when you had trouble seeing a different point of view or taking multiple perspectives. Why do you think it was difficult for you, and what could you have done differently?

8. How did you respond to the questions about intellectual humility? Where do you have room to grow?

Assessment

Complete the humility assessment from the scale items discussed earlier.[83]

Instructions

As you respond to each item, be honest with yourself. Although you may *intend* to exhibit a behavior or trait in the future, respond to the item based on who you are and how you behave *today*.

Scale

1	Strongly disagree
2	Disagree
3	Slightly disagree
4	Slightly agree
5	Agree
6	Strongly agree

Item		Rating
1.	I seek out the truth about myself, even if it highlights my weaknesses.	1 2 3 4 5 6
2	I identify the contributions and inherent worth of others around me.	1 2 3 4 5 6
3.	I view myself as a good partner to those I interact with (family members, coworkers, friends).	1 2 3 4 5 6
4.	I am open to new information about myself.	1 2 3 4 5 6
5.	I am aware that others have contributed to my accomplishments.	1 2 3 4 5 6
6.	I view myself as a good member to a larger community (my local community, my workplace, other groups).	1 2 3 4 5 6
7.	I do not react defensively toward criticism.	1 2 3 4 5 6
8.	I appreciate the reality of being one person in a larger community.	1 2 3 4 5 6
9.	What is important to me is working to improve the welfare of the community(ies) I value and/or belong to (my local community, my workplace, other groups).	1 2 3 4 5 6
10.	I actively seek out information about my strengths.	1 2 3 4 5 6
11.	My accomplishments don't make me more valuable than others.	1 2 3 4 5 6
12.	I feel my fate is intertwined with the fate of those around me.	1 2 3 4 5 6
13.	I actively seek out information about my weaknesses.	1 2 3 4 5 6
14.	I feel connected to a purpose greater than myself.	1 2 3 4 5 6
15.	I feel good when I cooperate with others.	1 2 3 4 5 6

Scoring

Understanding yourself: #1, 4, 7, 10, 13

Relating to others: #3, 6, 9, 12, 15

Perspective: #2, 5, 8, 11, 14

Add together the numbers you chose for the "understanding yourself" items only (#1, 4, 7, 10, 13). Now, add together the numbers you chose for the "relating to others" items only (#3, 6, 9, 12, 15). Finally, add together numbers you chose for the "perspective" items only (#2, 5, 8, 11, 14). The interpretation of the scores are for each dimension of humility (understanding yourself, relating to others, and perspective) rather than for humility as a whole. In this way, the measure gives you the opportunity to pinpoint where you might further develop your ability to exercise humility.

Interpretation

If you scored 0–10 on any dimension, you are low on this dimension. If you scored 11–20 on any dimension, you are medium on this dimension. For example, this means that sometimes you are exhibiting "understanding yourself" and sometimes you are not. If you scored 21–30 on any dimension, you are high on this dimension. For example, this means that you generally exercise "understanding yourself."

Mini-Cases

Consider the following scenarios. On your own or with a partner, discuss the best course of action in each case. What would you do, and what factors into your decision?

Scenario 1

You were just awarded Employee of the Month, announced at a department meeting. Everyone is applauding you. How do you respond? What do you say when people congratulate you later?

Scenario 2

You're at a meeting about a new project, and you're feeling lost. After dividing up work, your team members seem clear about their responsibilities, but you are not. The meeting is wrapping up, and they're making plans to share completed work in three days. What will you do?

Scenario 3

An employee who reports to you asks for a meeting. He tells you that he and others in the department need clearer direction from you. They aren't sure what you need when you assign work. You're both uncomfortable during the meeting, but the employee says he thought it was important to tell you. How will you handle the situation with this employee and the rest of the team?

Team Activity

With a work or project team, discuss your answers to questions in Figure 8.6, how you respond to challenging feedback. What is useful for your team to know about you? Share your responses and discuss ways you can improve and ways the team can help you. For example, if you typically withdraw when you hear negative feedback, would it help if your teammates drew you out by asking you questions, or should they leave you alone for a while until you have time to internalize the feedback? Find ways to support each other and to become a team open to feedback and focused on continuous learning.

Team Activity

At the end of Chapter 2, you completed the Johari Window exercise. Revisit the model with your team now that some time has passed. What strategies have you used to move between quadrants (for example, observation, self-disclosure, self-awareness, and feedback)? How have the quadrants changed over time? Which strategies could the team use more to continue progressing?

Paired Activity

Meet with someone you know fairly well to ask for and receive feedback. This will give you practice in accepting feedback gracefully and giving feedback kindly.

Planning Questions

1. Who is an appropriate person for this activity? Consider someone who knows you fairly well and may offer you useful feedback.

2. How will you ask for and receive feedback? You might, for example, take turns discussing each other's strengths first and then move on to discussing potential areas for improvement or ways you can be more effective—for instance, in interpersonal relationships or project management.

3. Consider taking notes. Writing down key points that you hear will help you remember them and may put them in perspective, particularly if the feedback is difficult or painful to hear—of if you're likely to dismiss positive comments, as some of us do. At the same time, you don't want to be too tied to writing; this should be an interactive, participative conversation.

4. How will you give feedback? You can be direct, as we discussed in Chapter 7, but be kind and sensitive. Offer specific examples and suggestions to help the receiver accept the feedback and take action.

5. How will you respond to feedback you receive? You might try an "active listening" approach: repeat or paraphrase what you hear without judgment or interpretation—for example, "You suggest developing a project plan ahead of time, so the team would more likely stay on track," or "You appreciate when I meet deadlines."

6. Consider your typical reactions to feedback. If you sometimes get defensive, for example, how can you remain open? If you dismiss positive feedback, how can you accept it?

7. Depending on your relationship with your partner, schedule plenty of time and a private space. You may end up discussing something sensitive, and you'll want to give your full attention to each other.

8. As you're talking with each other, pay attention to what you're saying, of course, but also pay attention to your reactions, both obvious and subtle. How are you responding physically and emotionally?

Reflection Questions

1. What was easy or difficult about the conversation for each of you?

2. What did you learn?

3. How did you react physically and emotionally during the discussion? What observations did you have about each other's body language, tone of voice, and so on?

4. Based on the chapter reading, how would you assess your humility in responding to this feedback?

5. How can you use what you learn from this activity in other relationships in your life?

9

Compassion

Caring for Others and Ourselves

Chapter Overview

The movie Blackfish called on SeaWorld to respond to trainer deaths and criticism about its treatment of orcas. Company leaders missed this opportunity and others to respond with compassion. Compassionate leaders ease others' suffering by providing comfort and demonstrating empathy. Self-compassion is also an important part of alleviating distress.

SeaWorld Fails to Respond to the Movie *Blackfish*

Perhaps no company in the last few years was more oblivious to a crisis than SeaWorld, which ignored criticism from the movie *Blackfish*. The documentary filmmakers set out to understand the death of an experienced orca (killer whale) trainer, Dawn Brancheau (Photo 9.1). Captured in the wild in the 1983,[1] Tilikum, who had been swimming with Brancheau for years, pulled her underwater during a live show and killed her in front of a live audience.

Photo 9.1   Dawn Brancheau performs at SeaWorld

Source: Orlando Sentinel / Julie Fletcher via Getty Images

When *Blackfish* first came out, SeaWorld underestimated the impact, and the leaders never handled the crisis well. The company sent emails to about 50 critics calling *Blackfish* "a dishonest movie,"[2] which probably just brought more attention to the issue.[3] SeaWorld leaders were mostly silent for months as millions of people saw the movie, animal rights activists and celebrities fueled social media comments, customers boycotted the parks, and musical groups canceled performances (Figure 9.1).

Later, SeaWorld communicated more. The company posted "The Truth About *Blackfish*" on its website to contest the movie. Calling it propaganda instead of a documentary, SeaWorld disputed "emotionally manipulative sequences," the credibility of sources, and facts about Tilikum and about Brancheau's death. Yet SeaWorld refused to be interviewed for the film and declined media interviews.[4,5]

SeaWorld leaders lacked compassion for Bancheau and those affected by her death—and they lacked compassion for the orcas they kept.

Compassion Alleviates Suffering

With genuine concern, leaders show compassion to alleviate others' suffering. SeaWorld leaders reacted defensively instead of compassionately to Brancheau's death and failed to recognize their role.

Compassion Defined

Tragedies happen in everyone's life: we're diagnosed with an illness, face a financial hardship, or lose a loved one. Sometimes our suffering is from work itself: we miss performance goals, work for a jerk, or get laid off.[6] People help relieve our distress when they respond with compassion.

Crossan and her colleagues identified humanity as an important leadership character dimension. Their definition includes the descriptors *considerate, empathic, compassionate, magnanimous*, and *forgiving*.[7] We see some overlap with forgiveness, discussed in Chapter 6.

Figure 9.1   SeaWorld's *Blackfish* crisis unfolds

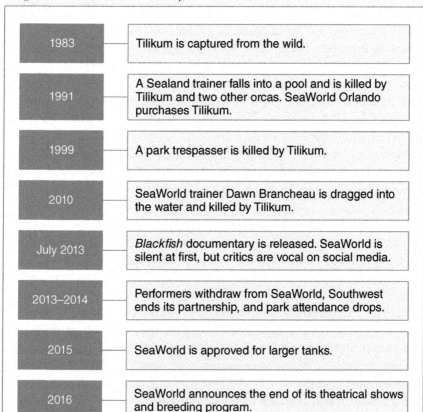

1983	Tilikum is captured from the wild.
1991	A Sealand trainer falls into a pool and is killed by Tilikum and two other orcas. SeaWorld Orlando purchases Tilikum.
1999	A park trespasser is killed by Tilikum.
2010	SeaWorld trainer Dawn Brancheau is dragged into the water and killed by Tilikum.
July 2013	*Blackfish* documentary is released. SeaWorld is silent at first, but critics are vocal on social media.
2013–2014	Performers withdraw from SeaWorld, Southwest ends its partnership, and park attendance drops.
2015	SeaWorld is approved for larger tanks.
2016	SeaWorld announces the end of its theatrical shows and breeding program.

Sources: Amy Newman, "SeaWorld's Response to the Movie *Blackfish*," Cornell University case, August 1, 2014; Will Coldwell, "Brancheau, Blackfish and San Diego Shutdown: A SeaWorld in Turmoil Timeline," *The Guardian*, November 11, 2015, https://www.theguardian.com/travel/2015/nov/11/brancheau-blackfish-san-diego-shutdown-seaworld-timeline, accessed July 7, 2017; SeaWorld Parks & Entertainment, "*Blackfish* Crisis: An Assessment of *Blackfish* Effect on SeaWorld," Arthur W. Page Society, 2016 Case Study Competition, January 15, 2016, http://csic.georgetown.edu/wp-content/uploads/2016/12/SeaWorld-Parks-Entertainment-Case-Study.pdf, accessed July 7, 2017.

We use the term *compassion* to reflect other academic research focusing on interpersonal relationships. Scholars define compassion as "an interpersonal process involving the noticing, feeling, sensemaking, and acting that alleviates the suffering of another person." The focus is on reacting to others' hardships with care and concern.[8] When people demonstrate compassion, they take the time to be with others.

SeaWorld's Lack of Compassion for Trainers

From this definition, we see how SeaWorld fell short. As we have seen in other situations, SeaWorld leadership didn't take full responsibility for Dawn Brancheau's death. The VP and general manager of SeaWorld Orlando said, "We extend our deepest sympathies to the family and friends and of the trainer and will do everything possible to assist them in this difficult time."[9] But they did little to demonstrate compassion to alleviate the suffering of Brancheau's family and coworkers. The short statement doesn't even reference Dawn by name.

Most of us know how to address a physical injury. When trainers are hurt, SeaWorld leaders will readily apply bandages, but what about mental health? Compassion is step one in providing first aid when people are experiencing sorrow.[10]

Instead, SeaWorld seemed to blame Brancheau for her death. At first, the Orange County Sheriff's Office reported, "She apparently slipped or fell into the tank and was fatally injured by one of the whales."[11] When witnesses contradicted this story, a company representative blamed Brancheau's ponytail for her death: "That ponytail had swung in front of him. He grabbed her by the hair and pulled her underwater and held her underwater."[12]

This story, too, was contradicted by people who say Tilikum pulled her underwater by her arm, although the method is still debated. Either way, the forensic reports of brutal injuries prove it wasn't a mere drowning as SeaWorld first claimed.

Brancheau wasn't Tilikum's only death. Based on two previous deaths involving Tilikum and other incidents, the Occupational Safety and Health Administration (OSHA) warned of the danger of working with orcas:

> The contributing factors to the accident, in the simplest of terms, is that swimming with captive orcas is inherently dangerous, and if someone hasn't been killed already, it is only a matter of time before it does happen.[13,14]

After Brancheau's death, for violations OSHA referred to as "serious" and "willful," including failing to protect trainers from "struck-by and drowning hazards," SeaWorld paid $7,500.[15]

SeaWorld's resistance to safety measures, including continuing to allow Tilikum to perform, showed a lack of compassion for Brancheau, for her friends and family, for other trainers, and for witnesses—parents and their children visiting the park for a holiday or celebration. Tilikum was the park's largest and most famous orca—and one of the most prolific breeders.

Critics say leaders put park revenue above trainer safety. One parkgoer expressed compassion in a way that SeaWorld leaders failed to:

> My heart goes out to [her coworkers] too. They work with her every day, I mean, it must have been hard to stand there.[16]

SeaWorld's Lack of Compassion for Orcas

Our focus is on leadership character, and compassion as an interpersonal experience, but is SeaWorld compassionate toward orcas? Orcas are highly social animals and live in small groups, each with its own culture and communication for maintaining group cohesion.[17,18]

Former SeaWorld trainers report terrible conditions for orcas at SeaWorld. Living in small tanks, being deprived of food, suffering abuse from other whales, getting punished for not performing "behaviors," and spending most of the time in isolation are some of the examples of life for orcas in captivity.[19] Former trainer Samantha Berg says SeaWorld managers told employees, "The love you're giving makes up for what they're missing in the wild."[20] People for the Ethical Treatment of Animals (PETA) compared their tanks to bathtubs and argued, "It's not surprising when these huge, smart animals lash out."[21]

SeaWorld has improved conditions—slowly. Over nearly three years since *Blackfish*, the park has increased the size of its tanks, focused more on "encounters" than "entertainment," invested more in conservation—and, finally, promised to stop breeding orcas,[22] so the whales they currently have will be their last.[23]

Former trainers believe the company could have done more. Releasing the orcas into the wild is controversial because of their ability to adapt, but trainers believe parks could have put them in an animal sanctuary. They also could have changed their business model to focus on conservation and education instead of entertainment.[24]

More compassion toward SeaWorld trainers and orcas may have prevented a death. At a minimum, it may have eased suffering when the death occurred.

Responding With Compassion Involves Four Steps

When we demonstrate compassion, we typically follow four steps. How people respond to others may depend on demographic factors. In a

Facebook example, we see aspects of compassion and where people could have done more.

Four Steps

Scholars have identified a four-step process for responding with compassion:

- Noticing that suffering is present in an organization
- Making meaning of suffering in a way that contributes to a desire to alleviate it
- Feeling empathic concern for the people suffering
- Taking action to alleviate suffering[25]

In their book *Awakening Compassion at Work*, Monica Worline and Jane Dutton offer questions for us to assess our capacity for compassion at each stage (Figure 9.2). The questions are for a workgroup but can be used for any group.

Differences in Responses

How people respond to suffering varies. Research shows that people of lower socioeconomic status (SES) respond with more compassion to others'

Figure 9.2   Questions help us explore our capacity for compassion

Noticing	I feel comfortable knowing about people's suffering and see this awareness as an important aspect of my work.
Noticing	In this group, I often have conversations in which I notice another person's suffering.
Interpreting	In this group, I tend to see people who get behind or make mistakes in their work as in need of help, and I approach them.
Interpreting	In this group, if I find out that someone is having difficulty in his or her life, I tend to ask about it and focus on the person's well-being.
Feeling	I often feel concern for others in this group.
Feeling	I find it easy to take the perspective of others in this group.
Acting	I often find myself taking action to help others in this group.
Acting	If I found out that people in this work group were suffering, I would very likely know what to do to comfort them.

Source: Monica C. Worline and Jane E. Dutton, *Awakening Compassion at Work* (Oakland, CA: Berrett-Koehler, 2017), p. 5.

suffering than do people of higher SES. The reason may be that lower-income, socially marginalized people develop relationships to adapt to threats.[26] Role expectations, power relationships, and distractions also may play a part in how people respond to suffering in an organization.[27] We'll see these and other factors in an example at Facebook.

Research is mixed about sex differences and compassion.[28] As we discussed in Chapter 4, women's communications tend to focus on relationships and building connections.[29] On the other hand, recent research questions whether men are less empathic, as is typically assumed. Most research has been based on self-reports, which may not be the best measure. Women and men tend to rate themselves according to gender stereotypes instead of their own behavior, causing women to rate themselves as more empathic than men rate themselves. One large-scale experiment showed no difference in empathy between men and women.[30]

Facebook Example

Let's look at an example of how these factors may play out at Facebook for Chief Operating Officer Sheryl Sandberg. Sandberg is also the author of the best-selling book *Lean In* about women and leadership.

We're not used to hearing about company leaders' personal lives, but Sandberg has been open about a tragic loss: the unexpected death of her husband, Dave Goldberg, former CEO of SurveyMonkey. When sheloshim, the 30-day Jewish mourning period, ended, Sandberg posted about her loss on Facebook. In part of the post, she describes suffering and the need for compassion—and she demonstrates vulnerability:

> In the last thirty days, I have heard from too many women who lost a spouse and then had multiple rugs pulled out from under them. Some lack support networks and struggle alone as they face emotional distress and financial insecurity. It seems so wrong to me that we abandon these women and their families when they are in greatest need.[31]

In a new book, *Option B*, and on a PBS *NewsHour* interview, Sandberg has talked openly about her grief:

> It's not just the loss, or the cancer, or losing a job, or someone in your family going to jail. It's the silence that surrounds that. And so, when I lost Dave, I had this overwhelming grief, but also just this isolation I had never felt in my life. I had always felt really connected to my friends, neighbors and family, people I work with. But when I came back to work, people barely spoke to me. They looked at me like I was a deer in the headlights.

And I know they meant well. They were afraid to say the wrong thing, so they said nothing at all.[32]

Looking at the research, we can guess why Facebook employees didn't engage Sandberg. First—and we're generalizing here—Facebook employees are probably less likely to be of lower SES, and only 33% of them are female.[33] We might also assume that the company's focus on technical skills rather than relationship skills results in an employee profile less likely to demonstrate compassion. Perhaps the company's fast-paced environment also results in conflicting demands on their attention. Or maybe Sandberg expected something different based on her own background, experience, and needs?

Appraisals and Response

The decision to respond to suffering depends on appraisals (Figure 9.3). Observers may avoid compassion because they think the sufferer is to blame, they don't think a sufferer needs help, or they question their own ability to cope with the situation. It's unlikely that Facebook employees thought Sandberg was to blame, but maybe, because of her senior leadership role, they didn't think she needed help, or they felt unsure about their ability to offer it. Facebook's younger employee demographic may have had little experience with death—and how many were married? As Sandberg says, "They were afraid to say the wrong thing, so they said nothing at all." When you're trying to comfort your boss's boss's boss, the stakes may feel higher for unintentionally saying "the wrong thing."

This model may help us understand why SeaWorld's leaders weren't more compassionate about Dawn Brancheau's death. Her death jeopardized the business, so maybe they were angry, and it was easier to blame her and her ponytail.

As another example, let's look at Penn State, mired in a crisis when university administrators were accused of knowing for years that football coach Jerry Sandusky had been abusing young boys. For failing to take action, university president Graham Spanier was convicted of child endangerment. After the verdict, a trustee wrote in an email that he was "[r]unning out of sympathy for 35-year-old, so-called victims with seven-digit net worth. Do not understand why they were so prominent in trial."[34] The trustee apologized and resigned, but his anger—feeling that some victims didn't deserve help—stifled his compassion and left the university, which was trying to rebuild its image after the terrible scandal, looking worse.

Figure 9.3   People appraise a situation before deciding whether to respond with compassion

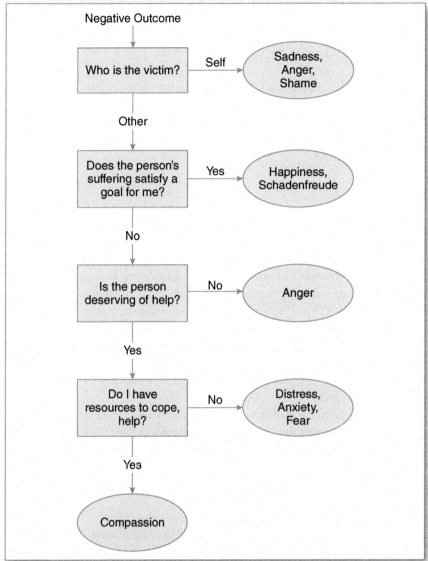

Source: Adapted from Jennifer L. Goetz, "Compassion: An Evolutionary Analysis and Empirical Review," *Psychological Bulletin*, Vol. 136, No. 3 (2010), pp. 351–374.

When faced with another's grief, we experience feelings of our own that influence how we respond. Practicing self-reflection, which we discussed as a strategy for managing failure, may help us observe our own reactions so they don't get in the way of responding when people need our compassion.[35]

Compassion Benefits People and Organizations

Like other leadership character dimensions, compassion has personal and business benefits. Some companies and schools recognize these benefits and look for compassion in future employees and students. When Tilikum died, SeaWorld missed another opportunity to demonstrate compassion and benefit the organization.

Personal Benefits

Compassion has tremendous individual benefits. For the person suffering, compassion reduces anxiety, improves physical recovery, and increases organizational commitment and feeling valued. Employees who see others expressing compassion feel proud of their organization and, in turn, are less punitive toward others.[36] Compassion leads to connections among colleagues, which is critical in times of stress and failure.

Imagine a situation where you're overwhelmed by work deadlines. A coworker demonstrates compassion and perhaps takes some of the work off your plate. With your coworker sharing your feelings and sharing the workload, you probably consider your job manageable and feel better about the organization overall.

In addition, research shows that people who demonstrate compassion feel good about themselves and are perceived as leaders.[37] By showing emotion, concern for others, and intentions to help, people are more likely to be categorized as leaders in research studies.[38]

Organizational Benefits

At the organizational level, compassion has significant and bottom-line effects. A study of department store workers found an association between compassion and job performance.[39] Studies of a financial services company showed that business units with more positive practices, including compassion, had lower turnover, better work climate, and better financial performance. In a health care company, positive practices were associated with lower turnover, higher quality care, and higher patient satisfaction.[40] Like vulnerability and forgiveness, compassion gives people space to make mistakes without fear, so innovation can happen.

Seeking Compassionate People

Businesses and college admissions officers are catching on to the value of compassion. LinkedIn CEO Jeff Weiner endorses what he calls "compassionate management,"[41] and he will ask candidates unusual interview questions— for example, what they would do if they were about to start a global meeting and heard that an employee at another location had been rushed to the hospital.[42]

The Harvard Graduate School of Education produced a report to influence who gets into college: "Turning the Tide: Inspiring Concern for Others and the Common Good Through College Admissions." The report encourages admissions officers to look for "ethical engagement" and applicants' "meaningful contributions to community service and engagement with the public good."[43] More colleges are weighing good citizenship over personal achievement and academics.[44]

As interest in character grows, so does interest in compassion. We want people around us who will genuinely express care and concern.

SeaWorld's Response to Tilikum's Death

SeaWorld's lack of compassion for suffering caused its own suffering. Known as the "*Blackfish* Effect," the movie and SeaWorld's failed response caused declining revenue and park attendance.[45] In addition, corporate partners, such as Southwest Airlines[46] and Mattel,[47] severed ties with the company; SeaWorld Trainer Barbie didn't have the same appeal after *Blackfish*.

When Tilikum died in 2017, SeaWorld may have missed another chance to demonstrate compassion—and help the business. Samantha Berg said they could have donated his body for forensic research: "They missed an opportunity to present themselves as a scientific organization." She suggested making Tilikum a "poster child" to promote more humane treatment of the animals.

Instead, when SeaWorld leaders announced Tilikum's death, they defended their practices. In a press release, the company focused on the care they provided, defended his age, reinforced that SeaWorld didn't capture him from the wild, and promoted the end of the orca-breeding program.[48] The statement does mention Dawn Brancheau, but the company doesn't take responsibility for her death, and critics note that more attention was given to Tilikum's death than to Brancheau's.

What if SeaWorld had been more grateful to *Blackfish*? What if the company had applauded the film for bringing some practices to light that needed to change? If leaders had participated in the film-making, could they have offered audiences a more balanced view and focused more on education and conservation? Could they have announced, as a result of the film, instead of years later by court orders, better conditions for the orcas and the end of their breeding program? We'll never know the impact on the company and whether the leaders would have been perceived as more compassionate.

Compassionate Leaders Respond With Small Gestures, Comfort, and Empathy

Now that we see the benefits of compassion, how can we communicate compassion to others? Making small gestures and offering comfort can help people in need. Part of providing comfort is expressing empathy, which goes beyond sympathy and listening.

Making Small Gestures

When coworkers suffer, we can express compassion in simple ways. A card, phone call, or visit can make a tremendous difference in how people recover from tragedy. If a coworker loses a family member, for example, a handwritten note or even an email communicates our care (Figure 9.4).

Notes of compassion signal our concern until we can spend time with the person and offer comfort.

Figure 9.4   A note expresses compassion

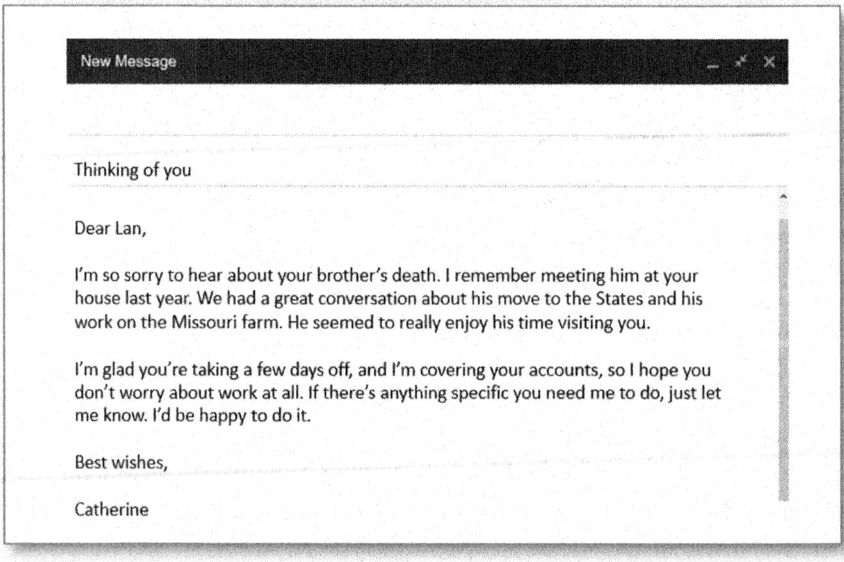

New Message   — ⤢ ✕

Thinking of you

Dear Lan,

I'm so sorry to hear about your brother's death. I remember meeting him at your house last year. We had a great conversation about his move to the States and his work on the Missouri farm. He seemed to really enjoy his time visiting you.

I'm glad you're taking a few days off, and I'm covering your accounts, so I hope you don't worry about work at all. If there's anything specific you need me to do, just let me know. I'd be happy to do it.

Best wishes,

Catherine

Offering Comfort

We don't always know the right thing to say or do when people are in pain, so we may avoid being compassionate. But if we push past the obstacles of whether the person "deserves" to be comforted and whether we feel equipped, we can make a big difference in others' lives and in the workplace.

In her book *The Art of Comforting*, Val Walker compared what we think we should do to comfort people (in U.S. mainstream culture) and what would actually help comfort people (Figure 9.5).

Figure 9.5   To offer comfort, we are open

Mainstream Culture	To Be Comforting
Avoiding Negative Emotions	
We like to cheer people up when they are down.	We don't try to take their pain away. We allow them to feel what they feel.
We like people to be strong and "hold up" under pressure.	We respect a person's right to be vulnerable. We can be a sanctuary, a safe person to be with, when someone falls apart.
We resort to platitudes and teachings from our favorite books, religions, and mentors. We offer popular sayings like "You'll be stronger for this" or "This too shall pass."	We avoid platitudes, which may feel impersonal and preachy. We try to focus on the specific loss.
Being Productive	
We like to feel useful and helpful.	We accept we may never know if we helped or how we helped.
We like to reassure the ones we are helping that we understand them.	We admit we do not fully understand their journey but offer to learn more about it with them.
We compare our struggles to theirs.	We relate to the shame and sorrow.
Getting Quick Results	
We like to be quick and efficient.	We offer our time, take our time, even just a few minutes. We don't rush.
We are always on the go, on the clock. We like to "get over" things quickly.	We allow someone's grief or trauma to take its own course, have its own pace.
We believe healing means to completely "get over" our losses.	Healing means learning to live with loss rather than getting over it completely.

(Continued)

(Continued)

Mainstream Culture	To Be Comforting
Organizing	
We like to know what is going to happen next. We like agendas and to-do lists.	We step into the present moment. We let go of expectations.
We like to have instructions explained for us.	We accept that comforting can be an unpredictable, disorganized process.
We hate not knowing what to do or say. We avoid silence.	We stay open and let the distressed person talk, even if he or she is upset.
We want to understand and categorize what we hear.	We approach others with curiosity, discovery, and awe.
Multitasking	
We do as much as we can, working with interruptions.	We give our undivided attention, with nothing in our hands and no distractions in the room.
We want to check our phones, not miss anything.	We communicate in a calm, quiet setting.
Finding Solutions	
We like to "fix it," get things working again.	We don't offer solutions but do offer our presence and experience as an equal.
We like to advise, to offer answers and remedies.	We listen closely.
We like to take a problem-solving approach.	We wait, letting the person find her or his own words.

Source: Adapted from Val Walker, *The Art of Comforting* (London: Penguin, 2010), pp. 6–8. Used by permission of Tarcher, an imprint of Penguin Publishing Group, a division of Penguin Random House LLC. All rights reserved

Our tendency is to fix things and solve people's problems, but we can't always do so. All we can do is let people know we care. Compassion is telling people. "I am with you. I am on your side." This may not be enough—everyone is different and needs something different at different times—but it's a start.

Avoiding Pity and Sympathy

Compassion is not pity, which implies one person is inferior to the other.[49] Compassion happens between equals, despite a leader's level in an organizational chart. In her book *The Places That Scare You*, Buddhist author and nun Pema Chodron writes,

> Compassion is not a relationship between the healer and the wounded. It's a relationship between equals. Only when we know our own darkness well can we be present with the darkness of others. Compassion becomes real when we recognize our shared humanity.[50]

Such compassion requires empathy, which is not quite the same as sympathy. Tinged with sadness, sympathy implies distance between people. In contrast, you have probably heard that empathy is "putting yourself in someone else's shoes."

Brené Brown describes the difference between empathy and sympathy: "Empathy fuels connection. Sympathy drives disconnection."[51] She says empathy is the more vulnerable choice because it means we're not only connecting with the other person but connecting with something in ourselves that may be painful. Val Walker further explains empathy:

> We can feel the sorrow of someone else, even if their life experience is nothing like ours, because we all know sorrow by having lived through loss in our own lives. Our commonality of human challenges and suffering is far greater than our separate ideologies, religions, cultures, or genders.[52]

When people are suffering or in distress, we resist the urge to judge negatively. When your friend loses a cat, even if you hate cats, you can still, as Sheryl Sandberg suggests, try to "acknowledge the pain."[53] Maybe you can relate because you have lost something that others wouldn't consider valuable?

Communicating Empathy

Listening with empathy, or empathic listening, is one way to communicate empathy. Empathic listening typically involves "being an attentive communicator and being other oriented."[54] Communication researcher Graham Bodie identifies what an empathic listener does during three stages of an interaction. During the *sensing* stage, we indicate that we are understanding the speaker's words as well as the emotional content of what is being said. During the *processing* stage, we remember what the speaker said, ask for clarification, and integrate points. During the *responding* stage, we may ask more questions, paraphrase what we heard, and use nonverbal behaviors to show our attention and interest.[55] We demonstrate empathy by listening attentively and without expressing negative judgments.

In her book *Listening*, Judi Brownell identifies "warm" and "cold" behaviors that communicate empathy. Cold behaviors include staring, looking away, fidgeting, and moving away from the speaker. Warm behaviors include making direct eye contact, nodding, keeping eyes wide open, and leaning forward.[56] Small utterances and expressions, such as "Uh-huh," "I see," and "I understand," also show that you're engaged and encourage people to continue talking.

When we communicate empathy, we avoid comparisons—for example, "He's upset that his brother is moving, but at least he has other family nearby. I don't have anyone." You can relate to another's feelings and maybe reveal something relevant about yourself ("It's painful when people close to you move away. My closest friend moved last year."), but be careful about taking over the conversation—it's not about you. You can be helpful by sharing your experience, but try not to compare. Everyone's sorrow is unique and should be honored.

Also try to avoid blaming: "Well, if she had worked harder, she would have passed the test." If someone hits our car and is hurt—even if he is at fault—we first offer compassion. We can address accountability later; first comes empathy.

Sometimes, the best comfort comes from simply taking the time to give someone your attention and listen. You can ask someone whether she wants to talk and then listen empathically, without interrupting.

These conversations may be uncomfortable, and that's okay. You can even say, "I'm not sure what to say, but I wanted you to know that I was thinking of you."

Communication About a Suicide Offers a Model of Compassion

When a student died at Western Washington University, the president wrote a message to the community (Figure 9.6).[57] In this example, we see many principles of compassion, providing comfort, and empathy.

The president shares his own pain to empathize with the pain of others. He is vulnerable talking about his son's suicide and encourages people to make a difference in each other's lives by showing compassion when people are suffering.

Self-Compassion and Gratitude Ease Suffering

As we care for others, we must care for ourselves. Research shows the importance of self-compassion to well-being and the benefits of gratitude.

Figure 9.6   University president writes a compassionate message

Members of Our Western Community:

This morning, you learned of the tragic death of a Western student. I know we all join in extending our heartfelt condolences and concerns for the student's family and friends as they now are grieving. We grieve, as well. And, Western's Counseling Center stands ready to assist any of you who might wish their support and guidance. They can be reached at 650-3164.

> Uses emotional language: "heartfelt," "grieving."

We have been advised by local law enforcement that the death is being investigated as a possible suicide. Suicide is not easy to talk about. You may not want to even read further. I ask that you do, for the well-being of us all.

> Uses explicit language and doesn't need to wait for official results when the suicide may have been obvious.

> Acknowledges the difficulty for some people.

I have written to campus before about this subject but we are a constantly changing community, and I think it critical to keep the subject of suicide prevention on all of our radars.

> Understands the audience's reaction to multiple messages.

I also want to offer an opportunity to join with many others tonight in positive campus action on the matter.

> Keeps the focus positive.

As uncomfortable as the topic may be, it is truly amazing how many of our lives have been or will be touched by suicide and the mental distress and disease that underlies it: family, friends, . . . Suicide is endemic among those in the typical college-age group. Actually, less so among those in college than those of similar age who are not in college. But, still, at Western, we feel this pain year in and year out.

> Provides brief context.

Can we change that?

> Takes a forward-looking approach.

Having lost a son away at college to this epidemic, my answer is simple: We must!

> Provides his own experience and the imperative.

Our reluctance to talk about such topics— suicide, depression, other mental distress and disease—was, I concluded, part of what can make ailments like depression the deadly diseases that they can be.

> Emphasizes openness.

(Continued)

(Continued)

Because of the stigma surrounding such topics, people do not bring the manifestations of a usually VERY treatable problem to the attention of others. In my layman's view, our brains are very powerful . . . but not always for good ends. Mental ailments can use that awesome brainpower, reinforced by fear of stigmas, to hide their very existence from the person with the ailment. Dire consequences can then result.

Admits his own embarrassment and fear.

So, I took a vow, no matter how personally painful it was, to never be too embarrassed or afraid to talk about these subjects. Or, about my son.

That is step one and I encourage you to consider joining me in that vow: break the stigma surrounding these topics by being willing to discuss them just as you would any other ailment to which we beautifully complex human beings are sometimes vulnerable.

Acknowledges vulnerability.

Step two is to reinforce a culture in which we care about each other. That is a hallmark of what it means to be Western. Do pay attention to signs that might indicate that a person you know may do harm to themselves. Or, to others. If you, yourself, are feeling at a loss with no solutions in sight, reach out for we will be there for you.

Encourages compassion and seeking help.

Step three logically follows: If you see a friend or associate manifesting problems, certainly speak to them if you are comfortable so doing. But, don't stop there: alert those trained on our campus to provide help. Give the alert, share what you are comfortable sharing, and you may do so knowing that professionals will confidentially and sensitively proceed.

Repeats resources mentioned up front.

Whom do you call to pass on a "heads up"? Again, the Counseling Center can help at 650-3164. They are trained to assess and provide direction to faculty, staff, and students with referrals and, if appropriate, engagement of our suicide prevention team.

We cannot be 100% successful so another step is, again, about taking care of ourselves when tragedy does strike: to feel and share our grief and our loss as we are today over yesterday's death.

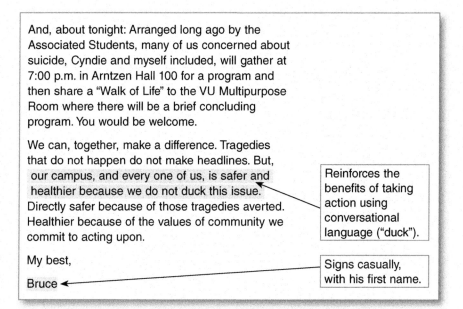

And, about tonight: Arranged long ago by the Associated Students, many of us concerned about suicide, Cyndie and myself included, will gather at 7:00 p.m. in Arntzen Hall 100 for a program and then share a "Walk of Life" to the VU Multipurpose Room where there will be a brief concluding program. You would be welcome.

We can, together, make a difference. Tragedies that do not happen do not make headlines. But, our campus, and every one of us, is safer and healthier because we do not duck this issue. Directly safer because of those tragedies averted. Healthier because of the values of community we commit to acting upon.

> Reinforces the benefits of taking action using conversational language ("duck").

My best,

Bruce

> Signs casually, with his first name.

Showing Compassion Toward Ourselves

Self-compassion—feeling positive and caring toward yourself during times of failure and suffering—is correlated with psychological well-being and may contribute to emotional resilience.[58] Caring for ourselves may protect us from getting crushed by failure so we can learn from it.

Researchers have identified three components of self-compassion:

- Self-Kindness: the ability to treat oneself with care rather than harsh self-judgment.
- Common Humanity: recognizing that imperfection is a shared aspect of the human experience rather than feeling isolated by one's failures.
- Mindfulness: holding one's experience in balanced perspective rather than exaggerating the dramatic storyline of suffering.[59]

Self-compassion scale items help us understand how we care for ourselves. Although recent research has questioned some items,[60] they are useful to see how we might be kinder to ourselves (Figure 9.7).

Practicing Gratitude

One way to improve self-compassion is to practice gratitude—recognizing goodness in your life and acknowledging that at least part of that goodness is outside yourself. Research demonstrates the positive effects of gratitude for well-being. In one study, people who focused on blessings instead of hassles or

Figure 9.7   Self-compassion scale items help us see how to be kinder
to ourselves

1. When I fail at something important to me, I become consumed by feelings of inadequacy.   2. I try to be understanding and patient toward those aspects of my personality I don't like.   3. When something painful happens, I try to take a balanced view of the situation.   4. When I'm feeling down, I tend to feel like most other people are probably happier than I am.   5. I try to see my failings as part of the human condition.   6. When I'm going through a very hard time, I give myself the caring and tenderness I need.
7. When something upsets me, I try to keep my emotions in balance.   8. When I fail at something that's important to me, I tend to feel alone in my failure.   9. When I'm feeling down, I tend to obsess and fixate on everything that's wrong.   10. When I feel inadequate in some way, I try to remind myself that feelings of inadequacy are shared by most people.   11. I'm disapproving and judgmental about my own flaws and inadequacies.   12. I'm intolerant and impatient toward those aspects of my personality I don't like.

Source: Filip Raes, Elizabeth Pommier, Kristin D. Neff, and Dinska Van Gucht, "Construction and Factorial Validation of a Short Form of the Self-Compassion," *Clinical Psychology and Psychotherapy*, Vol. 18 (2011), pp. 250–255. You'll find a more extensive assessment at Kristin Neff, "Test How Self-Compassionate You Are," Self-Compassion website, http://self-compassion .org/test-how-self-compassionate-you-are/, accessed June 18, 2017.

complaints felt better about their lives and were more optimistic. In another study, people completing daily gratitude exercises had a better outlook and were more likely to help someone else. In other words, "counting our blessings" makes us happier and improves interpersonal relations.[61,62]

Studies also show positive effects of writing and giving someone a thank-you letter, writing down three good things in one's life every day and providing a cause for them, and writing about a time when a personal strength was used.[63] Sheryl Sandberg learned the value of gratitude during her grief:

I have learned gratitude. Real gratitude for the things I took for granted before—like life. As heartbroken as I am, I look at my children each day and rejoice that they are alive. I appreciate every smile, every hug. I no longer take each day for granted. When a friend told me that he hates birthdays and so he was not celebrating his, I looked at him and said through tears, "Celebrate your birthday, goddammit. You are lucky to have each one." My next birthday will be depressing as hell, but I am determined to celebrate it in my heart more than I have ever celebrated a birthday before.

I can't even express the gratitude I feel to my family and friends who have done so much and reassured me that they will continue to be there. In the brutal moments when I am overtaken by the void, when the months and years stretch out in front of me endless and empty, only their faces pull me out of the isolation and fear. My appreciation for them knows no bounds.[64]

Sandberg shows us the value of gratitude with a deep, personal example from her own life. Being grateful, even during times of immense pain, helps us practice kindness toward ourselves and toward others.

SUMMARY

SeaWorld's business took a hit because leaders failed to offer compassion to trainers and orcas. The *Blackfish* movie and Tilikum's death were opportunities for the company to show their concern and care, but they prioritized the business and defended their practices.

SeaWorld is slowly moving toward a different model, partly by necessity because of declining business. The new president has taken some action, but activists want to see more and still call on company leaders to focus more on conservation and education than on entertainment.

Suffering is painful but doesn't have to be a solitary condition. At work, leaders at all levels demonstrate compassion to those in distress, resulting in healthier employees and a better place to work. Even though it may be difficult, people push past their own resistance and feelings of inadequacy. Compassionate leaders follow a four-step process of noticing, interpreting, feeling, and acting and find ways to demonstrate comfort and empathy.

Finally, we practice self-compassion. Being gentle with ourselves and practicing gratitude are essential to personal growth and character development.

EXERCISES

Concept Review Questions

1. What is the value of compassion to individuals and to an organization?

2. What is the four-step process for responding with compassion?

3. How do appraisals affect how we respond to others?

4. What are some ways we can offer others comfort?

5. How is empathy different from sympathy or pity?

Self-Reflection Questions

1. Think of a time when someone successfully comforted you when you were in distress. What did the person say or do that was helpful? What else, if anything, would have been helpful? Was anything not helpful?

2. When have you noticed someone in distress? How could you tell?

3. Can you think of another time when you may have missed cues that someone was in distress? What got in the way of your noticing?

4. In Figure 9.5, we see several reasons people might avoid giving comfort, for example, focusing too much on productivity and multitasking, wanting to avoiding negative emotions, and emphasizing fixing problems. Which do you think is most prevalent for you or for an organization where you worked?

5. Have you ever noticed someone suffering but didn't act? What were the circumstances? If you had a chance to replay the situation, would you do anything differently?

6. Overall, how well equipped do you feel giving comfort to others? What could help you feel more skilled?

Mini-Cases

Consider the following scenarios. On your own or with a partner, discuss the best course of action in each case. What would you do, and what factors into your decision?

Scenario 1

One of your coworkers appears to be in distress. Her eyes are red, and she seems anxious—fidgeting and getting up from her desk every few minutes to get coffee or go to the restroom. You don't know her that well because she just started with the company a month ago, but she works in the cubicle next to yours. You overhear another coworker say to her, "You OK?" She responds in a clipped voice, "Yeah, I'm fine." You want to offer compassion. What will you do? How does your relationship and her response to your co-worker affect how you approach the situation?

Scenario 2

One of your employees is upset because he lost a report he had been working on for a week. He accidentally overwrote a file, and the technology support group is trying to recover it, but it doesn't look good. You're frustrated because you have stressed many times that people should regularly back up their work. If he had created a backup file, he could retrieve an older version and not start from scratch. How might your appraisal of the situation affect your response? How can you offer compassion anyway?

Scenario 3

Your manager sent an email to the group that his mother died suddenly. The group has been working together for more than two years, and people know each other well and sometimes socialize together outside of work. How will you respond? Consider how you might respond as a group as well.

Self-Assessment: Capacity for Compassion

Think of a group to which you belong and complete the assessment in Figure 9.2. Use a five-point scale, where 1 is *strongly disagree*, 3 is *neutral*, and 5 is *strongly agree*. There is no scoring for this assessment, but your answers will help you understand your capacity for compassion during each of the four steps.

Team Activity

With your group, discuss your responses to the assessment in Figure 9.3. What did you learn from the items? What, if anything, surprised you about your responses? In which of the four steps could you improve your capacity for compassion? What did you learn about your teammates from this activity?

Self-Assessment: Self-Compassion

Complete a Self-Compassion Assessment online at the website, Self-Compassion (http://self-compassion.org/test-how-self-compassionate-you-are/).[65] This is a more extensive version of the items listed in Figure 9.7. After you rate each item, read the score interpretations. Note that some categories are reversed: higher scores in self-judgment, isolation, and overidentification reflect lower self-compassion, and lower scores reflect higher self-compassion.

Paired or Team Activity

Discuss your scores from the Self-Compassion assessment. What did you learn from the questions? What, if anything, surprised you about your scores? What does your overall self-compassion score indicate about your self-compassion? What are your scores in the subscales—self-kindness, self-judgment, common humanity, isolation, mindfulness, and overidentification? In which areas could you be more compassionate to yourself? What else do you want your partner or team members to know about you?

Paired Activity

Prepare to role-play a situation with a partner to practice listening with empathy. Imagine that one is the manager and the other is the employee. The employee took a day off because of a house fire.[66] The next day, the manager meets with the employee to check in. Let's assume you've known each other for about six months and have a good working relationship.

Planning Questions for the Manager's Role

1. What do you hope to achieve by having the conversation?

2. What are your concerns about how the conversation could go?

3. How will you set the stage? Where will you meet, and where will each of you sit? Try to avoid having a table or desk as a barrier, and consider sitting catty-corner (at an angle) rather than directly opposite each other, which could feel more like an interview.

4. How will you start the conversation?

5. What can you do or say to comfort the employee in this situation?

Planning Questions for the Employee's Role

1. How might you benefit from the conversation?

2. What are your concerns about talking with a manager in this way about something potentially personal?

3. How will you describe what happened and the impact on you and your family? (You can invent details.)

4. What might you avoid saying?

Role Play or Video Activity

Prepare to role-play the situation described above. Consider video-recording the interaction.

Practice and Reflection

After you complete the role play, reflect on how it went:

1. What was realistic—or not—about the situation?

2. Regardless, from the employee's perspective, how well did the manager demonstrate compassion? What was done well, and what could have been improved?

3. From the manager's perspective, how did you feel? What was comfortable or uncomfortable? Do you agree with the employee's feedback?

4. Now watch the video together if you recorded the interaction. What other observations do you have? Pay attention to body language—for example, eye contact, facial expressions, and gestures.

5. What did you learn about yourselves—in both roles—from doing this activity?

If you have time, switch roles and practice another situation: this time, an employee got in a car accident. Although there were no serious injuries, the employee's car was unexpectedly sideswiped and the experience was fairly traumatic.

Summary

B*uilding Leadership Character* is a tool for developing our character strengths over time. We have opportunities throughout our careers to make good decisions and to do well by others. In this section, we'll see examples that summarize learning from failing and each character dimension. Next, we'll see how organizations and individuals can choose leadership character.

We Choose Leadership Character Throughout Our Career

We have seen many paradoxes throughout the book. We are vulnerable, yet strong; humble, yet willful; courageous, yet careful; and authentic, yet adaptable. Leadership character is complex, and developing character is as challenging as it is rewarding. Character is cultivated in decisions big and small throughout our lives.

At all stages of your career, you will face decisions that shape your character, and you will find occasions to communicate your character to others through your choices. We'll look at examples throughout the career life cycle to illustrate learning from failure and our seven character dimensions.

Learning From Failure

You applied for several jobs but haven't received any offers yet, and you're worried about getting a position that suits you. How will you handle the stress? Will you be able to push through your fears and spend time reflecting on what you could be doing differently? Can you be observant about your intellectual, emotional, and physical reactions to maintain perspective and to learn how to improve your job search?

Authenticity

When you apply for a job, what are you hoping to accomplish? Are you more concerned with external rewards, such as status and money, or do you seek intrinsic rewards? Do you focus more on how the job will look on your résumé or more on the impact you will have?

When you begin your new job, what will you do to fit in? We all want to feel a sense of belonging, but what individual sacrifices are you willing and not willing to make? Will you cut your hair, wear a suit, downplay your religion? Or do you feel comfortable being your authentic self and talking about who you really are and what's most important to you?

Humility

What will define your contribution to the organization and to your coworkers? Are you more concerned with being smart and outpacing others, or are you more interested in learning? Can you be humble—willing to admit what you don't know and ask for feedback?

When employees join the organization after you, how will you ensure they're successful? Do you make space for new people by giving them your time and by showing them patience?

Vulnerability

When you get passed up for a promotion, how will you handle the situation? Will you be angry and rely on false bravado, or can you be open about your disappointment without feeling resentful?

When you make a mistake, will you risk exposure and apologize? Can you be vulnerable in order to build connections with others who can support and challenge you?

Accountability

Also when you make a mistake, will you accept ownership for making things right? Can you stand up publicly and take accountability?

When you do get that promotion and you're leading others, do you hold yourself accountable in the same way you hold those reporting to you accountable? Do you give employees enough authority to do their work and enough leeway to make mistakes? When they do inevitably mess up, do you tend to be more blaming or more forgiving? Can you also admit your own role in the failing?

Integrity

When people at work depend on you, will you be trustworthy? Will you be consistent in your behavior, and will you be whole, by upholding worthy goals of the organization and by challenging them when they fall short?

Will you also place your trust in others? Over time, will you build relationships where people can rely on each other to accomplish good work?

Compassion

When someone in your group is dealing with a personal tragedy, will you offer comfort and demonstrate empathy? Will you also offer compassion when people are feeling pressure at work? Can you manage your own feelings of blame or inadequacy so they don't prevent you from reaching out to comfort others?

When you're experiencing stress, fear, or panic, are you kind to yourself? Can you express gratitude even when you're in distress?

Courage

When you're promoted again, this time to a senior-level position, will you report wrongdoing of your colleagues or of people more senior than you? Are you willing to wrestle with the ambiguity, face the exposure, and handle the potential loss of compensation, status, and relationships?

Throughout your career, can you make tough choices for the good of others? When faced with conflicting work demands, relationships, and personal needs, what will guide you to become, over time, a person of strong leadership character?

Organizations Set the Stage for Cultivating Leadership Character

We are fortunate that leadership character can be developed over time. No one expects us to be perfect, and expecting it from ourselves is futile. We are all works in progress—and so are our organizations. The next two sections summarize the ways our organizations and we, as individuals, can cultivate leadership character.

Organizations decide who they want to hire and how they will model and reward good character. As a group, leaders make decisions every day about the behaviors that sustain the organization to provide jobs, products and services, and shareholder returns.

Hiring for Leadership Character

Selecting the right people is key to building an organization that encourages and rewards good leadership character. Several company executives talk about hiring for character over skills. Bill Marriott quotes his father, who opened his first hotel in 1957:

> He hired for character. In fact, one of his 12 rules for success was, "It's more important to hire people with the right qualities than with specific experience."[1]

Companies like Southwest and ING prefer to hire from outside the industry.[2] This might avoid some of the character failures we learned about in the book, for example, when veterans from the auto and banking industries perpetuated bad habits from former leaders.

The difficulty is in assessing character. We can more easily evaluate accomplishments than what's in someone's heart or mind. To select leaders, we may need to spend more time getting to know them and gathering feedback from former colleagues.

Behavioral interview questions are one strategy for assessing someone's character. For example, rather than asking, "Do you think ethics is important?" (who would say no?), we might ask, "Tell me about a time you faced an ethical dilemma. What did you do, and how did it turn out?" Or, more specifically, "Tell me about a time when you challenged the status quo," "Tell me about a time you made a mistake that affected others," "When have you stood up for someone who couldn't or wouldn't stand up for himself or herself?" or "Tell me about a risk you took." Such questions encourage candidates to demonstrate vulnerability and authenticity in addition to other character dimensions. How candidates tackle these questions also tells a recruiter about their willingness to learn.

Modeling Good Leadership Character

Throughout the book, we talked about the importance of going beyond a list of core values or a code of ethics. We know this isn't enough—and prescriptive procedures may deny people the chance to use their judgment and make better decisions. Leaders model character for others and create a culture that supports and values strong character.

Leadership character certainly starts at the top. We saw many examples of how leaders who demonstrate vulnerability, courage, accountability, integrity, and other character dimensions have positive impacts on the people they lead and on their organizations. We look to leaders to set the tone for the organization and for clues about what is acceptable and rewarded. Some of us aspire to be them.

Being a leader presents both an opportunity and responsibility. Leaders can make or break employees' experience at an organization—coaching and guiding them to be the best they can be or torturing them until they quit.

By definition, leadership character considers the effect we have on others. Of course, leaders face constraints at all levels of the organization, but having strong character means leaders prioritize people when they make decisions, and this encourages others in the organization to do the same. We hope for participation from all parts of the organization to improve the working environment for everyone.

Rewarding Good Leadership Character

In the book introduction, we saw examples of rewarding short-term performance. When companies take a longer-term view, leaders may be less likely to take ethical shortcuts and may be more likely to take measured risks—and fail, which we learned builds character.

As with most organizational change, taking a longer view is easier said than done. Corporate boards of directors, CEOs, and shareholders need to sacrifice immediate financial rewards to emphasize good character over quick results.

Of course, rewarding good character means openly addressing bad behavior. Employees need to see negative consequences when people demonstrate self-interest over the good of the team. We may have to sacrifice privacy to make employment decisions public. The termination disguised as an individual "layoff" or executive "resignation" may not serve the organization in the long run.

Finally, we learned the limitations of rewards and regulations. We cannot force people to have stronger character; our incentives and rules may result in specific behaviors, but developing leadership character requires personal discipline for self-development.

Individuals Choose Leadership Character

Context matters, but everyone in an organization chooses the type of leader—and the type of person—they want to be. Developing leadership character is a lifelong journey and requires practicing new approaches and behaviors to replace old habits. Our focus is on leadership character, but your choices at work, home, and in the community collectively form your character.

Practicing Self-Awareness

From the beginning the book, we saw the critical role of self-awareness on character development. People need time and space to reflect openly and honestly on how they present themselves and serve others. To learn from failure, to be vulnerable, to be humble—all paths lead to continuous improvement.

Self-awareness doesn't happen in a vacuum. We know and develop ourselves through our relationships with others. Leaders build character by being open to feedback from others, particularly when it conflicts with their own views.

At the same time, we strive to be authentic. As we mature, we know ourselves better and feel good about who we are. We bring our whole selves to work because we like who we are and don't want to "fake it" to impress others or to fill a role.

Practicing Good Character

We often know the right thing to do, but we have to choose to do it. In her book *Giving Voice to Values*, Mary Gentile describes a new way of teaching ethics in college.[3] Rather than asking students, "What would you do?" in the case of an ethical dilemma, students assume they choose the ethical path and then focus on how to get it done: how to communicate the decision and persuade others.

The idea is that most people want to do the right thing, but they need experience to build skills. As discussed in the Introduction, *practicing* making better decisions leads to *making* better decisions. The choice gets easier and easier until it becomes a reflex—how we normally operate.

Choosing Wisely

Just as recruiters should choose job candidates who demonstrate elements of good character, we choose where and with whom we work. Associating with people of strong character makes our own path easier.

During the selection process, you have many ways to determine whether the organization is a "good" choice: review news stories about the company; ask people from your social networks about working there, particularly about any difficult situations they have encountered; read reviews on company review sites, such as Glassdoor; try to meet many of your prospective colleagues; and ask questions during the hiring interviews about the culture and expectations.

If you're bold, you might try one or two behavioral interview questions of your own, for example, "When has the organization [company or department] faced an ethical dilemma, and how was it resolved?" or "What types of conflicts usually come up within the department?" or "I'd like to know how failures are managed. Can you please tell me about a mistake an employee made and how it was handled?" or "How is performance measured?" or "How are people held accountable in the department?"

We are fortunate when we can choose our employer. Of course, that isn't always the case: when job prospects are limited and people are tied to a location, changing organizations is difficult and may be impossible. But when we have the freedom to choose where, how, and with whom we want to spend our time, we can leave if an organization doesn't align with our values or puts our self-worth or character in jeopardy.

Cultivating leadership character is a challenging path. Leaders who want to develop character continuously try to do better and learn that change is incremental and not a straight line. Difficult situations litter their path, and leaders tackle some more successfully than others.

Leaders with strong character may find financial success, but that isn't their goal. They aren't motivated by awards or accolades. They are nourished by seeing their own development and by doing well by others. Their reward is in living a good life and inspiring others to do the same.

Notes

Introduction

1. Nelson D. Schwartz, "Route to Air Travel Discomfort Starts on Wall Street," *New York Times*, May 28, 2017, https://www.nytimes.com/2017/05/28/business/corporate-profit-margins-airlines.html, accessed June 4, 2017.
2. Daphne A. Jameson, "Economic Crises and Financial Disasters: The Role of Business Communication," *Journal of Business Communication*, Vol. 46, No. 4 (2009), pp. 499–509.
3. Mary Crossan, Daina Mazutis, Gerard Seijts, and Jeffrey Gandz, "Developing Leadership Character in Business Programs," *Academy of Management Learning and Education*, Vol. 12, No. 2 (2013), pp. 285–305.
4. Mary C. Gentile, "Giving Voice to Values: A Pedagogy for Behavioral Ethics," *Journal of Management Education*, Vol. 41, No. 4 (2017), pp. 469–479.

Chapter 1

1. U.S. Bureau of Labor Statistics, "Unemployment Level (UNEMPLOY)," FRED Economic Data, May 5, 2017, https://fred.stlouisfed.org/graph/?id=UNEMPLOY, accessed May 9, 2017.
2. "The Great Recession: Over but Not Gone? IPR researchers document ongoing effects," Northwestern University Institute for Policy Research, 2014, http://www.ipr.northwestern.edu/about/news/2014/IPR-research-Great-Recession-unemployment-foreclosures-safety-net-fertility-public-opinion.html, accessed May 9, 2017.
3. Jennifer von Pohlmann, "Less Than 1 Percent of Seriously Underwater U.S. Properties Qualify for Principal Reduction Under New FHFA Program," *Realty Trac*, May 4, 2016, http://www.realtytrac.com/news/foreclosure-trends/q1-2016-u-s-home-equity-and-underwater-report/, accessed May 9, 2017.
4. E. Scott Reckard, "Mozilo Gets Flak Over an E-mail Misfire," *Los Angeles Times*, May 21, 2008, http://articles.latimes.com/2008/may/21/business/fi-mozilo21, accessed May 9, 2017.
5. Max Abelson, "Angelo Mozilo Speaks: No Regrets at Countrywide," *Bloomberg*, September 2, 2014, https://www.bloomberg.com/news/articles/2014-09-02/angelo-mozilo-speaks-no-vil lainy-at-countrywide, accessed May 9, 2017.

6. "Feds Won't File Fraud Suit Against Countrywide's Mozilo," *Chicago Tribune*, June 17, 2016, http://www.chicagotribune.com/business/ct-countrywide-angelo-mozilo-feds-20160617-story.html, accessed August 3, 2017.

7. "Bank of America to Pay Nearly $17 Bn to Settle Mortgage Claims," *Philadelphia Herald*, August 2, 2014, http://www.philadelphiaherald.com/news/224972439/bank-of-america-to-pay-nearly-17-bn-to-settle-mortgage-claims, accessed August 4, 2017.

8. Mary Crossan, Gerard Seijts, and Jeffrey Gandz, *Developing Leadership Character* (New York: Routledge, 2016), pp. 4–5.

9. Ibid.

10. Mary Crossan, Daina Mazutis, Gerard Seijts, and Jeffrey Gandz, "Developing Leadership Character in Business Programs," *Academy of Management Learning and Education*, Vol. 12, No. 2 (2013), pp. 285–305.

11. "Leadership Character Insight Assessment," Leader Report for Sam Sample, November 26, 2015, SIGMA Assessment Systems, Inc.

12. Christopher Peterson and Martin Seligman, *Character Strengths and Virtues: A Handbook and Classification* (Oxford University, 2004), https://teaching psychology.files.wordpress.com/2011/11/character-strengths-and-virtues.pdf, accessed August 4, 2017.

13. Martin Seligman's *Learned Optimism* preceded *Character Strengths and Virtues: A Handbook and Classification* with Christopher Peterson.

14. Crossan et al., *Developing Leadership Character*, pp. 6–7.

15. Ibid., p. 7.

16. Mary Gentile, *Giving Voice to Values* (New Haven: Yale University Press, 2010), p. 28.

17. Rushworth M. Kidder, *Moral Courage* (New York: HarperCollins, 2005), pp. 39–64.

18. Crossan et al., *Developing Leadership Character*, p. 7.

19. David Brooks, *The Road to Character* (New York: Random House, 2015), p. 21.

20. James Bartholomew, "The awful rise of 'virtue signaling,'" *The Spectator*, April 18, 2015, https://www.spectator.co.uk/2015/04/hating-the-daily-mail-is-a-sub-stitute-for-doing-good/, accessed August 4, 2017.

21. Peter G. Northouse, *Leadership: Theory and Practice, 7th edition* (Thousand Oaks, CA: SAGE, 2016).

22. Kevin Kruse, "What Is Leadership?" *Forbes*, April 9, 2013, https://www.forbes.com/sites/kevinkruse/2013/04/09/what-is-leadership/#4122be135b90, accessed August 4, 2017.

23. Judi Brownell, "Leadership in the Service of Hospitality," *Cornell Hospitality Quarterly*, Vol. 51, No. 3 (2010), pp. 363–378.

24. Gregory A. Stone, Robert F. Russell, and Kathleen Patterson, "Transformational Versus Servant Leadership: A Difference in Leader Focus," *Leadership and Organization Development Journal*, Vol. 24, No. 4 (2004), pp. 349–361.

25. J. Bruce Tracey and Timothy R. Hinkin, "Transformational Leadership or Effective Managerial Practices?" *Group and Organization Management*, Vol. 23, 1998, pp. 220–236.

26. Stone et al., "Transformational Versus Servant Leadership."

27. Ibid.

28. Rynetta R. Washington, Charlotte D. Sutton, and Hubert S. Field, "Individual Differences in Servant Leadership: The Roles and Values and Personality," *Leadership and Organization Development Journal*, Vol. 27, No. 8 (2006), pp. 700–716.

29. "How Mary Barra Led GM Through Crisis," *Fortune*, October 21, 2015, http://fortune.com/video/2015/10/21/mary-barra-gm-crisis/, accessed June 6, 2017.

30. Bill George, *Discover Your True North, 2nd Edition* (Hoboken, NJ: John Wiley & Sons, 2015).

31. Ibid., p. 3.

32. Mary M. Crossan, Alyson Byrne, Gerard H. Seijts, Mark Reno, Lucas Monzani, and Jeffrey Gandz, "Toward a Framework of Leader Character in Organizations," *Journal of Management Studies* (2017), doi: 10.1111/joms.12254.

33. Vera Leonard, "Leadership Is a Matter of How to Be, Not How to Do: A Conversation With Frances Hesselbein," Wayne County Community College District publication *Great Leadership*, Vol. 3, No. 2, August 2009, http://www.wccd.edu/news/pdfs/August%202009%20WEB.pdf, accessed August 3, 2017.

34. Mary Crossan, Jeffrey Gandz, and Gerard Seijts, "Developing Leadership Character," *Ivey Business Journal*, January 2012, http://www.charactercommunity.org/site/charactercommu nity/assets/pdf/developing_leadership_character_-_ivey_business_journal.pdf, accessed May 9, 2017.

35. Crossan et al., "Toward a Framework of Leader Character in Organizations."

36. Jason Slotkin, "Adidas Apologizes for Congratulating 2017 Boston Marathon 'Survivors,'" *NPR*, April 19, 2017, http://www.npr.org/sections/thetwo-way/2017/04/19/524692534/adidas-apologizes-for-congratulating-2017-boston-mar athon-survivors, accessed May 9, 2017.

37. Adidas (@adidasUS), Twitter, April 18, 2017, https://twitter.com/adidasUS/status/854422872944771073?ref_src=twsrc%5Etfw&ref_url=http%3A%2F%2Fwww.npr.org%2Fsections%2Fthetwo-way%2F2017%2F04%2F19%2F5246925 34%2Fadidas-apologizes-for-congratulating-2017-boston-marathon-survivors, accessed May 9, 2017.

38. Ahiza Garcia, "Adidas Executive on Navigating Politics (and That Boston Marathon Tweet)," *CNN*, April 27, 2017, http://money.cnn.com/2017/04/27/news/companies/adidas-mark-king-interview/, accessed June 4, 2017.

39. Paul A. Argenti, "Building Trust through Reputation Management," Tuck School of Business at Dartmouth, http://exec.tuck.dartmouth.edu/images/uploads/CMS/751/argenti_building_trust_chapter_final.pdf, accessed June 4, 2017.

40. W. Timothy Coombs and Sherry J. Holladay, "Helping Crisis Managers Protect Reputational Assets," *Management Communication Quarterly*, Vol. 16, No. 2 (2016), pp. 165–186.

41. "The CEO Reputation Premium: Gaining Advantage in the Engagement Era," KRC Research and Weber Shandwick, http://www.webershandwick.com/uploads/news/files/ceo-reputation-premium-executive-summary.pdf, accessed June 4, 2017.

42. "The Company Behind the Brand: In Reputation We Trust," Weber Shandwick, http://www.webershandwick.com/uploads/news/files/InRepWeTrust_ExecutiveSummary.pdf, accessed June 4, 2017.

43. Fred Kiel, *Return on Character: The Real Reason Leaders and Their Companies Win* (Boston: Harvard Business Review Press, 2015).

44. Read or listen to Fred Kiel's interview with Sarah Green, *Harvard Business Review*, "Ethical CEOs Finish First," April 30, 2015, https://hbr.org/ideacast/2015/04/ethical-ceos-finish-first.htm, accessed May 25, 2017.

45. Fred Kiel, "Measuring the Return on Character," *Harvard Business Review*, April 2015, https://hbr.org/2015/04/measuring-the-return-on-character, accessed May 9, 2017.

46. Crossan et al., "Toward a Framework of Leader Character in Organizations."

47. Kiel, *Return on Character*.

48. Charles' Fav Movie Clips, "The Buble [*sic*] in Florida and the Mortgage Brokers—*The Big Short*," YouTube, March 5, 2017, https://www.youtube.com/watch?v=PgGLgygsqus, accessed May 9, 2017.

49. Stacy Cowley and Jessica Silver-Greenberg, "Loans 'Designed to Fail': States Say Navient Preyed on Students," *New York Times,* April 9, 2017, https://www.nytimes.com/2017/04/09/business/dealbook/states-say-navient-preyed-on-students.html, accessed May 9, 2017.

50. Michael Lewis, "Occupational Hazards of Working on Wall Street," *Bloomberg*, September 24, 2014, https://www.bloomberg.com/view/articles/2014-09-24/occupational-hazards-of-working-on-wall-street, accessed May 9, 2017.

51. For an overview, see Dennis Gentilin, *The Origins of Ethical Failures: Lessons for Leaders* (Abingdon, Oxon: Routledge, 2016), Chapter 1.

52. Crossan et al., "Developing Leadership Character in Business Programs."

53. Judi Brownell, "Ethics From the Bottom Up," *Cornell Hospitality Report*, Vol. 17, No. 10 (2017), pp. 3–13.

54. "Leadership Character Insight Assessment."

55. Crossan et al., *Developing Leadership Character*.

56. "Leadership Character Insight Assessment."

57. Crossan et al., "Developing Leadership Character," *Ivey Business Journal*.

58. James Rest, Muriel Bebeau, and J. Volker, "An Overview of the Psychology of Morality," in J. R. Rest (Ed.), *Moral Development: Advances in Research and Theory* (New York: Praeger, 1986), as cited in Ralph W. Jackson, Charles M. Wood, and James J. Zboja, "The Dissolution of Ethical Decision-Making in Organizations: A Comprehensive Review and Model," *Journal of Business Ethics*, Vol. 116, No. 2 (2013), pp. 233–250.

59. Kevin Lehnert, Yung-hwal Park, and Nitish Singh, "Research Note and Review of the Empirical Ethical Decision-Making Literature: Boundary Conditions and Extensions," *Journal of Business Ethics*, Vol. 129, No. 1 (2015), pp. 195–219.

60. Stephen Cohen, "Promoting Ethical Judgment in an Organisational Context," *Journal of Business Ethics*, Vol. 117, No. 3 (2013), pp. 513–523.

61. "United CEO Oscar Munoz Defends Employees in Letter," *Chicago Tribune*, April 10, 2017, http://www.chicagotribune.com/business/ct-united-ceo-oscar-munoz-letter-20170410-story.html, accessed May 9, 2017.

62. Roomy Khan, "United Airlines Customer Dragging Drama: Are Corporate Mandates Killing the Conscience?" *Forbes*, April 19, 2017, https://www.forbes.com/sites/roomykhan/2017/04/19/united-airlines-customer-dragging-drama-are-corporate-mandates-killing-the-conscience/, accessed May 9, 2017.

63. Susan Carey, "Behind United's Fateful Move to Call Police," *Wall Street Journal*, April 16, 2017, https://www.wsj.com/articles/behind-united-airlines-fateful-decision-to-call-police-1492384610, accessed June 9, 2017.

64.   Oscar Munoz, "Actions Speak Louder Than Words," United Airlines email, April 28, 2017, http://bit.ly/2oSYEaA, accessed April 29, 2017.

65.   Ashley Lutz, "Nordstrom's Employee Handbook Has Only One Rule," *Business Insider*, October 13, 2014, http://www.businessinsider.com/nordstroms-employee-handbook-2014-10, accessed June 9, 2017.

66.   Ralph W. Jackson, Charles M. Wood, and James J. Zboja, "The Dissolution of Ethical Decision-Making in Organizations: A Comprehensive Review and Model," *Journal of Business Ethics*, Vol. 116, No. 2 (2013), pp. 233–250.

67.   Dennis Gentilin, *The Origins of Ethical Failures: Lessons for Leaders* (New York: Routledge, 2016), p. 164.

68.   Most of the featured company leaders are white men who are leading major organizations and whose crisis situations are public. Each chapter includes additional examples and a more representative sample of leaders.

69.   This activity is adapted from Mary Gentile, *Giving Voice to Values* (New Haven: Yale University Press, 2010), pp. 51–53.

Chapter 2

1.   Eugene Kim, "How Amazon CEO Jeff Bezos Has Inspired People to Change the Way They Think About Failure," *Business Insider*, May 29, 2016, http://www.businessinsider.com/how-amazon-ceo-jeff-bezos-thinks-about-failure-2016-5/#bezos-is-a-big-fan-of-failure-1, accessed August 6, 2017.

2.   Ibid.

3.   Brooke Obie, "5 Lessons From Shonda Rhimes' New Book *Year of Yes*," *NBC News*, November 24, 2015, http://www.nbcnews.com/news/nbcblk/5-lessons-new-shonda-rhimes-book-year-yes-n464246, accessed June 6, 2017.

4.   Shonda Rhimes, "A Year of Saying Yes to Everything," TED Talk, March 9, 2016, https://www.youtube.com/watch?v=gmj-azFbpkA, accessed June 4, 2017.

5.   Andrew Beaujon, "Woman Hides Under Desk for Half-Hour to Dodge TV Reporter," *Poynter*, February 13, 2016, http://www.poynter.org/2013/woman-hides-under-desk-for-half-hour-to-dodge-tv-reporter/204220/, accessed June 4, 2017.

6.   Frank Landry, "Cookie-Eating Health Boss Loses Job," *Toronto Sun*, November 24, 2010, http://www.torontosun.com/news/canada/2010/11/24/16303161.html, accessed June 4, 2017.

7.   Coursera, Lecture 11: "Who Should Learn Character?" Interview with Dominic Randolph, https://www.coursera.org/learn/teaching-character/lecture/4IlZA/who-should-learn-character-interview-with-dominic-randolph, accessed June 7, 2017.

8.   "Our Approach," KIPP website, http://www.kipp.org/kipp-foundation/history/, accessed August 6, 2017.

9.   Paul Tough, *How Children Succeed: Grit, Curiosity, and the Hidden Power of Character* (New York: Houghton Mifflin Harcourt, 2012).

10.   The quote is attributed to William Edward Hickson, sometimes with an additional "try." See https://www.goodreads.com/author/quotes/4298891.William_Edward_Hickson, accessed June 4, 2017.

11.   Bill George, Peter Sims, Andrew N. McLean, and Diana Mayer, "Discovering Your Authentic Leadership," *Harvard Business Review*, February 2007, https://hbr.org/2007/02/discovering-your-authentic-leadership, accessed August 8, 2017.

12.   Tim Harford, *Adapt: Why Success Always Starts With Failure* (New York: Farrar, Straus and Giroux, 2011).

13.   Amy Edmondson, "Strategies for Learning From Failure," *Harvard Business Review*, April 2011, https://hbr.org/2011/04/strategies-for-learning-from-failure, accessed June 4, 2017.

14.   Julian Birkinshaw and Martine Haas, "Increase Your Return on Failure," *Harvard Business Review*, May 2016, https://hbr.org/2016/05/increase-your-return-on-failure, accessed June 4, 2017.

15.   Laurence G. Weinzimmer and Candace A. Esken, "Learning From Mistakes: How Mistake Tolerance Positively Affects Organizational Learning and Performance," *Journal of Applied Behavioral Science*, Vol. 1, No. 27 (2017).

16.   Erika Hayes James and Lynn Perry Wooten, "Orientations of Positive Leadership in Times of Crisis," in Gretchen M. Spreitzer and Kim S. Cameron (Eds.), *The Oxford Handbook of Positive Organizational Scholarship* (Oxford University Press, 2011).

17.   Ibid.

18.   David Brooks, "The Moral Bucket List," *New York Times*, April 11, 2015, https://www.nytimes.com/2015/04/12/opinion/sunday/david-brooks-the-moral-bucket-list.html, accessed May 9, 2017.

19.   Francesca Gino and Gary P. Pisano, "Why Leaders Don't Learn From Success," *Harvard Business Review*, April 2011, https://hbr.org/2011/04/why-leaders-dont-learn-from-success, accessed June 7, 2017.

20.   Francisco Polidoro Jr., "Why Organizations Forget What They Learn From Failures," *Harvard Business Review*, February 2016, https://hbr.org/2016/02/why-organizations-forget-what-they-learn-from-failures, accessed June 7, 2017.

21.   Jon Gertner, "The Truth About Google X: An Exclusive Look Behind the Secretive Lab's Closed Doors," *Fast Company*, April 15, 2014, https://www.fastcompany.com/3028156/the-google-x-factor, accessed June 4, 2017.

22.   NASA, "Nasa's Innovation Awards," https://nasapeople.nasa.gov/awards/eligibility.htm, accessed June 7, 2017.

23.   Grey, "Culture," Grey.com/us/culture, accessed June 4, 2017.

24.   Associated Press, "Sweden's Museum of Failure Highlights Products That Flopped," *Washington Post*, June 12, 2017, https://www.washingtonpost.com/lifestyle/kidspost/swedens-museum-of-failure-highlights-products-that-flopped/2017/06/12/3f24cd48-4ba7-11e7-9669-250d0b15f83b_story.html, accessed August 6, 2017.

25.   Johannes Haushofer, "CV of Failures," https://www.princeton.edu/~joha/Johannes_Haushofer_CV_of_Failures.pdf, accessed August 6, 2017.

26.   George et al., "Discovering Your Authentic Leadership."

27.   Daniel Goleman, "What Makes a Leader?" *Harvard Business Review*, January 2004, https://xa.yimg.com/kq/groups/17881575/601861488/name/1246794.pdf, accessed June 4, 2017.

28.   For more, see Peter M. Senge, C. Otto Scharmer, Joseph Jaworski, and Betty Sue Flowers, *Presence: Human Purpose and the Field of the Future* (New York: Doubleday, 2008).

29.   Laura Billiter, Alex Koyl, Tiffany Mellor, Amanda Nogaki, and Victoria Sanchez, *JetBlue Crisis Communication Plan*, https://pressfolios-production.s3.amazonaws.com/uploads/story/story_pdf/80607/806071400003445.pdf, accessed June 7, 2017.

30. "After-Action Review: Technical Guidance," USAID from the American People, http://pdf.usaid.gov/pdf_docs/PNADF360.pdf, accessed June 4, 2017.

31. Eric Kail, "Leadership Character: The Role of Reflection," *Washington Post*, March 9, 2012, https://www.washingtonpost.com/blogs/guest-insights/post/leadership-character-the-role-of-reflection/2011/04/04/gIQAdJOr1R_blog.html, accessed May 9, 2017.

32. Francesca Gino and Bradley Staats, "Why Organizations Don't Learn," *Harvard Business Review*, November 2015, https://hbr.org/2015/11/why-organizations-dont-learn, accessed June 7, 2017.

33. Ibid.

34. Daniel Goleman, "On Self-Awareness," November 15, 2012, http://www.danielgole man.info/on-self-awareness/, accessed June 4, 2017.

35. Fung Kei Cheng, "What Does Meditation Contribute to Workplace? An Integrative Review," *Journal of Psychological Issues in Organizational Culture*, Vol. 6, No. 4 (2016), pp. 18–34.

36. Aslak Hjeltnes, Per-Elnar Binder, Christian Moltu, and Ingrid Dundas, "Facing the Fear of Failure: An Explorative Qualitative Study of Client Experiences in a Mindfulness-Based Stress Reduction Program for University Students With Academic Evaluation Anxiety," *International Journal of Qualitative Studies on Health and Well-Being*, Vol. 10, No. 1 (2015).

37. Cheng, "What Does Meditation Contribute to Workplace?"

38. Kimberly Schaufenbuel, "Why Google, Target, and General Mills Are Investing in Mindfulness," *Harvard Business Review*, December 2015, https://hbr.org/2015/12/why-google-target-and-general-mills-are-investing-in-mindfulness, accessed June 7, 2017.

39. Margaret Chapman-Clarke, *Mindfulness in the Workplace: An Evidence-Based Approach to Improving Wellbeing and Maximizing Performance* (London: Kogan Page, 2016).

40. Drake Baer, "Here's What Google Teaches Employees in Its 'Search Inside Yourself' Course," *Business Insider*, August 5, 2014, http://www.businessinsider.com/search-inside-yourself-googles-life-changing-mindfulness-course-2014-8, accessed June 7, 2017.

41. Profanity omitted.

42. Jo Confino, "Google's Head of Mindfulness: 'Goodness Is Good for Business,'" *The Guardian*, May 14, 2014, https://www.theguardian.com/sustainable-business/google-meditation-mindfulness-technology, accessed June 4, 2017.

43. Drake Baer, "Here's What Google Teaches Employees in Its 'Search Inside Yourself' Course," *Business Insider*, August 5, 2014, http://www.businessinsider.com/search-inside-yourself-googles-life-changing-mindfulness-course-2014-8, accessed June 7, 2017.

44. Temple Grandin, *Animals Make Us Human: Creating the Best Life for Animals* (Mariner Books, 2010).

45. Amy Cuddy, *Presence* (New York: Little, Brown, and Company, 2015), p. 190.

46. Amy Cuddy's research on "Power Poses" made famous in her TED Talk has been discounted by a coauthor, but Cuddy stands by the work—and her book is still a worthy read.

47. Matthew A. Stults-Kolehmainen and Rajita Sinha, "The Effects of Stress on Physical Activity and Exercise," *Sports Medicine*, Vol. 44, No. 1 (2014), pp. 81–121.

48. Cindy L. Carmack, Carl de Moor, Edwin Boudreaux, Marta Amaral-Melendez, and Phillip J. Brantley, "Aerobic Fitness and Leisure Physical Activity as Moderators of the Stress–Illness Relation," *Annals of Behavioral Medicine*, Vol. 21, No. 3 (1999), pp. 251–257.

49. Rebecca Rueggeberg, Carsten Wrosch, and Gregory E. Miller, "The Different Roles of Perceived Stress in the Association Between Older Adults' Physical Activity and Physical Health," *Health Psychology*, Vol. 31, No. 2 (2012), pp. 164–171.

50. Jonathan D. Brown, "Staying Fit and Staying Well: Physical Fitness as a Moderator of Life Stress," *Journal of Personality and Social Psychology*, Vol. 60, No. 4 (1991), pp. 555–561.

51. Jonathan D. Brown, "Exercise as a Buffer of Life Stress: A Prospective Study of Adolescent Health," *Health Psychology*, Vol. 7, No. 4 (1988), pp. 341–353.

52. This is a true story, and the candidate didn't get the job.

53. Adapted from Mary Crossan, Gerard Seijts, and Jeffrey Gandz, *Developing Leadership Character* (New York: Routledge, 2016), p. 184.

54. For example, "Breathing Meditation With Thich Nhat Hanh," YouTube, January 9, 2008, https://www.youtube.com/watch?v=E7XJdkL4j3Y, accessed June 4, 2017.

55. The Greater Good Science Center at the University of California, Berkeley, "Mindful Breathing," http://ggia.berkeley.edu/practice/mindful_breathing, accessed June 4, 2017.

Chapter 3

1. Jeff S. Bartlett, Michelle Naranjo, and Jeff Plungis, "Guide to the Volkswagen Emissions Recall," *Consumer Reports*, January 6, 2017, http://www.consumerreports .org/cro/cars/guide-to-the-volkswagen-dieselgate-emissions-recall-, accessed June 13, 2017.

2. Federal Trade Commission, "Complaint for Permanent Injunction and Other Equitable Relief," Case 3:16-cv-01534 *Federal Trade Commission v. Volkswagen Group of America, Inc.*, March 29, 2016, https://www.ftc.gov/system/files/documents/cases/160329volkswagen_cmpt.pdf, accessed June 13, 2017.

3. Federal Trade Commission, "Complaint for Permanent Injunction."

4. Brené Brown, "The Power of Vulnerability," YouTube, January 3, 2011, https://www.youtube.com/watch?v=iCvmsMzlF7o&t=651s, accessed June 12, 2017.

5. Brené Brown, "Shame Resilience Theory: A Grounded Theory Study on Women and Shame," *Families in Society*, Vol. 87, No. 1, p. 43.

6. Ibid.

7. "Honda Motor Company Retains Strongest Corporate Reputation Among Automakers; Volkswagen Group's Reputation Plunges," The Harris Poll, February 18, 2016, http://www.theharrispoll.com/business/Auto-Industry-Reputation.html, accessed April 21, 2017.

8. Jack Ewing, "Inside VW's Campaign of Trickery," *New York Times*, May 6, 2017, https://www.nytimes.com/2017/05/06/business/inside-vws-campaign-of-trickery.html, accessed June 10, 2017.

9. Kartikay Mehrotra, "VW Reaches $1.2 Billion Settlement Over Audi, Porsche Diesels," *Bloomberg*, February 1, 2017, https://www.bloomberg.com/news/articles/2017-02-01/vw-u-s-drivers-agree-final-1-2-billion-diesel-settlement, accessed June 10, 2017.

10. Ewing, "Inside VW's Campaign of Trickery."

11. Ibid.

12. Bill Vlasic and Aaron M. Kessler, "It Took E.P.A. Pressure to Get VW to Admit Fault," *The New York Times*, September 21, 2015, https://www.nytimes.com/2015/09/22/business/it-took-epa-pressure-to-get-vw-to-admit-fault.html, accessed June 10, 2017.

13. Ewing, "Inside VW's Campaign of Trickery."

14. Of course, consumers also have some responsibility to protect themselves.

15. Brené Brown, *Daring Greatly: How the Courage to Be Vulnerable Transforms the Way We Live, Love, Parent, and Lead* (New York: Penguin, 2012).

16. Volkswagen Group, "Video Statement Prof. Dr. Martin Winterkorn," YouTube, September 22, 2015, https://www.youtube.com/watch?v=wMPX98_H0ak, accessed April 21, 2017.

17. Volkswagen Press Release, "Statement by Prof. Dr. Martin Winterkorn," https://www.volkswagen-media-services.com/en/detailpage/-/detail/Statement-by-Prof-Dr-Winterkorn/view/2721302/7a5bbec13158edd433c6630f5ac445da?p_p_auth=y1muovrJ, accessed June 12, 2017.

18. Jack Ewing, "VW Engineers Wanted O.K. From the Top for Emissions Fraud, Documents Show," *New York Times*, May 17, 2017, https://www.nytimes.com/2017/05/17/business/volkswagen-muller-diesel-emissions.html, accessed June 10, 2017.

19. Tom Schoenberg, Christoph Rauwald, and David McLaughlin, "Volkswagen Agrees to Plead Guilty in Diesel-Emissions Scandal," *Bloomberg*, January 11, 2017, www.bloomberg.com/news/articles/2017-01-11/volkswagen-agrees-to-pay-4-3-billion-plead-guilty-in-u-s-case, accessed April 21, 2017.

20. Müller is being investigated by German authorities for not notifying shareholders early enough about the scandal. Ewing, "VW Engineers Wanted O.K."

21. Sonari Glinton, "'We Didn't Lie,' Volkswagen CEO Says of Emissions Scandal," *NPR*, January 11, 2016, www.npr.org/sections/thetwo-way/2016/01/11/462682378/we-didnt-lie-volkswagen-ceo-says-of-emissions-scandal, accessed April 21, 2017.

22. Ibid.

23. Timothy W. Coombs and Sherry J. Holladay, "Comparing Apology to Equivalent Crisis Response Strategies: Clarifying Apology's Role and Value in Crisis Communication," *Public Relations Review*, Vol. 34 (2008), pp. 252–257.

24. "Volkswagen TDI Goodwill Package," http://vwgoodwillpackage.com/, accessed June 14, 2017.

25. "Timeline: Volkswagen's Long Road to a U.S. Dieselgate Settlement," *Reuters*, January 11, 2017, http://www.reuters.com/article/us-volkswagen-emissions-timeline-idUSKBN14V100, accessed June 14, 2017.

26. Brené Brown, "Listening to Shame," TED Talk, March 2012, www.ted.com/talks/brene_brown_listening_to_shame#t-852434, accessed April 21, 2017.

27. "Volkswagen: 'We Have Totally Screwed Up,'" *New York Times*, September 22, 2015, www.nytimes.com/video/business/international/100000003928968/volkswagen-we-have-totally-screwed-up.html, accessed April 21, 2017.

28. "Testimony of Michael Horn, President and CEO of Volkswagen Group of America, Inc. Before the House Committee on Energy and Commerce Subcommittee on Oversight and Investigations," U.S. House of Representatives Document Repository,

October 8, 2015, http://docs.house.gov/meetings/IF/IF02/20151008/104046/HHRG-114-IF02-Wstate-HornM-20151008.pdf, accessed April 21, 2017.

29. "Volkswagen's Emissions Cheating Allegations: Initial Questions," U.S. House of Representatives Document Repository, October 8, 2015, http://docs.house.gov/meetings/IF/IF02/20151008/104046/HHRG-114-IF02-Transcript-20151008.pdf, accessed April 21, 2017.

30. David Brooks, *The Road to Character* (New York: Random House, 2015).

31. Blue Bell, "Blue Bell Voluntarily Expands Recall," http://cdn.bluebell.com/the_little_creamery/press_releases/all-product-recall, accessed April 21, 2017.

32. Ann Lauricello, "After Listeria Recall, Blue Bell Ice Cream Return," Fox31 Denver, http://kdvr.com/2017/03/22/after-listeria-recall-blue-bell-ice-cream-returns/, accessed August 8, 2017.

33. Steven Fink, *Crisis Communications: The Definitive Guide to Managing the Message* (New York: McGraw-Hill, 2013), p. 12.

34. Ibid., p. 174.

35. Ibid., p. 179

36. Ibid., p. 132.

37. Alan Alda, "The First Time I Was Stabbed in the Face," *The New York Times*, May 30, 2017, https://www.nytimes.com/2017/05/30/books/alan-alda-the-first-time-i-was-stabbed-in-the-face.html, accessed June 10, 2017.

38. "The Michigan Model: Medical Malpractice and Patient Safety at UMHS," *Michigan Medicine*, May 2016, www.uofmhealth.org/michigan-model-medical-malpractice-and-patient-safety-umhs, accessed April 21, 2017.

39. Richard C. Boothman, "Full Disclosure of Medical Errors Reduces Malpractice Claims and Claim Costs for Health System," *AHRQ Health Care Innovations Exchange*, https://innovations.ahrq.gov/profiles/full-disclosure-medical-errors-reduces-malpractice-claims-and-claim-costs-health-system, accessed April 21, 2017.

40. "The Michigan Model."

41. Michelle M. Mello, Richard C. Boothman, Timothy McDonald, Jeffrey Driver, Alan Lembitz, Darren Bouwmeester, Benjamin Dunlap, and Thomas Gallagher, "Communication-and-Resolution Programs: The Challenges and Lessons Learned From Six Early Adopters," *Health Affairs*, Vol. 33, No. 1 (2014), pp. 20–29.

42. Megan A. Adams, Joseph B. Elmunzer, and James M. Scheiman, "Effect of a Health System's Medical Error Disclosure Program on Gastroenterology-Related Claims Rates and Costs," *American Journal of Gastroenterology*, Vol. 109, Issue 4 (2014), pp. 460–464.

43. Alexandra Stevenson, "Valeant Bet Was a 'Huge Mistake,' Hedge Fund Chief Ackman Says," *New York Times*, March 29, 2017, https://www.nytimes.com/2017/03/29/business/dealbook/valeant-bet-was-a-huge-mistake-hedge-fund-chief-ackman-says.html, accessed June 10, 2017.

44. Stephen Gandel, "Valeant: A Timeline of the Big Pharma Scandal," *Fortune*, October 31, 2015, http://fortune.com/2015/10/31/valeant-scandal/, accessed June 10, 2017.

45. William A. Ackman, "Letter to Shareholders," Pershing Square Holdings, 2016 Annual Report, https://assets.pershingsquareholdings.com/media/2014/09/28204101/PSH-Annual-Report_12.31.16.pdf, accessed July 12, 2017.

46.   Dov Seidman, "Calling for an Apology Cease-Fire," Deal Book, *New York Times*, February 3, 2014, https://dealbook.nytimes.com/2014/02/03/calling-for-an-apology-cease-fire/, accessed June 10, 2017.

47.   Brown, "Listening to Shame."

48.   Brown, *Daring Greatly*, pp. 34–35.

49.   T. Rees Shapiro, "Key Elements of *Rolling Stone*'s U-Va. Gang Rape Allegations in Doubt," *Washington Post*, December 4, 2014, www.washingtonpost.com/local/education/u-va-fraternity-to-rebut-claims-of-gang-rape-in-rolling-stone/2014/12/05/5fa5f7d2-7c91-11e4-84d4-7c896b90abdc_story.html, accessed April 21, 2017.

50.   T. Rees Shapiro, "Jury Finds Reporter, *Rolling Stone* Responsible for Defaming U-Va. Dean With Gang Rape Story," *Washington Post*, November 4, 2016, www.washingtonpost.com/local/education/jury-finds-reporter-rolling-stone-responsible-for-defaming-u-va-dean-with-gang-rape-story/2016/11/04/aaf407fa-a1e8-11e6-a44d-cc2898cfab06_story.html, accessed April 21, 2017.

51.   Sheila Coronel, Steve Coll, and Derek Kravitz, "*Rolling Stone*'s Investigation: 'A Failure That Was Avoidable,'" *Columbia Journalism Review*, April 5, 2015, www.cjr.org/investigation/rolling_stone_investigation.php, accessed April 21, 2017.

52.   Sheila Coronel, Steve Coll, and Derek Kravitz, "Rolling Stone & UVA: Columbia School of Journalism's Report," *Rolling Stone*, April 5, 2015, www.rollingstone.com/culture/features/a-rape-on-campus-20141119, accessed April 21, 2017.

53.   Dan Whitcomb, "How Two Teens in Leggings Became a PR Mess for United Airlines," *Reuters*, March 28, 2017, www.reuters.com/article/us-unitedairlines-leggings-idUSKBN16Y2HY, accessed April 21, 2017.

54.   Abby Ohlheiser, "Just How Offensive Did Milo Yiannopoulos Have to Be to Get Banned From Twitter?" *Washington Post*, July 21, 2016, www.washingtonpost.com/news/the-intersect/wp/2016/07/21/what-it-takes-to-get-banned-from-twitter, accessed April 21, 2017.

55.   Bill Maher, *Real Time With Bill Maher*, HBO, Episode 415, February 17, 2017, www.hbo.com/real-time-with-bill-maher/episodes/15/415-episode/index.html, accessed April 21, 2017.

56.   David D. Luxton, Jennifer D. June, and Jonathan Fairall, "Social Media and Suicide: A Public Health Perspective," *American Journal of Public Health*, Vol. 102, Suppl. 2 (2012), pp. S195–S200.

57.   Ohlheiser, "Just How Offensive Did Milo Yiannopoulos Have to Be."

58.   Bradley Honan, "What Is CEO Reputation Premium, and Why Does It Matter for Your Organization?" KRC Research, August 16, 2016, www.krcresearch.com/what-is-ceo-reputation-premium-and-why-does-it-matter-for-your-organization/, accessed April 21, 2017.

59.   Ryan Holmes, "Yes, Even CEOs Need to Use Social Media—and They Need to Do It Well," *Fast Company*, March 23, 2016, www.fastcompany.com/3056970/yes-even-ceos-need-to-use-social-media-and-do-it-well, accessed April 21, 2017.

60.   Weber Shandwick, "The Company Behind the Brand: In Reputation We Trust," http://www.webershandwick.com/uploads/news/files/InRepWeTrust_ExecutiveSummary.pdf, accessed April 21, 2017.

61.   Bertel Schmitt, "General Motors Is World's Third Largest, and Nearly Landed in #4," *Forbes*, February 7, 2017, https://www.forbes.com/sites/bertel-schmitt/2017/02/07/general-motors-is-worlds-third-largest/#5493815587da, accessed August 15, 2017.

62. Christoph Rauwald, "VW Says It's 'Back on Track' After Restructuring," *BloombergTechnology*, March 14, 2017, https://www.bloomberg.com/news/articles/2017-03-14/vw-recovery-makes-progress-as-namesake-car-brand-s-margins-widen, accessed August 15, 2017.

63. Justin Huggler, "German Car Giants 'May Have Colluded on Emissions,'" *The Telegraph*, July 17, 2017, http://www.telegraph.co.uk/business/2017/07/21/german-car-giants-may-have-colluded-emissions/, accessed August 15, 2017.

64. Bill George, *Discover Your True North, 2nd edition* (Hoboken, NJ: John Wiley & Sons, 2015).

Chapter 4

1. Jeff Bennett, "GM to Recall 8.45 Million More Vehicles in North America," *Wall Street Journal*, June 30, 2014, https://www.wsj.com/articles/gm-to-recall-7-6-million-more-vehicles-in-u-s-1404153705, accessed July 1, 2014.

2. David Shepardson, "GM Compensation Fund Completes Review With 124 Deaths," *Detroit News*, August 24, 2015, http://www.detroitnews.com/story/business/autos/general-motors/2015/08/24/gm-ignition-fund-completes-review/32287697/, accessed May 8, 2017.

3. Jennifer Liberto, "Two Died in 2006 Cobalt Crash. But GM Counts Only One," *CNN Money*, May 28, 2014, http://money.cnn.com/2014/05/28/news/companies/gm-recall-death/index.html, accessed May 28, 2014.

4. Nathan Bomey, "GM Pays $1M SEC Fine Over Ignition-Switch Scandal," *USA Today*, January 18, 2017, https://www.usatoday.com/story/money/cars/2017/01/18/general-motors-securities-and-exchange-commission-sec-ignition-switch/96717570/, accessed May 8, 2017.

5. Danielle Ivory and Bill Vlasic, "$900 Million Penalty for G.M.'s Deadly Defect Leaves Many Cold," *New York Times*, September 17, 2015, https://www.nytimes.com/2015/09/18/business/gm-to-pay-us-900-million-over-ignition-switch-flaw.html, accessed May 8, 2017.

6. Melvin Seeman, *Social Status and Leadership: The Case of the School Executive* (Columbus: Bureau of Educational Research and Service, Ohio State University, 1960), as cited in Bruce J. Avolio and William J. Gardner, "Authentic Leadership Development: Getting to the Root of Positive Forms of Leadership," *Leadership Quarterly*, Vol. 16, No. 3 (2005), pp. 315–338.

7. "A Look at Mary Barra, GM's First Female CEO," *Wall Street Journal*, December 10, 2013, https://blogs.wsj.com/corporate-intelligence/2013/12/10/a-look-at-mary-barra-gms-first-female-ceo/, accessed June 13, 2017.

8. General Motors Company, "Leadership: Mary T. Barra Chairman and Chief Executive Officer, General Motors Company," www.gm.com, accessed May 8, 2017.

9. Fun fact: Akio Toyoda was confirmed as the president of Toyota in June 2009 and delivered his apology to Congress about vehicle recalls in February 2010.

10. Energy and Commerce Committee, "The GM Ignition Switch Recall: Why Did It Take So Long?" April 1, 2014, https://energycommerce.house.gov/hearings-and-votes/hearings/gm-ignition-switch-recall-why-did-it-take-so-long, accessed May 8, 2017.

11. General Motors Company, "CEO Mary Barra's Written Congressional Testimony Now Available," www.gm.com, accessed May 8, 2017.

12. Matthew L. Wald, "Highlights From Senate Hearing on G.M. Defects," *New York Times*, The Lede Blogging the News With Robert Mackey, April 2, 2014, https://thelede.blogs.nytimes.com/2014/04/02/live-video-from-senate-hearing-on-g-m-defects, accessed May 8, 2017.

13. *Note:* Some "authentic leadership" definitions include more general leadership functioning and are broader than what we're discussing here as a character dimension.

14. Bill George and Sarah Green Carmichael, "Becoming a More Authentic Leader," *Harvard Business Review*, December 10, 2015, https://hbr.org/ideacast/2015/12/becoming-a-more-authentic-leader.html, accessed May 8, 2017.

15. Michael Kernis and Brian Goldman, "A Multicomponent Conceptualization of Authenticity: Theory and Research," *Advances in Experimental Social Psychology*, Vol. 38 (2006), pp. 283–357.

16. Chris Isidore, "Barra on Recall: 'Terrible Things Happened,'" *CNN*, March 18, 2014, http://money.cnn.com/2014/03/17/news/companies/gm-recall-barra, accessed May 8, 2017.

17. General Motors Company, "GM CEO Addresses Employees in Town Hall Meeting," www.gm.com, September 17, 2015, http://media.gm.com/media/us/en/gm/news.detail.html/content/Pages/news/us/en/2015/sep/0917-barra.html, accessed May 8, 2017.

18. Alex Wood, Alex Linley, John Maltby, Michael Baliousis, and Joseph Stephen, "The Authentic Personality: A Theoretical and Empirical Conceptualization and the Development of the Authenticity Scale," *Journal of Counseling Psychology*, Vol. 55, No. 3 (2008), pp. 385–399.

19. Daniel M. Cable, Francesca Gino, and Bradley R. Staats, "Breaking Them In or Eliciting Their Best? Reframing Socialization Around Newcomers' Authentic Self-Expression," *Administrative Science Quarterly*, Vol. 58, No. 1 (2013), pp. 1–36.

20. Michael D. McGee, "Authenticity and Healing," *Journal of Religion and Health*, Vol. 53, No. 3 (2014), pp. 725–730.

21. Jeffrey Pfeffer, *Leadership BS: Fixing Workplaces and Careers One Truth at a Time* (New York: Harper Business, 2015).

22. Herminia Ibarra, "The Authenticity Paradox," *Harvard Business Review*, January 2015, https://hbr.org/2015/01/the-authenticity-paradox.com/uploads/3/8/1/3/38138031/hbr--authenticity_paradox.pdf, accessed May 8, 2017.

23. Herminia Ibarra, "The Authenticity Paradox."

24. Oliver C. Robinson, Frederick G. Lopez, Katherine Ramos, and Sofya Nartova-Bochaver, "Authenticity, Social Context, and Well-Being in the United States, England, and Russia: A Three Country Comparative Analysis," *Journal of Cross-Cultural Psychology*, Vol. 44, No. 5, pp. 719–737.

25. Alison P. Lenton, Martin Bruder, Letitia Slabu, and Constantine Sedikides, "How Does 'Being Real' Feel? The Experience of State Authenticity," *Journal of Personality*, Vol. 31, No. 3 (2013), pp. 276–289.

26. Herminia Ibarra, "The Authenticity Paradox," *Harvard Business Review*, January 2015, https://hbr.org/2015/01/the-authenticity-paradox, accessed May 8, 2017.

27. Bill George, "Authentic Leadership Rediscovered," Harvard Business School, November 10, 2015, http://hbswk.hbs.edu/item/authentic-leadership-rediscovered, accessed May 8, 2017.

28. David Brooks, *The Road to Character* (New York: Random House, 2016), pp. 249–260.

29. Ibid., pp. 249, 257.

30. Ibid., p. 253.

31. Lenton et al., "How Does 'Being Real' Feel?"

32. Ralph Van den Bosch and Toon W. Taris, "Authenticity at Work: Development and Validation of an Individual Authenticity Measure at Work," *Journal of Happiness Studies*, Vol. 15, Issue 1 (2014), pp. 1–18.

33. Fred Walumbwa, Bruce Avolio, William Gardner, Tara Wernsing, and Suzanne Peterson, "Authentic Leadership: Development and Validation of a Theory-Based Measure," *Journal of Management*, Vol. 34, No. 1 (2008), pp. 89–126.

34. Hannes Leroy, Michael E. Palanski, and Tony L. Simons, "Authentic Leadership and Behavioral Integrity as Drivers of Follower Commitment and Performance," *Journal of Business Ethics*, Vol. 107, No. 3 (2012), pp. 255–264. *Note:* The connection here is behavioral integrity, which we'll discuss in the next chapter.

35. Ralph Van den Bosch and Toon W. Taris, "Authenticity at Work: Development and Validation of an Individual Authenticity Measure at Work," *Journal of Happiness Studies*, Vol. 15, No. 1 (2014), pp. 1–18.

36. Vanessa Buote, "Most Employees Feel Authentic at Work, but It Can Take a While," *Harvard Business Review*, May 11, 2016, https://hbr.org/2016/05/most-employees-feel-authentic-at-work-but-it-can-take-a-while, accessed June 12, 2017.

37. Cable et al., "Breaking Them In or Eliciting Their Best?"

38. Annamarie Mann and Jim Harter, "The Worldwide Employee Engagement Crisis," *Gallup*, January 7, 2016, http://www.gallup.com/businessjournal/188033/worldwide-employee-engagement-crisis.aspx, accessed June 11, 2017.

39. "Indra Nooyi's Leadership Lessons: Head, Heart & Hands," *Enactus Career Connections*, January 2, 2014, www.enactuscareerconnections.com/indra-nooyis-leadership-lessons-head-heart-hands/, accessed April 28, 2015.

40. "GM's New Chief Officer on Being in the Driver's Seat," *CBS Sunday Morning*, May 3, 2015, https://www.youtube.com/watch?v=5pdQZXBjics, accessed May 8, 2017.

41. Nina Easton, "GM CEO Mary Barra Learned This Important Lesson From the Recall Crisis," *Fortune* video, September 16, 2016, http://fortune.com/2016/09/15/mary-barra-gm-lesson/, accessed May 8, 2017.

42. Ibid.

43. Buote, "Most Employees Feel Authentic at Work."

44. *Note:* Some argue that organizational or cultural fit conflicts with diversity and inclusion goals. See, for example, Erika Andersen, "Is 'Cultural Fit' Just a New Way to Discriminate?" *Forbes*, March 17, 2015, https://www.forbes.com/sites/erikaandersen/2015/03/17/is-cultural-fit-just-a-new-way-to-discriminate/#6796e9813923, accessed June 13, 2017.

45. Mark Snyder, *Public Appearances, Private Realities: The Psychology of Self-Monitoring*, Series of Books in Psychology (W.H. Freeman & Company, September 1986).

46. Adrian Furnham, "Monitoring the Self: Are You a High or Low Self-Monitor?" *Psychology Today*, January 26, 2017, https://www.psychologytoday.com/blog/sideways-view/201701/moni toring-the-self-are-you-high-or-low-self-monitor, accessed May 8, 2017.

47. Brené Brown, *Daring Greatly: How the Courage to Be Vulnerable Transforms the Way We Live, Love, Parent and Lead* (New York: Avery, 2015), p. 232.

48.   Eric Clay, "The Made of Clay Report," WRFI Radio Show, Interview with Aloja Airewele, June 15, 2014, http://madeofclay.org/aloja-airewele-and-eric-clay/, accessed April 28, 2015.

49.   Buote, "Most Employees Feel Authentic at Work."

50.   Brooks, *The Road to Character*, p. 211.

51.   Helen Coffey, "Why 'Admitting' You Are a Christian at Work Is So Very Hard," *Telegraph*, March 31, 2014, http://www.telegraph.co.uk/women/womens-life/10733863/Why-admitting-you-are-a-Christian-at-work-is-so-very-hard.html, accessed June 12, 2017.

52.   F. Warner, "With Their Blessing (Religion at Work)," *Human Resource Management International Digest*, Vol. 90, No. 4 (2011), pp. 20–23.

53.   John Coleman, Daniel Gulati, and W. Oliver Segovia, *Passion & Purpose* (Boston: Harvard Business Review Press, 2012).

54.   Fred Luthans, "Inspiring Leaders," in Steve Norman and Larry Hughes, *Authentic Leadership: A New Approach for a New Time* (London: Routledge, 2006).

55.   Alex Wood, Alex Linley, John Maltby, Michael Baliousis, and Joseph Stephen, "The Authentic Personality: A Theoretical and Empirical Conceptualization and the Development of the Authenticity Scale," *Journal of Counseling Psychology*, Vol. 55, No. 3 (2008), pp. 385–399.

56.   Bill George, *Discover Your True North, 2nd edition* (Hoboken, NJ: John Wiley & Sons, 2015), p. 87.

57.   Bill George, "Finding Your Sweet Spot as a Leader," Discover Your True North website, http://discoveryourtruenorth.org/finding-your-sweet-spot-as-a-leader/, accessed August 14, 2017.

58.   George, *Discover Your True North*, p. 99.

59.   Brené Brown, "The Power of Vulnerability," TED Talk, January 3, 2011, https://www.youtube.com/watch?v=iCvmsMzlF7o&t=768a, accessed May 8, 2017.

60.   "Most Powerful Women," *Fortune*, 2016, http://fortune.com/most-powerful-women, accessed June 5, 2017.

61.   Deborah Tannen, *You Just Don't Understand* (New York: HarperCollins, 2013).

62.   The company founder, Kiichiro Toyoda, named the company Toyota partly because it takes eight strokes to write instead of 10. Eight is a favorable number in Japanese. Yamasa Institute, "Toyota Motor Company," http://yamasa.org/japan/english/destinations/aichi/toyota.html, accessed June 5, 2017.

63.   Roxana D. Maiorescu, "Crisis Management at General Motors and Toyota: An Analysis of Gender-Specific Communication and Media Coverage," *Public Relations Review*, Vol. 42, No. 4 (2016), pp. 556–563.

64.   Beth Kowitt, "GM's Mary Barra to Staff: 'No More Crappy Cars,'" *Fortune*, October 16, 2013, http://fortune.com/2013/10/16/gms-mary-barra-to-staff-no-more-crappy-cars/, accessed June 11, 2017.

65.   Ibid.

66.   Kyle Stock, "GM's Mary Barra Fires 15, Says More Recalls Are Coming," *Bloomberg*, June 5, 2014, https://www.bloomberg.com/news/articles/2014-06-05/gms-mary-barra-fires-15-says-more-recalls-are-coming, accessed May 8, 2017.

67.   Arthur W. Page Society, "General Motors' Corporate Culture Crisis: An Assessment of the Ignition Switch Recall," January 16, 2015, http://www

.awpagesociety.com/attachments/1edd5184509636aabbdc07ef0c3546e0facf5c0c/sto
re/00f8d9b37cec4d725c881b7235467635aeab21b4d2333398c819839d426b/
General-Motors-Case-Study-2015.pdf, accessed May 8, 2017.
    68. Stock, "GM's Mary Barra Fires 15."
    69. Katie Meyer, "Crisis Management 101: How Did DiGiorno Bounce Back
From a Cheesy Tweet?" *Medium*, October 27, 2015, https://medium.com/@crowd
babble/crisis-management-101-how-did-digiorno-bounce-back-from-a-cheesy-tweet-
e384a8c0839f, accessed May 7, 2017.
    70. "State of the American Consumer: Insights for Business Leaders," *Gallup*,
2014, http://products.gallup.com/171722/state-american-consumer.aspx, accessed
April 26, 2017.
    71. Matt Wilson, "American Airlines Responds to Every Tweet With Original,
Non-scripted Answers," *PR Daily*, August 1, 2012, www.prdaily.com/Main/
Articles/12296.aspx, accessed April 26, 2017.
    72. Melissa Fares, "Bernie Sanders' Ghost Tweeter Keeps His Brooklyn
Accent," *Reuters*, April 4, 2016, http://www.reuters.com/article/us-usa-election-
sanders-tweets-idUSKCN0X00NZ, accessed May 8, 2017.
    73. Hyojung Park and Glen T. Cameron, "Keeping It Real: Exploring the Roles
of Conversational Human Voice and Source Credibility in Crisis Communication
via Blogs," *Journalism and Mass Communication Quarterly*, Vol. 91, No. 3 (2014),
pp. 487–507.
    74. Mark Phelan, "CEO Mary Barra Shakes Up GM," *USA Today*, June 4, 2017,
https://www.usatoday.com/story/money/cars/2017/06/04/ceo-mary-barra-shakes-up-
gm/102484738/, accessed August 9, 2017.
    75. From George, *Discover Your True North*.

Chapter 5

    1. FIFA, "InfoPlus: Fédération Internationale de Football Association," https://
web.archive.org/web/20060915133001/http://access.fifa.com/infoplus/IP-199_01E_
big-count.pdf, accessed May 30, 2017.
    2. "FIFA Corruption Crisis: Key Questions Answered," *BBC News*, December 21,
2015, http://www.bbc.com/news/world-europe-32897066, accessed May 30, 2017.
    3. Leon Siciliano and Sophie Jamieson, "FIFA: A Timeline of Corruption—in
90 Seconds," *The Telegraph*, March 22, 2016, http://www.telegraph.co.uk/football/
2016/03/22/fifa-a-timeline-of-corruption—in-90-seconds/, accessed June 20, 2017.
    4. "FIFA Corruption Crisis."
    5. Austin Knoblauch and Barry Stavro, "A Timeline on the FIFA Scandal," *Los
Angeles Times*, June 2, 2015, http://www.latimes.com/sports/soccer/la-sp-fifa-scandal-
timeline-20150603-story.html, accessed June 20, 2017.
    6. Luke Matthews, "It's a Big Museum of Dinosaurs—Diego Mara-
dona Blasts FIFA," *Goal*, June 4, 2011, http://www.goal.com/en-gb/news/2557/
news/2011/06/04/2517750/its-a-big-museum-of-dinosaurs-diego-maradona-blasts-
fifa, accessed May 30, 2017.
    7. "FIFA 'Like Mafia Family,' Says Former FA Boss Triesman," *BBC News*, June
11, 2014, http://www.bbc.com/news/uk-politics-27801996, accessed May 30, 2017.

8.   AFP, "Blatter, Mbeki 'Discussed' $10 Mln World Cup Deal," *Times Live*, June 7, 2015, http://www.timeslive.co.za/local/2015/06/07/Blatter-Mbeki-discussed-10-mln-World-Cup-deal#, accessed May 30, 2017.

9.   Eliott C. McLaughlin and Greg Botelho, "FIFA Corruption Probe Targets 'World Cup of Fraud,' IRS Chief Says," *CNN*, http://edition.cnn.com/2015/05/27/football/fifa-corruption-charges-justice-department/, accessed May 30, 2017.

10.   Mary Crossan, Gerard Seijts, and Jeffrey Gandz, *Developing Leadership Character* (New York: Routledge, 2016).

11.   Tony Simons, *The Integrity Dividend: Leading by the Power of Your Word* (San Francisco: Jossey-Bass, 2008), p. 5.

12.   Daryl Koehn, "Integrity as a Business Asset," *Journal of Business Ethics*, Vol. 58, No. 1 (2005), pp. 125–136.

13.   Robert H. Moorman, Todd C. Darnold, Manuela Priesemuth, and Craig P. Dunn, "Toward a Measurement of Perceived Leader Integrity: Introducing a Multidimensional Approach," *Journal of Change Management*, Vol. 12, No. 4 (2012), pp. 383–398.

14.   Roger C. Mayer, James H. Davis, and F. David Schoorman, "An Integrative Model of Organizational Trust," *Academy of Management of Review*, Vol. 20, No. 3 (1995), pp. 709–734.

15.   Aneil K. Misha, "Organizational Responses to Crisis: The Centrality of Trust," in Roderick Kramer and Tom Tyler (Eds.), *Trust in Organizations: Frontiers of Theory and Research* (Thousand Oaks, CA: SAGE, 1996), http://sk.sagepub.com.proxy.library.cornell.edu/books/trust-in-organizations/n13.xml, accessed June 25, 2017.

16.   Tony Simons, "The Made of Clay Report," WRFI Radio Show, April 9, 2017, http://mad eofclay.org/tony-simons/, accessed April 25, 2017.

17.   FIFA, "FIFA Code of Ethics," 2012 edition, https://resources.fifa.com/mm/document/affederation/administration/50/02/82/codeofethics_v211015_e_neutral.pdf, accessed May 31, 2017.

18.   Diana-Maria Tinjala, Lavinia Mirela Pantea, and Alexandru Buglea, "Business Ethics and Integrity. A Case Study on 300 U.S. Listed Companies," *Studia Universitatis Vasile Goldiş, Arad—Seria Ştiinţe Economice*, Vol. 25, No. 2 (2015), pp. 63–80.

19.   Deloitte, "Culture of Purpose—Building Business Confidence; Driving Growth," 2014 Core Beliefs & Culture Survey, https://www2.deloitte.com/content/dam/Deloitte/us/Documents/about-deloitte/us-leadership-2014-core-beliefs-culture-survey-040414.pdf, accessed May 31, 2017.

20.   Bruce Rogers, "Purpose Drives Profits and Confidence, According to Latest Study From Deloitte," *Forbes*, April 8, 2014, https://www.forbes.com/sites/brucerogers/2014/04/08/purpose-drives-profits-and-confidence-according-to-latest-study-from-deloitte/, accessed May 30, 2017.

21.   Hannes Leroy, Michael E. Palanski, and Tony Simons, "Authentic Leadership and Behavioral Integrity as Drivers of Follower Commitment and Performance," *Journal of Business Ethics*, Vol. 107, No. 3 (May 2012), pp. 255–264.

22.   Tony Simons, Hannes Leroy, Veroniek Collewaert, and Stijn Masschelein, "How Leader Alignment of Words and Deeds Affects Followers: A Meta-analysis of Behavioral Integrity Research," *Journal of Business Ethics*, Vol. 132, No. 4 (2015), pp. 832–844.

23.   Simons, *The Integrity Dividend*.

24. Margaret Cording, Jeffrey S. Harrison, Robert E. Hoskisson, and Karsten Jonsen, "Walking the Talk: A Multistakeholder Exploration of Organizational Authenticity, Employee Productivity, and Post-Merger Performance," *Academy of Management Perspectives*, Vol. 28, No. 1 (2014), pp. 38–56.

25. Rob Harris, "US Attorney General Reveals FIFA Corruption Probe Is Ongoing as First Trial Approaches," *The Independent*, January 14, 2017, http://www.independent.co.uk/sport/football/international/us-attorney-general-reveals-fifa-corruption-probe-is-ongoing-as-first-trial-approaches-a7527766.html, accessed May 30, 2017.

26. Edelman, "Executive Summary," Edelman company website, http://www.edelman.com/executive-summary/, accessed May 30, 2017.

27. Ibid.

28. "20 Years Inside the Mind of the CEO . . . What's Next?" PwC Global, https://www.pwc.com/gx/en/ceo-agenda/ceosurvey/2017/gx.html, accessed May 31, 2017.

29. Paul J. Zak, "The Neuroscience of Trust," *Harvard Business Review*, January/February 2017, https://hbr.org/2017/01/the-neuroscience-of-trust, accessed May 14, 2017.

30. Paul J. Zak, *Trust Factor* (New York: AMACOM, 2017), p. 5.

31. Kees van den Bos and E. Allan Lind, "Uncertainty Management by Means of Fairness Judgments," *Advances in Experimental Psychology*, Vol. 34 (2002), pp. 1–60.

32. Roger C. Mayer, James H. Davis, and F. David Schoorman, "An Integrative Model of Organizational Trust," *Academy of Management of Review*, Vol. 20, No. 3 (1995), pp. 709–734.

33. John Gottman, "On Trust and Betrayal," *Greater Good*, October 29, 2011, http://greatergood.berkeley.edu/article/item/john_gottman_on_trust_and_betrayal, accessed May 30, 2017.

34. Ibid.

35. Tony Simons, *The Integrity Dividend: Leading by the Power of Your Word* (San Francisco: Jossey-Bass, 2008), p. 74.

36. Andrew K. Schnackenberg and Edward C. Tomlinson, "Organizational Transparency: A New Perspective on Managing Trust in Organization–Stakeholder Relationships," *Journal of Management*, Vol. 42, No. 7 (2016), pp. 1784–1810.

37. Matt Rizzetta, "How FIFA Can Revive Its Brand Image," *CNBC*, June 4, 2015, http://www.cnbc.com/2015/06/04/how-fifa-can-revive-its-brand-image-commentary.html, accessed June 1, 2017.

38. Schnackenberg and Tomlinson, "Organizational Transparency."

39. Jeffrey A. Trachtenberg, "Time Inc. Plans to Lay Off Over 100 Workers," *Wall Street Journal*, August 3, 2016, https://www.wsj.com/articles/time-inc-plans-to-lay-off-over-100-workers-1470243305, accessed May 30, 2017.

40. See Hugh Rank's model in Charles U. Larson, *Persuasion: Reception and Responsibility, 10th edition* (Belmont, CA: Wadsworth/Thomson Learning, 2004).

41. Boudewign de Bruin, "Pledging Integrity: Oaths as Forms of Business Ethics Management," *Journal of Business Ethics*, Vol. 136, No. 1 (2016), pp. 23–42.

42. Robert B. Cialdini and Noah J. Goldstein, "The Science and Practice of Persuasion," *Cornell Hotel and Restaurant Administration Quarterly*, Vol. 43, No. 2 (2002), pp. 40–50.

43. Chipotle, "Food With Integrity," https://www.chipotle.com/food-with-integrity, accessed June 11, 2017.

44. Lydia Wheeler, "Critics Launch Campaign Attacking Chipotle," *The Hill*, September 4, 2015, http://thehill.com/regulation/252774-critics-launch-campaign-attacking-chipotle, accessed June 12, 2017.

45. John Kell, "Here's Why Your Local Chipotle Is Closed for Lunch Today," *Fortune*, February 8, 2016, http://fortune.com/2016/02/08/chipotle-food-safety-meeting/, accessed June 11, 2017.

46. Ibid.

47. Kim B. Serota and Timothy R. Levine, "A Few Prolific Liars: Variation in the Prevalence of Lying," *Journal of Language and Social Psychology*, Vol. 34, No. 2 (2014), pp. 138–157.

48. Rony Halevy, Shaul Shalvi, and Bruno Verschuere, "Being Honest About Dishonesty: Correlating Self-Reports and Actual Lying," *Human Communication Research*, Vol. 40, No. 1 (2014), pp. 54–72.

49. Tomas Chamorro-Premuzic, "How and Why We Lie at Work," *Harvard Business Review*, January 2, 2015, https://hbr.org/2015/01/how-and-why-we-lie-at-work, accessed May 30, 2017.

50. Patricia Cohen, "Downfall of ITT Technical Institutes Was a Long Time in the Making," *New York Times*, September 7, 2016, https://www.nytimes.com/2016/09/08/business/downfall-of-itt-technical-institutes-was-a-long-time-in-the-making.html, accessed May 30, 2017.

51. Elizabeth Olson, "Law Graduate Who Sued Her School Loses at Trial," *New York Times*, March 24, 2016, https://www.nytimes.com/2016/03/25/business/dealbook/law-graduate-who-sued-her-school-loses-at-trial.html, accessed May 30, 2017.

52. Shannon Achimalbe, "The Anna Alaburda Aftermath: The Self-Righteous Celebration and Thomas Jefferson School of Law's Empty Victory," *Above the Law*, March 30, 2016, http://abovethelaw.com/2016/03/the-anna-alaburda-aftermath-the-self-righteous-celebration-and-thomas-jefferson-school-of-laws-empty-victory/, accessed August 29, 2017.

53. Emma Court, "Reynolds Can't Call Its Cigarettes 'Natural' Anymore," *Market Watch*, March 6, 2017, http://www.marketwatch.com/story/reynolds-will-have-to-remove-natural-and-additive-free-from-natural-american-spirit-cigarettes-2017-03-02, accessed May 30, 2017.

54. The charges were made despite language already required on packaging by the Federal Trade Commission: "No additives in our tobacco does NOT mean a safer cigarette."

55. Madeline Kennedy, "Are 'natural' cigarette smokers being misled?" *Reuters*, January 20, 2017, http://www.reuters.com/article/us-health-tobacco-additives-idUSKBN1542J0, accessed June 11, 2017.

56. Paul Brownfield, "Nature's Cancer Sticks," *Bloomberg Businessweek*, November 14, 2016, https://www.bloomberg.com/features/2016-natural-american-spirit-cigarettes/, accessed May 30, 2017.

57. Jana, "The 'Green' Cigarette?" *Care2*, January 14, 2009, http://www.care2.com/greenliv ing/the-green-cigarette.html, accessed November 7, 2017.

58. Brownfield, "Nature's Cancer Sticks."

59. Ibid.

60. Ibid.

61. Warren Buffett, "Integrity," YouTube, March 26, 2017, https://www.youtube.com/watch?v=tpmY1aK3jP8, accessed June 11, 2017.

62. Margaret Heffernan, "How Warren Buffett Defines Integrity," *CBS MoneyWatch*, November 13, 2013, http://www.cbsnews.com/news/how-warren-buffett-defines-integrity/, accessed June 11, 2017.

63. Warren Buffett, Berkshire Hathaway annual letter, http://www.berkshirehathaway.com/letters/2016ltr.pdf, accessed May 15, 2017.

64. Rachael Levy, "A Hot Investing Startup Wrote an Open Letter to Donald Trump, and Is Setting the Stage for a Battle on Wall Street," *Business Insider*, December 5, 2016, http://www.businessinsider.com/betterments-wall-street-journal-donald-trump-ad-on-fiduciary-rule-2016-12, accessed May 30, 2017.

65. "FIFA Statement on Recent Media Coverage Regarding the 'Garcia Report,'" FIFA media release, June 27, 2017, http://www.fifa.com/governance/news/y=2017/m=6/news=fifa-statement-on-recent-media-coverage-regarding-the-garcia-report-2898791.html, accessed July 10, 2017.

66. Tony L. Simons, Ray Friedman, Leigh Ann Liu, and Judi McLean Parks, "Racial Differences in Sensitivity to Behavioral Integrity: Attitudinal Consequences, In-Group Effects, and 'Trickle Down' Among Black and Non-Black Employees," Cornell University, School of Hospitality Administration website, http://scholarship.sha.cornell.edu/articles/722, accessed July 26, 2017.

Chapter 6

1. Wells Fargo, "2015 Annual Report," https://www08.wellsfargomedia.com/assets/pdf/about/investor-relations/annual-reports/2015-annual-report.pdf, accessed June 13, 2017.

2. Michael P. Regan, "Eight Rhymes With Separate for Wells Fargo," *Bloomberg*, September 20, 2016, https://www.bloomberg.com/gadfly/articles/2016-09-20/eight-rhymes-with-separate-for-critics-of-wells-fargo, accessed June 13, 2017.

3. Court Filing, Superior Court of California, County of Los Angeles, "The People of the State of California vs. Wells Fargo & Company," Complaint for Equitable Relief and Civil Penalties, May 4, 2015, https://assets.bwbx.io/documents/users/iqjWHBFdfxIU/rPxi_pVaKx2Y/v0, accessed May 7, 2017.

4. Matt Levine, "Wells Fargo Opened a Couple Million Fake Accounts," *Bloomberg*, September 9, 2016, https://www.bloomberg.com/view/articles/2016-09-09/wells-fargo-opened-a-couple-million-fake-accounts, accessed June 13, 2016.

5. Paul Blake, "Timeline of the Wells Fargo Accounts Scandal," *ABC News*, November 3, 2016, http://abcnews.go.com/Business/timeline-wells-fargo-accounts-scandal/story?id=42231128, accessed June 22, 2017.

6. "The Wells Fargo Fake Account Scandal: A Timeline," *Forbes*, https://www.forbes.com/pictures/fkmm45eegei/eight-is-great/#45ca29963d6b, accessed June 22, 2017.

7. Dictionary.com, "Responsible," www.dictionary.com/browse/responsible, accessed July 27, 2017.

8. Dictionary.com, "Accountable," www.dictionary.com/browse/accountable, accessed July 27, 2017.

9. Tracy Skousen, "Responsibility vs. Accountability," Partners in Leadership, April 12, 2016, https://www.partnersinleadership.com/insights-publications/responsibility-vs-accountability/, accessed June 13, 2017.

10. The others are forgiveness, compassion, and integrity.

11. Mary Crossan, Gerard Seijts, and Jeffrey Gandz, *Developing Leadership Character* (New York: Routledge, 2016).

12. Fred Kiel, *Return on Character* (Boston: Harvard Business Review Press, 2015).

13. Michael Corkery and Stacy Cowley, "Wells Fargo Warned Workers Against Sham Accounts, but 'They Needed a Paycheck,'" *New York Times*, September 16, 2016, https://www.nytimes.com/2016/09/17/business/dealbook/wells-fargo-warned-workers-against-fake-accounts-but-they-needed-a-paycheck.html, accessed June 13, 2017.

14. Ibid.

15. Ibid.

16. "Wells Fargo CEO John Stumpf Talks With CNBC's Cramer: 'I'm accountable,'" *CNBC*, September 18, 2016, http://www.cnbc.com/2016/09/18/wells-fargo-ceo-john-stumpf-talks-with-cnbcs-cramer-im-accountable.html, accessed June 13, 2017.

17. Wilfred Frost and Dawn Giel, "Wells Fargo Board Slams Former CEO Stumpf and Tolstedt, Claws Back $75million," *CNBC*, April 10, 2017, http://www.cnbc.com/2017/04/10/wells-fargo-board-slams-stumpf-and-tolstedt-claws-back-millions.html, accessed June 13, 2017.

18. Corkery and Cowley, "Wells Fargo Warned Workers."

19. Max Whittaker, "Voices From Wells Fargo: 'I Thought I Was Having a Heart Attack,'" *CNBC*, October 20, 2016, https://www.nytimes.com/2016/10/21/business/dealbook/voices-from-wells-fargo-i-thought-i-was-having-a-heart-attack.html, accessed June 13, 2017.

20. "Wells Fargo CEO John Stumpf."

21. "Unauthorized Wells Fargo Accounts," Senate Banking Committee, September 20, 2016, C-SPAN video, https://www.c-span.org/video/?415547-1/ceo-john-stumpf-testifies-unauthorized-wells-fargo-accounts, accessed May 9, 2017.

22. Stephen Cohen, "Promoting Ethical Judgment in an Organisational Context," *Journal of Business Ethics*, Vol. 117, No. 3 (2013), pp. 513–523.

23. William Bruce Cameron, *Informal Sociology: A Casual Introduction to Sociological Thinking* (New York: Random House, New York, 1963), p. 13. *Note:* A variation of this quote is sometimes attributed to Albert Einstein. See quoteinvestigator.com/2010/05/26/everything-counts-einstein, accessed July 20, 2017.

24. Cohen, "Promoting Ethical Judgment."

25. Ibid.

26. Ibid.

27. William S. Laufer, "Social Accountability and Corporate Greenwashing," *Journal of Business Ethics*, Vol. 43, No. 3 (2003), pp. 253–261.

28. Ibid.

29. Danielle Ivory, "Federal Auditor Finds Broad Failure at N.H.T.S.A.," *New York Times*, June 19, 2015, https://www.nytimes.com/2015/06/20/business/federal-auditor-finds-broad-failures-at-nhtsa.html, accessed June 13, 2017.

30. Jennifer Jones, "Many Employees Seen Trying to 'Pass the Buck,'" American Management Association website, June 27, 2013, http://www.amanet.org/news/8636.aspx, accessed June 13, 2017.

31. Michele J. Gelfand, Beng-Chong Lim, and Jana L. Raver, "Culture and Accountability in Organizations: Variations in Forms of Social Control Across Cultures," *Human Resource Management Review*, Vol. 14, No. 1 (2004), pp. 135–160.

32. Robert Steinbauer, Robert W. Renn, Robert R. Taylor, and Phil K. Njoroge, "Ethical Leadership and Followers' Moral Judgment: The Role of Followers' Perceived Accountability and Self-Leadership," *Journal of Business Ethics*, Vol. 120, No. 3 (2014), pp. 381–392.

33. Randy Pennington, "Building a Culture of Accountability," *Society for Human Resource Management*, September 1, 2015, https://www.shrm.org/hr-today/news/hr-magazine/pages/0915-building-an-accountable-culture.aspx, accessed June 14, 2017.

34. Melissa Burden, "GM CEO Barra: 'You Can't Fake Culture,'" *Detroit News*, May 4, 2015, http://www.detroitnews.com/story/business/autos/general-motors/2015/05/04/gm-ceo-barra-fake-culture/26900825/, accessed June 14, 2017.

35. Rachel Feintzeigh, "The Never-Ending Performance Review: Companies Are Transitioning to More Frequent Evaluations," *Wall Street Journal*, May 9, 2017, https://www.wsj.com/articles/the-never-ending-performance-review-1494322200, accessed May 11, 2017.

36. Feintzeigh, "The Never-Ending Performance Review."

37. Craig Redding, "Increasing Accountability," *Organization Development Journal*, Vol. 22, No. 1 (2004), pp. 56–66.

38. Redding, "Increasing Accountability."

39. Fiona Lee, Christopher Peterson, and Larissa Z. Tiedens, "Mea Culpa: Predicting Stock Prices From Organizational Attributions," *Personality and Social Psychology Bulletin*, Vol. 30, No. 12 (2004), pp. 1636–1649.

40. Andrew K. Schnackenberg and Edward C. Tomlinson, "Organizational Transparency: A New Perspective on Managing Trust in Organization-Stakeholder Relationships," *Journal of Management*, Vol. 42, No. 7 (2016), pp. 1784–1810.

41. Fred Kiel, *Return on Character* (Boston: Harvard Business Review Press, 2015).

42. Vincent R. Waldron and Douglas L. Kelley, *Communicating Forgiveness* (Thousand Oaks, CA: SAGE, 2008).

43. Kim Cameron and Arran Caza, "Organizational and Leadership Virtues in the Role of Forgiveness," *Journal of Leadership and Organizational Studies*, Vol. 9, No. 1 (2002), pp. 33–48.

44. Ibid.

45. Kim Cameron, David Bright, and Arran Caza, "Exploring the Relationship Between Organizational Virtues and Performance," *American Behavioral Scientist*, Vol. 47, No. 6 (2004), pp. 1–24.

46. Shann R. Ferch and Matthew M. Mitchell, "Intentional Forgiveness in Relational Leadership: A Technique for Enhancing Effective Leadership," *Journal of Leadership Studies*, Vol. 7, No. 4 (2001), p. 70.

47. Jen Wieczner, "How Wells Fargo's Carrie Tolstedt Went From Fortune Most Powerful Woman to Villain," *Fortune*, April 10, 2017, http://fortune.com/2017/04/10/wells-fargo-carrie-tolstedt-clawback-net-worth-fortune-mpw, accessed June 13, 2017.

48. Lucinda Shen, "Here's How Much Wells Fargo CEO John Stumpf Is Getting to Leave the Bank," *Fortune*, October 13, 2016, http://fortune.com/2016/10/13/wells-fargo-ceo-john-stumpfs-career-ends-with-133-million-payday/, accessed June 13, 2017.

49.   Dan Freed, Lauren Tara LaCapra, and Chizu Nomiyama, "Wells Fargo pauses annual meeting due to unruly shareholder," *Reuters*, April 25, 2017, http://www .reuters.com/article/us-wells-fargo-accounts-meeting-sharehol-idUSKBN17R202, accessed June 13, 2017.

50.   Jeff Cox, "A Nun Was Interrupted by a Shareholder at the Rowdy Wells Fargo Annual Meeting," *CNBC*, April 25, 2017, http://www.cnbc.com/2017/04/25/second-rowdy-shareholder-disrupts-wells-fargo-annual-meeting.html, accessed June 13, 2017.

51.   Wells Fargo, "Wells Fargo Announces Preliminary Voting Results of 2017 Annual   Meeting,"   https://www.wellsfargo.com/about/press/2017/shareholders-meeting_0425, accessed June 13, 2017.

52.   Stacy Cowley and Michael Corkey, "A Showdown Over Wells Fargo's Board of Directors Looms," *New York Times*, DealBook, April 24, 2017, https://www .nytimes.com/2017/04/24/business/dealbook/wells-fargo-board-election.html, accessed May 7, 2017.

53.   Gretchen Morgenson, "Meet the Shareholders? Not at These Shareholder Meetings," *New York Times*, March 31, 2017, https://www.nytimes.com/2017/03/31/business/corporate-virtual-shareholder-meetings.html, accessed June 13, 2017.

54.   Jeffrey A. Sonnenfeld, "What Makes Great Boards Great," *Harvard Business Review*, September 2002, https://hbr.org/2002/09/what-makes-great-boards-great, accessed June 12, 2017.

55.   Fun fact: Jeffrey Sonnenfeld called the Wells Fargo Banking Committee meetings "political theater" and said Stumpf was "completely unprepared." Yale School of Management, Chief Executive School of Leadership, September 21, 2016, http://som.yale.edu/news/2016/09/stumpf-completely-unprepared-sonnenfeld,   accessed July 20, 2017.

56.   Christopher Heine, "What Consumers Really Think About YouTube's Offensive Content Problem and Its Advertisers," *Adweek*, March 28, 2017, http://www .adweek.com/digital/what-consumers-really-think-about-youtubes-offensive-content-problem-and-its-advertisers/, accessed June 21, 2017.

57.   "YouTube Highlights Problems With Digital Advertising," *The Economist*, March 30, 2017, www.economist.com/news/business/21719840-big-brands-protest-about-ads-next-offensive-content-youtube-highlights-problems-digital, accessed June 15, 2017.

58.   Daisuke Wakabayashi and Sapna Maheshwari, "YouTube Advertiser Exodus Highlights Perils of Online Ads," *New York Times*, March 23, 2017, https://www .nytimes.com/2017/03/23/business/media/youtube-advertisers-offensive-content.html, accessed June 15, 2017.

59.   Kent Walker, "Four Steps We're Taking Today to Fight Terrorism Online," Google blog, June 18, 2017, https://blog.google/topics/google-europe/four-steps-were-taking-today-fight-online-terror/, accessed June 23, 2017.

60.   Farhad Manjoo, "Social Insecurity," *New York Times Magazine*, April 30, 2017.

61.   Mark Zuckerberg, "Community Standards and Reporting," April 18, 2017, Facebook website, https://newsroom.fb.com/news/h/community-standards-and-reporting, accessed May 9, 2017.

62.   Ibid.

63.   Ann Marsh, "Wells May Be Forced to Welcome Back Another Whistleblower," *American Banker*, April 5, 2017, https://www.americanbanker.com/news/feds-may-order-wells-fargo-to-rehire-a-second-whistleblower, accessed June 15, 2017.

64.   Ibid.

65.   Vicky Nguyen, Liz Wagner, and Felipe Escamilla, "OSHA Dismisses Majority of Whistleblower Cases Agency Investigates," NBC Bay Area, May 20, 2017, http://www.nbcbayarea.com/news/local/OSHA-Dismisses-Majority-of-Whistleblower-Cases-Agency-Investigates-332258162.html, accessed June 15, 2017.

66.   Ann Marsh, "Fired Federal Investigators Supported Adviser's Claim Against JPMorgan," *Financial Planning*, December 9, 2016, https://www.financial-planning.com/news/ex-federal-investigators-supported-rias-whistleblower-claim-against-jpmorgan, accessed June 15, 2017.

67.   Nguyen et al., "OSHA Dismisses Majority."

68.   Hyunjoo Jin, "Blowing the Whistle in South Korea: Hyundai Man Takes on Chaebol Culture," *Reuters*, May 15, 2017, http://www.reuters.com/article/us-hyundai-whistleblower-idUSKCN18B0J5, accessed June 22, 2017.

69.   Antoine Gara, "Wells Fargo Withholds $32 Million in Bonuses Due to Fake Account Scandal," *Forbes*, March 1, 2017, https://www.forbes.com/sites/antoinegara/2017/03/01/wells-fargo-withholds-32-million-in-bonuses-due-to-fake-account-scandal/#1a57f6e91f01, accessed June 21, 2017.

70.   Gretchen Morgenson, "Wells Fargo Needs to Make a Clean Break With the Past," *New York Times*, Fair Game, October 14, 2016, https://www.nytimes.com/2016/10/16/business/wells-fargo-needs-to-make-a-clean-break-with-the-past.html, accessed June 21, 2017.

71.   Jim Kane and Bill Chappell, "United Airlines Settles With Passenger Dragged From Plane," *NPR WSKG Public Radio*, April 27, 2017, http://www.npr.org/sections/thetwo-way/2017/04/27/525845287/united-airlines-will-now-pay-voluntarily-bumped-passengers-up-to-10-000, accessed June 16, 2017.

72.   Stacy Cowley, "Wells Fargo Review Finds 1.4 Million More Suspect Accounts," *New York Times*, DealBook, August 31, 2017, https://www.nytimes.com/2017/08/31/business/dealbook/wells-fargo-accounts.html, accessed September 4, 2017.

73.   "The Oz Principle® Individual Accountability Quiz," Partners in Leadership, https://info.partnersinleadership.com/individual-accountability-quiz, accessed July 26, 2017.

Chapter 7

1.   U.S. Department of Transportation, "DOT Bans All Samsung Galaxy Note7 Phones from Airplanes," October 14, 2016, https://www.transportation.gov/briefing-room/dot-bans-all-samsung-galaxy-note7-phones-airplanes, accessed June 16, 2017.

2.   Paul Mozur and Su-Hyun Lee, "Samsung to Recall 2.5 Million Galaxy Note 7s Over Battery Fire," *New York Times*, September 2, 2016, https://www.nytimes.com/2016/09/03/business/samsung-galaxy-note-battery.html, accessed June 16, 2017.

3.   Mark Sullivan, "Samsung Is Working Hard to Humanize Its Image," *Fast Company*, May 25, 2015, https://www.fastcompany.com/3059283/samsung-is-working-hard-to-humanize-its-image, accessed June 16, 2017.

4.   Mozur and Lee, "Samsung to Recall 2.5 Million."

5. Mark Sullivan, "How Did Samsung Botch the Galaxy Note 7 Crisis? It's a Failure of Leadership," *Fast Company*, October 12, 2016, https://www.fastcompany .com/3064569/how-did-samsung-botch-the-galaxy-note-7-crisis-its-a-failure-of-leadership, accessed June 16, 2017.

6. MS, "Samsung: About Half of Galaxy Note 7 Phones in the U.S. Have Been Replaced," *Fast Company*, September 23, 2016, https://news.fastcompany.com/samsung-about-half-of-galaxy-note-7-phones-in-the-us-have-been-replaced-4020065, accessed June 16, 2017.

7. "Galaxy Note 7: Timeline of Samsung's Phones Woes," *BBC News*, October 11, 2016, http://www.bbc.com/news/technology-37615496, accessed July 5, 2017.

8. *Note:* Not everyone agrees that stopping production would have been the best move, but delaying and replacing phones with more damaged devices certainly wasn't the best decision either.

9. Arjun Kharpal, "Samsung Permanently Halts Production of Its Galaxy Note 7; $18 Billion Wiped Off Shares," *CNBC*, October 11, 2016, http://www.cnbc .com/2016/10/11/samsung-permanently-halts-production-of-its-galaxy-note-7-18-billion-wiped-off-shares.html, accessed June 16, 2017.

10. Sullivan, "How Did Samsung Botch the Galaxy Note 7 Crisis?"

11. Ibid.

12. Monica C. Worline, "Courage in Organizations: An Integrative Review of the 'Difficult Virtue,'" in Gretchen M. Spreitzer and Kim S. Cameron (Eds.), *The Oxford Handbook of Positive Organizational Scholarship* (Oxford University Press, 2011).

13. Rushworth M. Kidder, *Moral Courage* (New York: HarperCollins, 2005), p. 7.

14. Mary M. Crossan et al., "Toward a Framework of Leader Character in Organizations," *Journal of Management Studies*, January 2017, doi: 10.1111/joms.12254.

15. Mary Crossan, Gerard Seijts, and Jeffrey Gandz, *Developing Leadership Character* (New York: Routledge, 2016).

16. Angela L. Duckworth, Christopher Peterson, Michael D. Matthews, and Dennis R. Kelly, "Grit: Perseverance and Passion for Long-Term Goals," *Journal of Personality and Social Psychology*, Vol. 92, No. 6 (2007), pp. 1087–1101.

17. Dictionary.com, "Encourage," http://www.dictionary.com/browse/encourage, accessed June 16, 2017.

18. Dictionary.com, "Discourage," http://www.dictionary.com/browse/discourage, accessed June 16, 2017.

19. Duckworth et al., "Grit."

20. Sean T. Hannah, Bruce J. Avolio, and Fred O. Walumbwa, "Relationships Between Authentic Leadership, Moral Courage, and Ethical and Pro-Social Behaviors," *Business Ethics Quarterly*, Vol. 21, No. 4 (October 2011), pp. 555–578.

21. Michael E. Palanski, Kristin L. Cullen, William A. Gentry, and Chelsea M. Nichols, "Virtuous Leadership: Exploring the Effects of Leader Courage and Behavioral Integrity on Leader Performance and Image," *Journal of Business Ethics* (2015), pp. 297–310.

22. Jack Mahoney, "Editorial Adieu: Cultivating Moral Course in Business," *Business Ethics: A European Review*, Vol. 7, No. 4, October 1998, pp. 188–198.

23. Kidder, *Moral Courage*.

24. Albert O. Hirschman, Exit, *Voice, and Loyalty: Responses to Decline in Firms, Organizations, and States* (Cambridge, MA: Harvard University Press, 1970).

25. Samsung might have learned a lesson from the classic crisis communication situation, Tylenol. See, for example, W. Timothy Coombs, "Impact of Past Crises on Current Crisis Communication: Insights From Situational Crisis Communication Theory," *Journal of Business Communication*, Vol. 41, No. 3 (2004), pp. 265–289.

26. More recently, Kevin Spacey has been accused of sexual assault and harassment, and Netflix has stopped working with him.

27. Huffpost, "Robin Wright Opens Up About Being Paid Less Than Kevin Spacey," YouTube, May 19. 2016, https://www.youtube.com/watch?v=TPVvoPh0 wcM, accessed June 21, 2017.

28. Laura Bradley, "Robin Wright Fought for Equal Pay on House of Cards," *Vanity Fair*, May 18, 2016, http://www.vanityfair.com/hollywood/2016/05/robin-wright-fought-for-equal-pay-on-house-of-cards, accessed June 21, 2017.

29. Stella Young, "I'm Not Your Inspiration, Thank You Very Much," TED Talk, June 9, 2014, https://www.youtube.com/watch?v=8K9Gg164Bsw, accessed June 21, 2017.

30. Ibid.

31. For further distinctions, see Jaak Panksepp, "Affective Consciousness: Core Emotional Feelings in Animals and Humans," *Consciousness and Cognition*, Vol. 14 (2005), pp. 30–80.

32. Brené Brown, "Listening to Shame," TED Talk, March 2012, https://www.ted .com/talks/brene_brown_listening_to_shame#t-292275, accessed June 16, 2017.

33. Brené Brown, "Choose Courage," Brené Brown website, August 14, 2014, http://brenebrown.com/2014/08/14/choose-courage/, accessed June 21, 2017.

34. Amy Newman, "How to Feel Confident for a Presentation . . . and Overcome Speech Anxiety," speaking.amynewman.com.

35. Karen Kangas Dwyer, "iConquer Speech Anxiety: A Workbook to Help You Overcome Your Nervousness About Public Speaking," KLD Publications, 2012. Also download a worksheet at http://bit.ly/2pZKgTx.

36. Alison Wood Brooks, "Get Excited: Reappraising Pre-performance Anxiety as Excitement," *Journal of Experimental Psychology*, Vol. 143, No. 3 (2015), pp. 1144–1158.

37. Benjamin Snyder, "Mark Zuckerberg Takes Facebook Workers to Task Over 'All Lives Matter' Graffiti," *Fortune*, February 25, 2016, http://fortune .com/2016/02/25/mark-zuckerberg-black-lives-matter/, accessed June 21, 2017.

38. Michael Nunez, "Mark Zuckerberg Asks Racist Facebook Employees to Stop Crossing Out Black Lives Matter Slogans," *Gizmodo*, February 25, 2016, http://gizmodo .com/mark-zuckerberg-asks-racist-facebook-employees-to-stop-1761272768, accessed June 21, 2017.

39. Rafi Letzter, "A Huge Group of Facebook Employees Took a Stand on the Black Lives Matter Movement," March 6, 2016, *Business Insider*, http://www.businessinsider .com/facebook-stands-up-for-blacklivesmatter-2016-3, accessed November 9, 2017.

40. Sapna Maheshwari, "Samsung's Response to Galaxy Note 7 Crisis Draws Criticism," *New York Times*, October 11, 2016, https://www.nytimes.com/2016/10/12/ business/media/samsungs-passive-response-to-note-7s-overheating-problem-draws-criticism.html, accessed June 22, 2017.

41. Yvonne Maher, "Lessons From Samsung's PR Fiasco: 6 Tips to Protect Your Reputation," *PR News*, October 26, 2016, http://www.prnewsonline.com/samsung-maher, accessed June 22, 2017.

42. Samsung Mobile USA, "#GalaxyNote7 Update . . . ," Facebook post, November 10, 2016, https://www.facebook.com/SamsungMobileUSA/photos/a .59297021785.81337.7224956785/10153841541076786, accessed June 22, 2017.

43. Maher, "Lessons From Samsung's PR Fiasco."

44. Karina Martin, "2,700 GM Venezuelan Employees Fired by Text Message After Government Takeover," *PanamPost*, April 25, 2017, https://panampost.com/ karina-martin/2017/04/25/2700-gm-venezuelan-employees-fired-by-text-message-after-government-takeover/, accessed June 22, 2017.

45. Angela M. Legg and Kate Sweeny, "Do You Want the Good News or the Bad News First? The Nature and Consequences of News Order Preferences," *Personality and Social Psychology Bulletin*, Vol. 40, No. 3 (2014), pp. 279–288.

46. Robert Bies, "The Delivery of Bad News in Organizations: A Framework for Analysis," *Journal of Management*, Vol. 39, No. 1 (2013), pp. 136–162.

47. Rana Tassabehji and Maria Vakola, "Business Email: The Killer Impact," *Communications of the ACM*, Vol. 48, No. 11 (November 2005), pp. 64–70.

48. Graham L. Bradley and Amanda C. Campbell, "Managing Difficult Workplace Conversations: Goals, Strategies, and Outcomes," *International Journal of Business Communication*, Vol. 53, No. 4 (2016), pp. 443–464.

49. Kerry Patterson, Joseph Grenny, Ron McMillan, and Al Switzler, *Crucial Conversations* (New York: McGraw-Hill, 2002).

50. "India's Turn Round Queen," *The Economist*, November 27, 2003, http:// www.economist.com/node/2245970, accessed June 22, 2017.

51. BW Online Bureau, "Courage Under Fire," *Business World*, November 2014, http://businessworld.in/article/Courage-Under-Fire/08-11-2014-68445/, accessed June 22, 2017.

52. "India's Turn Round Queen."

53. Cristina Alesci, "Xerox's Ursula Burns: Business Is Made for Men," *CNN Tech*, February 9, 2017, http://money.cnn.com/2017/02/03/technology/american-dream-ursula-burns/, accessed June 22, 2017.

54. Ibid.

55. Ibid.

56. Kim Scott, *Radical Candor: Be a Kick-Ass Boss Without Losing Your Humanity* (New York: St. Martin's Press, 2017), p. 40.

57. Scott, *Radical Candor*.

58. Ibid.

59. Melissa Burden, "GM CEO Barra: 'You Can't Fake Culture,'" *Detroit News*, May 4, 2015, http://www.detroitnews.com/story/business/autos/general-motors/2015/05/04/gm-ceo-barra-fake-culture/26900825/, accessed June 22, 2017.

60. Tiffany Gallicano, "Radical Transparency," *Public Relations Tactics*, September 1, 2015, http://apps.prsa.org/Intelligence/Tactics/Articles/view/11200/1115/Radical_ Transparency_Examining_Ghostwriting_and_So#.WXtboaL58Uo, accessed July 28, 2017.

61. Clive Thompson, "The See-Through CEO," *Wired*, April 1, 2017, https://www .wired.com/2007/04/wired40-ceo/, accessed June 22, 2017.

62. Ryan Smith and Golnax Tabibnia, "Why Radical Transparency Is Good Business," *Harvard Business Review*, October 11, 2012, https://hbr.org/2012/10/why-radical-transparency-is-good-business, accessed June 22, 2017.

63. Bridgewater, Inc., "Welcome," Bridgewater website, https://www.bridgewater.com/, accessed June 22, 2017.

64. Alexandra Stevenson and Matthew Goldstein, "Bridgewater's Ray Dalio Spreads His Gospel of 'Radical Transparency,'" *New York Times*, September 8, 2017, https://www.nytimes.com/2017/09/08/business/dealbook/bridgewaters-ray-dalio-spreads-his-gospel-of-radical-transparency.html, accessed September 16, 2017.

65. Worline, "Courage in Organizations."

66. Handwritten punctuation and repetition errors corrected.

67. Gavin Long, suicide note retrieved from car, July 17, 2016, released on June 30, 2017, https://www.scribd.com/document/352613999/Gavin-Long-Suicide-Note#fullscreen&from_embed, accessed July 8, 2017.

68. Starbucks, "Message From Howard Schultz to Starbucks Partners: Living Our Values in Uncertain Times," January 29, 2017, https://news.starbucks.com/news/living-our-values-in-uncertain-times, accessed June 21, 2017.

69. Douglas Ernst, "Starbucks Investor Booed After Grilling CEO on Politics, Refugee Hiring Process," *Washington Times*, March 24, 2017, http://www.washingtontimes.com/news/2017/mar/24/starbucks-investor-booed-after-grilling-ceo-howard/, accessed June 22, 2017.

70. Ibid.

71. Lisa Baertlein, "Starbucks CEO's Refugee Comments Sour Customer Views of Chain: Survey," March 9, 2017, http://www.reuters.com/article/us-starbucks-refugee-idUSKBN16H04P, accessed June 22, 2017.

72. Kate Taylor, "People Are Boycotting Starbucks After CEO Announces Plan to Hire Thousands of Refugees," *Business Insider,* January 30, 2017, http://www.businessinsider.com/starbucks-boycott-after-ceos-refugee-support-2017-1, accessed June 22, 2017.

73. Agence France-Presse, "Samsung to Overtake Apple With Record Profits Despite Scandals," *The Telegraph*, July 27, 2017, http://www.telegraph.co.uk/technology/2017/07/27/samsung-overtake-apple-record-profits-despite-scandals/, accessed July 27, 2017.

74. Arthur Ashe, http://www.arthurashe.org/in-his-words.html, accessed August 2, 2017.

Chapter 8

1. Dave Lee, "Uber Fires 20 Staff After Harassment Investigation," *BBC Business*, June 7, 2017, http://www.bbc.com/news/business-40179472, accessed June 28, 2017.

2. Dan Levine, "Uber Drivers Remain Independent Contractors as Lawsuit Settled," *Reuters*, April 22, 2016, http://www.reuters.com/article/us-uber-tech-drivers-settlement-idUSKCN0XJ07H, accessed June 28, 2017.

3. Mike Isaac, "Uber's CEO Plays With Fire," *New York Times*, April 23, 2017, https://www.nytimes.com/2017/04/23/technology/travis-kalanick-pushes-uber-and-himself-to-the-precipice.html, accessed June 28, 2017.

4. Ibid.

5. Tracey Lien, "Uber CEO's Right-Hand Man, Emil Michael, Is Out. It's Unclear If He Was Fired or Quit," *Los Angeles Times*, June 12, 2017, http://www.latimes.com/business/technology/la-fi-hy-uber-20170612-story.html, accessed November 9, 2017.

6. Ben Smith, "Uber Executive Suggests Digging Up Dirt on Journalists," *BuzzFeed*, November 17, 2014, https://www.buzzfeed.com/bensmith/uber-executive-suggests-digging-up-dirt-on-journalists?utm_term=.np0YvnBxo#.yaDzwaO1Q, accessed June 28, 2017.

7. Mark Moore, "Uber Slammed for Surge Pricing During London Attacks," *New York Post*, June 4, 2017, http://nypost.com/2017/06/04/uber-slammed-for-surge-pricing-during-london-attacks, accessed June 28, 2017.

8. Isaac, "Uber's CEO Plays With Fire."

9. Julia Carrie Wong and Olivia Solon, "Uber Accused of 'Calculated Theft' of Google's Self-Driving Car Technology," *The Guardian*, February 23, 2017, https://www.theguardian.com/technology/2017/feb/23/alphabet-sues-uber-self-driving-cars-technology-waymo-otto, accessed June 28, 2017.

10. Isaac, "Uber's CEO Plays With Fire."

11. Levine, "Uber Drivers Remain Independent Contractors."

12. Dave Lee, "Uber to Pay $20m to 'Misled' Drivers," *BBC News*, January 20, 2017, http://www.bbc.com/news/technology-38686787, accessed June 28, 2017.

13. Julia Carrie Wong, "Uber CEO Travis Kalanick Caught on Video Arguing With Driver About Fares," *The Guardian*, March 1, 2017, https://www.theguardian.com/technology/2017/feb/28/uber-ceo-travis-kalanick-driver-argument-video-fare-prices, accessed June 28, 2017.

14. Mike Isaac, "Inside Travis Kalanick's Resignation as Uber's C.E.O.," *New York Times*, June 21, 2017, https://www.nytimes.com/2017/06/21/technology/uber-travis-kalanick-final-hours.html, accessed November 9, 2017.

15. Mike Isaac, "Uber Founder Travis Kalanick Resigns as C.E.O.," *New York Times*, June 21, 2017, https://www.nytimes.com/2017/06/21/technology/uber-ceo-travis-kalanick.html, accessed November 9, 2017.

16. Although Kalanick resigned as CEO, he remains on the board of directors.

17. Jorge L. A. Garcia, "Being Unimpressed With Ourselves: Reconceiving Humility," *Philosophia*, Vol. 34 (2006), pp. 419–424.

18. June P. Tangney, "Humility," in Shane J. Lopez and C. R. Snyder (Eds.), *The Oxford Handbook of Positive Psychology, 2nd edition* (2009), http://www.oxfordhandbooks.com/view/10.1093/oxfordhb/9780195187243.001.0001/oxfordhb-9780195187243.

19. Mary Crossan, Gerard Seijts, and Jeffrey Gandz, *Developing Leadership Character* (New York: Routledge, 2016), p. 81.

20. Brené Brown, *Daring Greatly: How the Courage to Be Vulnerable Transforms the Way We Live, Love, Parent and Lead* (New York: Avery, 2015), p. 22.

21. Daryl R. Van Tongeren, Don E. Davis, and Joshua N. Hook, "Social Benefits of Humility: Initiating and Maintaining Romantic Relationships," *Journal of Positive Psychology*, Vol. 9, No. 4 (2014), pp. 313–321.

22. Bradley P. Owens, Michael D. Johnson, and Terence R. Mitchell, "Expressed Humility in Organizations: Implications for Performance, Teams, and Leadership," *Organization Science*, Vol. 24, No. 5 (2013), pp. 1517–1538.

23. Mary Crossan, Gerard Seijts, and Jeffrey Gandz, *Developing Leadership Character* (New York: Routledge, 2016), p. 27.

24.   Bradley P. Owens, Wade C. Rowatt, and Alan L. Wilkins, "Exploring the Relevance and Implications of Humility in Organizations," in Gretchen M. Spreitzer and Kim S. Cameron (Eds.), *The Oxford Handbook of Positive Organizational Scholarship* (Oxford University Press, 2011).

25.   Bradley P. Owens, Michael D. Johnson, and Terence R. Mitchell, "Expressed Humility in Organizations: Implications for Performance, Teams, and Leadership," *Organization Science*, Vol. 24, No. 5 (2013), pp. 1517–1538.

26.   Arménio Rego et al., "Leader Humility and Team Performance: Exploring the Mediating Mechanisms of Team PsyCap and Task Allocation Effectiveness," *Journal of Management* (January 2017), http://journals.sagepub.com/doi/abs/10.1177/0149206316688941, accessed November 9, 2017.

27.   Susan J. Fowler, "Reflecting on One Very, Very Strange Year at Uber," Susan J. Fowler blog, February 19, 2017, https://www.susanjfowler.com/blog/2017/2/19/reflecting-on-one-very-strange-year-at-uber, accessed November 9, 2017.

28.   Kia Kokalitcheva, "Uber CEO Responds to Claims of Workplace Sexism," *Axios*, February 19, 2017, https://www.axios.com/uber-ceo-responds-to-claims-of-workplace-sexism-2272950757.html, accessed June 28, 2017.

29.   Eric Newcomer, "Uber Fires More Than 20 Employees in Harassment Probe," *Bloomberg Technology*, June 6, 2017, https://www.bloomberg.com/news/articles/2017-06-06/uber-said-to-fire-more-than-20-employees-in-harassment-probe, accessed June 28, 2017.

30.   Kara Swisher and Johana Bhuiyan, "In His 2013 'Miami Letter,' Uber CEO Kalanick Advised Employees on Sex Rules for a Company Celebration," *CNBC*, June 8, 2017, http://www.cnbc.com/2017/06/08/in-his-2013-miami-letter-uber-ceo-kalanick-advised-employees-on-sex-rules-for-a-company-celebration.html, accessed June 28, 2017.

31.   Kerry Flynn, "From 'Boober' to #DeleteUber, the 12 Times Uber Disgusted All of Us," *Mashable*, February 21, 2017, http://mashable.com/2017/02/21/uber-disgusting-examples/#liD9Lkrymmq0, accessed June 28, 2017.

32.   Heather Somerville, "Uber President Jeff Jones Quits, Deepening Turmoil," *Reuters*, March 20, 2017, http://www.reuters.com/article/us-uber-jeffjones-idUSKBN16Q0X3, accessed June 28, 2017.

33.   Travid Kalanick, "A Profound Apology," Uber Newsroom, February 28, 2017, https://newsroom.uber.com/a-profound-apology/, accessed July 7, 2017.

34.   Jim Collins, "Level 5 Leadership: The Triumph of Humility and Fierce Resolve," *Harvard Business Review*, July/August 2005, https://hbr.org/2005/07/level-5-leadership-the-triumph-of-humility-and-fierce-resolve, accessed June 28, 2017.

35.   *Good to Great* received criticism because some of the companies Collins research eventually closed. See, for example, "*Good to Great* Is a Flawed Book," Young Money blog, April 21, 2015, http://y0ungmoney.blogspot.com/2015/04/good-to-great-is-flawed-book.html, accessed July 12, 2017.

36.   Jim Collins, "Level 5 Leadership: The Triumph of Humility and Fierce Resolve," *Harvard Business Review*, July/August 2005, https://hbr.org/2005/07/level-5-leadership-the-triumph-of-humility-and-fierce-resolve, accessed June 28, 2017.

37.   Bradley Honan, "What Is CEO Reputation Premium, and Why Does It Matter for Your Organization?" KRC Research, http://www.krcresearch.com/what-is-ceo-reputation-premium-and-why-does-it-matter-for-your-organization/, accessed June 28, 2017.

38.   Online Etymology Dictionary, "Humility," http://www.etymonline.com/index.php?allowed_in_frame=0&search=humility, accessed June 28, 2017.

39.   Eric Clay, email, July 8, 2017. Clay also says, "In religious teachings, humility is 'rightsizing the self.' We aren't so big that we take advantage of others, and we aren't so small that we're taken advantage of. Both are considered sins."

40.   Karl Albrecht, "The Paradoxical Power of Humility," *Psychology Today*, January 8, 2015, https://www.psychologytoday.com/blog/brainsnacks/201501/the-paradoxical-power-humility, accessed June 29, 2017.

41.   David Brooks, *The Road to Character* (New York: Random House, 2015), pp. 249–251.

42.   For an interesting take, see Fareed Zakaria, "The Try-Hard Generation," *The Atlantic*, June 10, 2015, https://www.theatlantic.com/education/archive/2015/06/in-defense-of-a-try-hard-generation/394535, accessed July 4, 2017.

43.   TMZ, "Reese Witherspoon Arrest Video—Crazier Than You Thought!" YouTube, May 2, 2013, https://www.youtube.com/watch?v=g9fwe_NEerE, accessed June 29, 2017.

44.   Berkeley Lovelace Jr., "Cramer on 'Arrogant' Snap CEO Spiegel: Take My Advice, 'Humility Is a Fabulous Thing," *CNBC*, May 11, 2017, http://www.cnbc.com/2017/05/11/cramer-on-snap-ceo-spiegel-humility-is-a-fabulous-thing.html, accessed June 28, 2017.

45.   Ibid.

46.   Kevin Roose, "As Uber Stumbles, Lyft Sees an Opening, and Bites Its Tongue," *New York Times*, June 27, 2017, https://www.nytimes.com/2017/06/27/business/lyft-uber-john-zimmer.html, accessed June 29, 2017.

47.   Ibid.

48.   Adam Bryant, "Lyft's John Zimmer on Empowering Others to Help Them Grow," interview with John Zimmer, *New York Times*, Corner Office, July 21, 2017, https://www.nytimes.com/2017/07/21/business/corner-office-lyft-president-john-zimmer.html, accessed August 31, 2017.

49.   Bill George, *Discover Your True North*, 2nd edition (Hoboken, NJ: John Wiley & Sons, 2015), p. 159.

50.   For an extensive discussion about whether one can be proud of one's humility, see James Kellenberger, "Humility," *American Philosophical Quarterly*, Vol. 47, No. 2, (2010), pp. 321–336.

51.   Michael C. Ashton, Kibeom Lee, and Reinout E. de Vries, "The HEXACO Honesty-Humility, Agreeableness, and Emotionality Factors," *Personality and Social Psychology Review*, Vol. 18, No. 2 (2014), pp. 139–152.

52.   HEXACO is an acronym for Honesty-Humility, Emotionality, eXtraversion, Agreeableness (versus Anger), Conscientiousness, Openness to Experience.

53.   "The Hexaco Personality Inventory—Revised," Scale Descriptions, Honesty-Humility, http://hexaco.org/scaledescriptions, accessed July 4, 2017.

54.   Ibid.

55.   Jocelyn Wiltshire, Joshua S. Bourdage, and Kibeom Lee, "Honesty-Humility and Perceptions of Organizational Politics in Predicting Workplace Outcomes," *Journal of Business and Psychology*, Vol. 29, No. 2 (2014), pp. 235–251.

56.   "Goldman Takes Too Narrow a View to Be Doing God's Work," *Evening Standard*, November 23, 2009, http://www.standard.co.uk/business/goldman-takes-too-narrow-a-view-to-be-doing-god-s-work-6764598.html, accessed June 29, 2017.

57. "Blankfein Says He's Just Doing 'God's Work,'" *New York Times*, DealBook, November 9, 2009, https://dealbook.nytimes.com/2009/11/09/goldman-chief-says-he-is-just-doing-gods-work/, accessed June 29, 2017.

58. Alex Hern, "Uber Employees 'Spied on Ex-Partners, Politicians and Beyoncé,'" *The Guardian*, December 13, 2016, https://www.theguardian.com/technology/2016/dec/13/uber-employees-spying-ex-partners-politicians-beyonce, accessed November 9, 2017.

59. Greg Smith, "Why I Am Leaving Goldman Sachs," *New York Times*, Opinion, March 14, 2012, http://www.nytimes.com/2012/03/14/opinion/why-i-am-leaving-goldman-sachs.html, accessed August 31, 2017.

60. Salvatore Zappalà, "Perspective Taking in Workplaces," *Journal for Perspectives of Economic, Political, and Social Integration*, Vol. 19, Nos. 1–2 (2014), pp. 55–70.

61. For a summary, see ibid.

62. Michelle Williams, "Building and Rebuilding Trust: Why Perspective Taking Matters," Cornell University, ILR School, 2012, http://digitalcommons.ilr.cornell.edu/cgi/viewcontent.cgi?article=2027&context=articles, accessed June 29, 2017.

63. The booklet is from 1996, and there's something simple and quaint about the approach and writing.

64. David W. Bracken, Dale S. Rose, and Allan H. Church, "The Evolution and Devolution of 360° Feedback," *Industrial and Organizational Psychology*, Vol. 9, No. 4 (2016), pp. 761–794.

65. Rob Nielsen, Jennifer A. Marrone, and Holly S. Ferraro, *Leading With Humility* (New York: Routledge, 2014), p. 77.

66. Paul J. Zak, "The Neuroscience of Trust," *Harvard Business Review*, January/February 2017, https://hbr.org/2017/01/the-neuroscience-of-trust, accessed May 14, 2017.

67. Kerry Flynn, "Airbnb CEO Teases Updates for 2017 on Twitter," *Mashable*, December 26, 2016, http://mashable.com/2016/12/26/airbnb-ceo-updates/#xUt1E7XamaqN, accessed June 30, 2017.

68. Brian Chesky (@bchesky), "Love this. I'll look into feasability," Twitter, December 26, 2016, https://twitter.com/bchesky/status/813261138267750400, accessed July 10, 2017.

69. Marty Swant, "Twitter CEO Jack Dorsey Asks Users How to Improve the Company in 2017," *Adweek*, December 29, 2016, http://www.adweek.com/digital/jack-dorsey-asked-users-what-changes-they-want-twitter-implement-175326/, accessed June 29, 2017.

70. "SMRT CEO Asks Staff for Frank Feedback on How to Forge Forward—Some Feel He Should Just Quit," *The Independent*, October 2, 2016, http://www.theindependent.sg/smrt-ceo-asks-staff-for-frank-feedback-on-how-to-forge-forward-some-feel-he-should-just-quit/, accessed June 30, 2017.

71. Mark R. Leary et al., "Cognitive and Interpersonal Features of Intellectual Humility," *Personality and Social Psychology Bulletin*, Vol. 43, No. 6 (2017), pp. 793–813.

72. Ibid.

73. Samantha A. Deffler, Mark R. Leary, and Rick H. Hoyle, "Knowing What You Know: Intellectual Humility and Judgments of Recognition Memory," *Personality and Individual Differences*, Vol. 96 (2016), pp. 255–259.

74. Leary et al., "Cognitive and Interpersonal Features."

75.   Ibid.

76.   Spencer Harrison, "Organizing the Cat? Generative Aspects of Curiosity in Organizational Life," in Gretchen M. Spreitzer and Kim S. Cameron (Eds.), *The Oxford Handbook of Positive Organizational Scholarship* (Oxford University Press, 2011).

77.   Julia Galef, "Why You Think You're Right—Even If You're Wrong," TED Talk, February 2016, https://www.ted.com/talks/julia_galef_why_you_think_you_re_right_even_if_you_re_wrong, accessed July 1, 2017.

78.   Pete Wells, "At Momofuku Nishi, David Chang's Magic Shows a Little Wear," *New York Times*, May 17, 2016, https://www.nytimes.com/2016/05/18/dining/momofuku-nishi-review.html, accessed July 1, 2017.

79.   Pete Wells, "At Thomas Keller's Per Se, Slips and Stumbles," *New York Times*, January 12, 2016, https://www.nytimes.com/2016/01/13/dining/pete-wells-per-se-review.html, accessed November 9, 2017.

80.   Ian Parker, "Pete Wells Has His Knives Out," *The New Yorker*, September 12, 2016, http://www.newyorker.com/magazine/2016/09/12/pete-wells-the-new-york-times-restaurant-critic, accessed November 9, 2017.

81.   Gabe Ulla, "Thomas Keller on That *New York Times* Review and the Future of Per Se," *Town and Country Magazine*, September 8, 2016, http://www.townandcountrymag.com/leisure/arts-and-culture/a7685/thomas-keller-per-se-new-york-times-review, accessed July 1, 2017.

82.   Bryant, "Lyft's John Zimmer on Empowering Others."

83.   Adapted from Nielsen et al., *Leading With Humility*, pp. 113–115.

Chapter 9

1.   SeaWorld did not capture Tilikum and hasn't captured any orca from the wild in more than 35 years. See https://seaworldcares.com/the-facts/truth-about-blackfish/#1, which disputes this implication from *Blackfish*.

2.   Bilge Ebiri, "SeaWorld Fights Back at the Critical Documentary 'Blackfish,'" *Bloomberg Business*, July 19, 2013, http://www.businessweek.com/articles/2013-07-19/seaworld-fights-back-at-the-critical-documentary-blackfish, accessed July 14, 2014.

3.   Kim Ventre (sister of Dr. Jeffrey Ventre, former SeaWorld trainer), quoted by Samantha Berg, guest speaker, Cornell SC Johnson College of Business, School of Hotel Administration, HADM 3640, Corporate Communication, April 27, 2017.

4.   Eric Kohn, "Sundance Interview: 'Blackfish' Director Gabriela Cowperthwaite Discusses Suffering Orcas, Trainer Death, and Why SeaWorld Hasn't Seen the Movie," *IndieWire*, January 26, 2014, http://www.indiewire.com/article/sundance-interview-blackfish-director-gabriela-cowperthwaite-discusses-suffering-orcas-trainer-death-and-why-seaworld-hasnt-seen-the-movie, accessed June 16, 2017.

5.   Brancheau's family also chose not to participate in *Blackfish* and wrote a statement. Jason Garcia, "Family of Dawn Brancheau Chastises 'Blackfish,'" *Orlando Sentinel*, January 21, 2014, http://articles.orlandosentinel.com/2014-01-21/business/os-dawn-brancheau-blackfish-statement-20140121_1_killer-whales-blackfish-orca-tilikum, accessed June 16, 2017.

6.   For some employees during layoffs, keeping the job can be worse than losing it. See, for example, Lori Conkling and Marvin Gottlieb, *Managing the Workplace*

Survivors: Organizational Downsizing and the Commitment Gap (Westport, CT: Quorum Books, 1995).

7.   Mary Crossan, Gerard Seijts, and Jeffrey Gandz, *Developing Leadership Character* (New York: Routledge, 2016), p. 69.

8.   Jane E. Dutton, Kristina M. Workman, and Ashley Hardin, "Compassion at Work," *Annual Review of Organizational Psychology and Organizational Behavior*, Vol. 1, No. 1 (2014), pp. 277–304.

9.   Jason Garcia and Susan Jacobson, "Animal Trainer Killed at SeaWorld," *Los Angeles Times*, February 25, 2010, http://articles.latimes.com/2010/feb/25/nation/la-na-seaworld-death25-2010feb25, accessed June 19, 2017.

10.   Mental Health First Aid is a concept described in a booklet by the same name, Mental Health Association of Maryland, 2013.

11.   John Couwels and Brian Todd, "SeaWorld Trainer Killed by Killer Whale," February 25, 2010, *CNN*, http://www.cnn.com/2010/US/02/24/killer.whale.trainer.death/index.html, accessed June 16, 2017.

12.   Lee Ferran and Russell Goldman, "SeaWorld Curator: Ponytail Likely Caused Fatal Killer Whale Attack," *ABC News*, February 25, 2010, http://abcnews.go.com/GMA/AmazingAnimals/seaworld-curator-dawn-brancheau-ponytail-caused-fatal-killer-whale-attack/story?id=9934382, accessed June 16, 2017.

13.   "Anderson Cooper 360 Degrees," *CNN* transcripts, March 1, 2010, http://www.cnn.com/TRANSCRIPTS/1003/01/acd.01.html, accessed June 16, 2017.

14.   Tim Zimmerman, "The Killer in the Pool," *Outside*, July 30, 2010, https://www.outsideonline.com/1924946/killer-pool, accessed June 16, 2017.

15.   Secretary of Labor v. SeaWorld of Florida, LLC, OSHRC Docket No. 10-1705, Occupational Safety and Health Review Commission, June 11, 2012, https://www.oshrc.gov/decisions/pdf_2012/10-1705.pdf, accessed June 17, 2017.

16.   WMUR-TV, NH Family Shares Video of Deadly Sea World Show, YouTube, February 25, 2010, https://www.youtube.com/watch?v=kIndSG9oeYQ, accessed June 16, 2017.

17.   National Oceanic and Atmospheric Administration, NOAA Fisheries, "Killer What," http://www.nmfs.noaa.gov/pr/species/mammals/whales/killer-whale.html, accessed June 18, 2017.

18.   Whale and Dolphin Conservation, "Facts About Orcas," http://us.whales.org/wdc-in-action/facts-about-orcas, accessed June 18, 2017.

19.   *Blackfish*, 2013, and Samantha Berg, guest speaker, Cornell SC Johnson College of Business, School of Hotel Administration, HADM 3640, Corporate Communication, April 27, 2017.

20.   Samantha Berg, guest speaker, Cornell SC Johnson College of Business, School of Hotel Administration, HADM 3640, Corporate Communication, April 27, 2017.

21.   Garcia and Jacobson, "Animal Trainer Killed at SeaWorld."

22.   SeaWorld Parks and Entertainment, "SeaWorld Cares," https://seaworldcares.com/en/Future/Educational-Encounters, accessed June 17, 2017.

23.   Ann O'Neill, "SeaWorld Can Expand Tank but Not Breed Whales, Board Rules," *CNN*, October 11, 2015, http://www.cnn.com/2015/10/08/us/seaworld-orca-tank-expansion-plan-hearing/index.html, accessed November 9, 2017.

24.   Samantha Berg, guest speaker, Cornell SC Johnson College of Business, School of Hotel Administration, HADM 3640, Corporate Communication, April 27, 2017.

25. Jane E. Dutton, Kristina M. Workman, and Ashley Hardin, "Compassion at Work," *Annual Review of Organizational Psychology and Organizational Behavior*, Vol. 1, No. 1 (2014), pp. 277–304; Monica C. Worline and Jane E. Dutton, *Awakening Compassion at Work* (Oakland, CA: Berrett-Koehler, 2017), p. 5.

26. Jennifer E. Stellar, Vida M. Manzo, Michael W. Kraus, and Dacher Keltner, "Class and Compassion: Socioeconomic Factors Predict Responses to Suffering," *Emotion*, Vol. 12, No. 3 (2012), pp. 449–459.

27. Dutton et al., "Compassion at Work."

28. Ibid.

29. Deborah Tannen, *You Just Don't Understand* (New York: HarperCollins, 2013).

30. Sandra Baez et al., "Men, Women . . . Who Cares? A Population-Based Study on Sex Differences and Gender Roles in Empathy and Moral Cognition," *PLoS ONE*, Vol. 12, No. 6 (2017), http://journals.plos.org/plosone/article?id=10.1371/journal.pone.0179336, accessed July 7, 2017.

31. Sheryl Sandberg, Facebook post, June 3, 2015, https://www.facebook.com/sheryl/posts/10155617891025177:0, accessed June 16, 2017.

32. Judy Woodruff and Sheryl Sandberg, "After Life-Shattering Loss, Sheryl Sandberg Reaches Out to Others in Grief," PBS *NewsHour*, April 24, 2017, http://www.pbs.org/newshour/bb/life-shattering-loss-sheryl-sandberg-reaches-others-grief/, accessed June 15, 2017.

33. Biz Carson and Skye Gould, "Uber's Diversity Numbers Aren't Great, but They're Not the Worst Either—Here's How They Stack Up to Other Tech Giants," *Business Insider*, March 28, 2017, http://www.businessinsider.com/uber-diversity-report-comparison-google-apple-facebook-microsoft-twitter-2017-3, accessed June 15, 2017.

34. Jack Stripling, "Seeking Closure in Verdict, Penn State Finds More Discord," *Chronicle of Higher Education*, March 30, 2017, http://www.chronicle.com/article/Seeking-Closure-in-Verdict/239637, accessed November 9, 2017.

35. Paul W. B. Atkins and Sharon K. Parker, "Understanding Individual Compassion in Organizations: The Role of Appraisals and Psychological Flexibility," *Academy of Management Review*, Vol. 37, No. 4 (2012), pp. 524–546.

36. Jane E. Dutton, Kristina M. Workman, and Ashley Hardin, "Compassion at Work," *Annual Review of Organizational Psychology and Organizational Behavior*, Vol. 1, No. 1 (2014), pp. 277–304.

37. Sadly, those who express contempt in this study were also categorized as leaders.

38. Shimul Melwani and Jennifer S. Mueller, "Looking Down: The Influence of Contempt and Compassion on Emergent Leadership Categorizations," *Journal of Applied Psychology*, Vol. 97, No. 6 (2012), pp. 1171–1185.

39. Won-Moo Hur, Taewon Moon, and Seung-Yoon Rhee, "Exploring the Relationships Between Compassion at Work, the Evaluative Perspective of Positive Work-Related Identity, Service Employee Creativity, and Job Performance," *Journal of Services Marketing*, Vol. 30, No. 1 (2016), pp. 103–114.

40. Kim Cameron, Carlos Mora, Trevor Leutscher, and Margaret Calarco, "Effects of Positive Practices on Organizational Effectiveness," *Journal of Applied Behavioral Science*, Vol. 47, No. 3 (2011), pp. 266–308.

41. Tanya Staples, LinkedIn Official Blog, January 31, 2017, https://blog.linkedin.com/2017/january/31/linkedin-ceo-jeff-weiner-teaches-how-to-manage-compassionately-learning-course, accessed June 16, 2017.

42. Worline and Dutton, *Awakening Compassion at Work*, p. 5.

43. Making Caring Common: A Project of the Harvard Graduate School of Education, "Turning the Tide Inspiring Concern for Others and the Common Good Through College Admissions," http://mcc.gse.harvard.edu/files/gse-mcc/files/20160120_mcc_ttt_execsummary_interactive.pdf, accessed June 16, 2017.

44. Lisa Heffernan and Jennifer Wallace, "To Get Into College, Harvard Report Advocates for Kindness Instead of Overachieving," *Washington Post*, January 30, 2016, https://www.washingtonpost.com/news/parenting/wp/2016/01/20/to-get-into-college-harvard-report-advocates-for-kindness-instead-of-overachieving, accessed June 16, 2017.

45. Michael Calia, "SeaWorld Attendance, Revenue Continue to Decline," *Wall Street Journal*, February 26, 2017, https://www.wsj.com/articles/seaworld-attendance-revenue-continue-to-decline-1424956041, accessed June 17, 2017.

46. Lauren Raab, "Southwest, SeaWorld End Partnership a Year After 'Blackfish' Backlash," *Los Angeles Times*, July 31, 2014, http://www.latimes.com/business/la-fi-seaworld-southwest-airlines-20140731-story.html, accessed November 9, 2017.

47. Ben Popken, "Mattel Dumps 'SeaWorld Trainer Barbie' After Animal Rights Backlash," *NBC News*, April 25, 2015, http://www.nbcnews.com/business/consumer/mattel-pulls-seaworld-trainer-barbie-after-animal-rights-backlash-n347756, accessed November 9, 2017.

48. SeaWorld Parks and Entertainment, "Saddened to Announce Death of Orca Tilikum," https://seaworld.com/orlando/media-room/press-releases/saddened-to-announce-death-of-orca-tilikum/, accessed June 17, 2017.

49. Jennifer L. Goetz, "Compassion: An Evolutionary Analysis and Empirical Review," *Psychological Bulletin*, Vol. 136, No. 3 (2010), pp. 351–374.

50. Pema Chodron, *The Places That Scare You: A Guide to Fearlessness in Difficult Times*, as quoted in Spirituality and Practice, http://www.spiritualityandpractice.com/book-reviews/excerpts/view/13661, accessed November 9, 2017.

51. Brené Brown, "Brené Brown on Empathy," YouTube, https://www.youtube.com/watch?v=1Evwgu369Jw&t=9s, accessed June 17, 2017.

52. Val Walker, *The Art of Comforting* (London: Penguin, 2010), p. 21.

53. Woodruff and Sandberg, "After Life-Shattering Loss."

54. Elizabeth S. Parks, "Listening With Empathy in Organizational Communication," *Organizational Development Journal*, Vol. 33, No. 3 (2015), pp. 9–22.

55. Graham D. Bodie, "The Active-Empathic Listening Scale (AELS): Conceptualization and Evidence of Validity Within the Interpersonal Domain," *Communication Quarterly*, Vol. 59, No. 3 (2011), pp. 277–295.

56. Judi Brownell, *Listening: Attitudes, Principles, and Skills, 6th edition* (Boston: Pearson, 2017).

57. Bruce Shepard, "President Shepard Sends Message Regarding Student Death," Western Washington University, January 26, 2012, https://westerntoday.wwu.edu/news/president-shepard-sends-message-regarding-student-death, accessed July 10, 2017.

58. Filip Raes, Elizabeth Pommier, Kristin D. Neff, and Dinska Van Gucht, "Construction and Factorial Validation of a Short Form of the Self-Compassion Scale," *Clinical Psychology and Psychotherapy*, Vol. 18 (2011), pp. 250–255.

59. Filip Raes, Elizabeth Pommier, Kristin D. Neff, and Dinska Van Gucht, "Construction and Factorial Validation of a Short Form of the Self-Compassion," *Clinical Psychology and Psychotherapy*, Vol. 18 (2011), pp. 250–255.

60.   See, for example, Rachel E. Brenner, Patrick J. Heath, David L. Vogel, and Marcus Credé, "Two Is More Valid Than One: Examining the Factor Structure of the Self-Compassion Scale (SCS)," *Journal of Counseling Psychology*, March 30, 2017, https://www.ncbi.nlm.nih.gov/pubmed/28358523, accessed November 11, 2017.

61.   Robert A. Emmons and Michael E. McCullough, "Counting Blessings Versus Burdens: An Experimental Investigation of Gratitude and Subjective Well-Being in Daily Life," *Journal of Personality and Social Psychology*, Vol. 84, No. 2 (2003), pp. 377–389.

62.   Robert A. Emmons, *Thanks! How the New Science of Gratitude Can Make You Happier* (New York: Houghton Mifflin, 2007).

63.   Martin Seligman, Tracy Steen, Nansook Park, and Christopher Peterson, "Positive Psychology Progress: Empirical Validation of Interventions," *American Psychologist*, Vol. 60, No. 5 (2005), pp. 410–421.

64.   Sandberg, Facebook post.

65.   Kristin Neff, "Test How Self-Compassionate You Are," Self-Compassion website, http://self-compassion.org/test-how-self-compassionate-you-are/, accessed July 30, 2017.

66.   If this situation doesn't work well for you, choose a different one.

Conclusion

1.   Bill Marriott, "Hiring for Character," Marriott on the Move blog, October 24, 2016, http://www.blogs.marriott.com/marriott-on-the-move/2016/10/hiring-for-character.html, accessed July 16, 2017.

2.   Bill Taylor, "Hire for Attitude, Train for Skill," *Harvard Business Review*, February 1, 2011, https://hbr.org/2011/02/hire-for-attitude-train-for-sk, accessed July 18, 2017.

3.   Mary C. Gentile, *Giving Voice to Values* (New Haven, CT: Yale University Press, 2010).

Company Index

Subject Index

Figures and photos are indicated by f or p following the page number. Organizations are in a separate index.

About the Author

Since 2004, **Amy Newman** has been a senior lecturer at the Cornell SC Johnson College of Business, in the School in Hotel Administration. Prior to her academic experience, Amy worked for 18 years as an internal manager and external consultant for major corporations, such as Canon, Reuters, Scholastic, and The New York Times. Most of her experience has been in developing communication and leadership skills and improving employee performance. Her business experience gives her a practical view of communication in the workplace, which she brings into the classroom every day when teaching courses in organizational behavior, business writing, persuasive written and oral communication, and corporate communication, including crisis communication. Amy is author of the textbook *Business Communication, In Person, In Print, Online*, now in its 10th edition. She has a bachelor's degree from Cornell University in Human Development and a master's degree in human resources management from the Milano School of International Affairs, Management, and Urban Policy at the New School in New York City. Amy is a director-at-large for the Association for Business Communication, for which she is a frequent presenter. In 2015, she won the organization's prestigious Meada Gibbs Outstanding Teacher-Scholar Award. In addition, she has won eight faculty teaching awards since joining Cornell. Since 2010, Amy has managed a blog of current examples for instructors to use in their classes. Visit Leadership Character and Communication at amynewman.com.